THE SEVEN AGES

OF YOUR

DOG

THE SEVEN AGES
OF YOUR
DOG

A COMPLETE GUIDE TO UNDERSTANDING AND CARING
FOR YOUR DOG FROM PUPPYHOOD TO OLD AGE

JAN FENNELL

HarperCollins*Entertainment*
An Imprint of HarperCollins*Publishers*

HarperCollins*Entertainment*
An Imprint of HarperCollins*Publishers*
77–85 Fulham Palace Road,
Hammersmith, London W6 8JB

www.harpercollins.co.uk

Published by HarperCollins*Entertainment* 2005

1 3 5 7 9 8 6 4 2

ISBN 0 00 719920 1

Designed and set by Butler and Tanner
Set in Grotesque and New Baskerville

Printed and bound in Great Britain by Butler and Tanner, Frome

To Tony, Ellie, David and Ronnie, my love always

The general information on canine health and veterinary matters contained in The Seven Ages of Your Dog has been read and approved by a leading veterinary surgeon. Readers should be aware, however, that this book is not a substitute for advice from a qualified vet. If you have specific queries in relation to your pet's health you are advised always to consult your veterinary surgeon or other appropriate expert.

CONTENTS

Picture Credits   x
Acknowledgments   xi
Introduction   **13**
From Wolf to Wolfhound: **16**
    The Evolution of the Modern Dog

PUPPY: 0–8 WEEKS   **22**
In the Wild   24
The First Age: Overview   26
The Early Hours – Birth and Beyond   26
Suckling Machines – The First Ten Days   27
The First Turning Point – Ten Days Onwards   28
Three Weeks – The Extended Pack Forms   29
    Handling the Puppy   31
    Teaching Recognition – Give a Dog   33
      a Good Name
    The Power of Play   34
    Cutting the Apron Strings – Weaning 36
      and Toilet Training
    Weaning   36
    Toilet Training: When, Where and How? 49
    Personality Testing   51
Wellbeing   55
    A Healthy Start: Protecting Your   55
      Puppy from Illness
    Internal Parasites: Worming   55
    Eye Testing   58

PIONEER: 8–12 WEEKS   **64**
In the Wild   66
The Second Age: Overview   68
Feeling at Home in the Human World: 68
    The Young Dog's Needs
A Safe Haven: What the Dog is Looking   70
    for in its New Den
    The First 48 Hours   70
    A Space of its Own   71

Making the Home Safe and Secure   72
A Place to Play   73
'No Go' Zones   73
A Place to Toilet   74
Diet   75
Canine Companionship   76
The Dog's Senses – And How to Use   77
    Them to Your Advantage
    Smell   78
    Sound   79
Breed's Apart – What Different Dogs   80
    Demand from their Owners
    Physical Demands   80
    Spatial Demands   81
    Grooming Demands   81
    Dogs with Medical / Lifespan Demands 87
Laying the Boundaries: Providing the   87
    Structure and Security a Young
      Dog Needs
    Training – Laying the Foundations   87
    The Art of Canine Communication: 88
      An Introduction
    Food Power   94
Typical Problems   95
    Teething Troubles: Dealing with Biting 95
    Independence Anxiety   96
    Crying at Night   98
    Canine Rivalries   99
    Rivalries with Other Animals   101
Wellbeing   102
    Vaccinations   102
    Grooming: The Key to Good Health   105
    The Home Vet: Checking on Your Dog's 112
      Health While Grooming

PLAYBOY: 3–9 MONTHS   **128**
In the Wild   130

The Third Age: Overview   132
Growing Up Fast: The Physical Change   132
  Watching Your Dog's Weight   133
  Body Scoring: How to Monitor Your
    Dog's Weight and Condition   134
  Dealing with Weight Problems   136
Pushing the Boundaries   137
  Heel Work and Preparing for the Walk   138
  First Steps: Going Out on the Walk   143
Moving into the Wider World –   157
  Typical Problems
  Canine Confrontations   157
  Fear of Noises on the Walk   158
  Introducing Dogs to Other Breeds   159
  Travelling: Getting Used to the Car   160
Wellbeing   162
  Grooming / Healthcare   162
Puberty   162
  How to Tell When Your Dog has
    Entered Puberty   162
  Neutering   165
  When Not to Neuter   165
  Single-Litter Mothers   166
  Overheated Hormones: Dealing with   166
    an Over-Amorous Dog

PROTÉGÉ: 9–18 MONTHS   **168**
In the Wild   170
The Fourth Age: Overview   172
The Apprentice   172
The Stay and Recall   173
Off the Leash: Letting Your Dog Run Free   175
  on the Walk
Freedom: First Time Off the Leash   176
  Accidents Will Happen   177
  Diagnosing the Problem   178
  Specific Injuries   179
  Useful Tip: Playing in the Snow: 184
    How to Avoid Ice Balls

Dogs Behaving Badly: How to Deal with   185
  'Difficult' Dogs
  Taking Charge of the Four Key Areas   187
  How to Establish Leadership when   189
    Reuniting: Step by Step
  How to be an Effective Leader   200
Wellbeing   202
  Hip and Elbow Scoring   202

PRETENDER: 18–28 MONTHS   **208**
In the Wild   210
The Fifth Age: Overview   212
Challenging Times   212
Leadership Challenges   213
  Challenges on the Walk   214
  Challenges at Mealtimes   216
The Ultimate Sanction: Countering
  Challenges to Your Leadership   217
  When and How to Banish a Dog   218
Breeding   219
  To Breed or Not to Breed?   219
  Finding the Right Partner for Your Dog   221
  Successful Mating – Getting It Right   223
  Making a Detailed Birth Plan   225
Pregnancy   225
  The Pup's Progress   225
  The Mother's Progress   228
  Phantom Pregnancies   231
  The Final Countdown   232
Delivery Day – Helping Your Dog
  Through Whelping   233
  Items to Have to Hand   233
  How to Spot That Whelping is About
    to Begin   234
  Whelping   234
  Litter Sizes   236
  Problem Deliveries   236
  When to Call the Vet   237
  Helping Out: How to Help the Mother   239

PROTECTOR: 28 MONTHS TO AROUND 7 YEARS 242

In the Wild 244

The Sixth Age: Overview 246

The Die is Cast 246

The Best Days of Their Lives: Helping 247
   Your Dog Enjoy Its Prime
   Field and Working Trials 248
   Agility 248
   Flyball 249
   Obedience Competitions 250
   Dog Shows 250
   Doing What Comes Naturally 251

Muddled Up Dogs 251

Potential Behavioural Problems 252
   Severe Aggression 252
   Separation Anxiety 255
   Nervous Aggression at Mealtimes 257
   Toilet Troubles 258
   Car Chaos 261

Rescue Dogs 262
   Living With a Rescue Dog 263

Wellbeing 265

Middle-Aged Spread – Overweight Dogs 265
   How to Tell if Your Dog is Overweight 265
   Dieting: How to Help Your Dog 266
     Lose Weight
   Problems Associated with Obesity 267

PENSIONER: AROUND 7 YEARS AND BEYOND 270

In The Wild 272

The Seventh Age: Overview 274

Longevity – How Long Will My Dog Live? 274
   Average Lifespans by Breed 275

Your Dog's Age in Human Terms 276
   According to Size – A Guide
   Emotional Old Age 276
   Interacting with other Dogs 278

Growing Old Gracefully – Looking After 279
   an Aging Dog
   Patience 279
   Comfort 279
   Routine 280
   Companionship 280
   Exercise 281

Diet 281
   Adapting the Dog's Diet to Old Age 281
   Overweight and Underweight Dogs 282
   Coaxing Old Dogs to Eat 282
   Special Needs 283

An Elder Dog's Best Friend – 283
   The Importance of the Vet

Grooming 284
   What to Look For 285

Wellbeing 287

Medical Problems 287
   Cancer 288
   Senility 289
   Heart Conditions 290
   Bowel and Bladder Problems 290

Sight and Sound – The Senses Fade 292
   Loss of Hearing 292
   Loss of Sight 294

The Final Farewell 297
   Euthanasia 297
   A Fitting Farewell: What to Do with 300
     Your Dog

A Fresh Start 300

Further Information 302

Contacts in the UK 302

Overseas Contacts/Kennel Clubs 303

Index 308

Picture Credits

The author and publisher are grateful to the following for
use of photographic material reproduced on pages:

Acknowledgments

Researching and writing this book was a major undertaking, and I would not have been able to complete it without the help of a number of people.

First, I'd like to thank Trevor Dolby and Monica Chakraverty at HarperCollins for their enthusiasm for the project when it was first conceived. Since then, I have had the pleasure of working with Jane Bennett and picture researcher Caroline Hotblack, who have been exceptional in their dedication to making the book a success.

Professor Peter Bedford, BVetMed, PhD, FRCVS, DVOphthal, DipECVO, ILTM, Emeritus Professor of Veterinary Ophthalmology, The Royal Veterinary College, University of London, provided an invaluable service by casting an editorial eye over the medical and veterinary sections of the manuscript. The book would have been much the poorer, without his input. Thanks Pete.

A very special thanks must go to Tracy-Ane Brooks at Mission Wolf in Westcliff, Colorado, not just for allowing us to use her fabulous photographs but also for her friendship and generosity in allowing me to roam free amongst the wolves at the sanctuary. It proved every bit as inspirational an experience as I thought it would. I'd also like to thank her husband Kent Weber for his kindness and knowledge. The work they do together is priceless. (Anyone interested should visit their website www.missionwolf.com)

Other special friends are Bob and Frances Jackson, who provided assistance often above and beyond the call of duty in helping with photography, while Geoff and Tony Sutton were generous in providing the use of their house in Kent.

As always, thanks go to the staff at Gillon Aitken Associates, who have done so much to help me: to Mary Pachnos, Dea Brovig and Sally Riley, who have helped spread my work around the world.

Last, but certainly not least, I am indebted to my own team, for without them this book probably would never have become a reality. Their love, support and encouragement, especially when the pressure was on, was remarkable: Glenn Miller, my friend and watchdog, whose constant devotion and protection I so often take for granted; Tony Knight, my son and fellow Dog Listener – professionally he is all I could wish for in the future of our work; Charlotte (Charlie) Medley, a young lady whose dedication to our team is outstanding, and the quality of care she gives to our dogs, horses, cats and wild birds is truly first class. One other person I wish to thank is my daughter Ellie, as her little pep-talks were fabulous. I know I am a very blessed person to have so many special people in my life.

'*Man in his time plays many parts,*
His acts being seven ages.'

William Shakespeare, *As You Like It*

INTRODUCTION

I've harboured the idea of writing a comprehensive guide to a dog's life – following its journey from puppyhood to old age – for a long time now. As a long-time dog lover and owner, as well as an occasional breeder, I've faced all the diverse problems canine life throws up – from weaning and toilet-training, neutering and whelping, to grooming and obedience. Yet even though I've come across countless books and guides on these individual issues, I've never found a single volume that has satisfactorily told me all I felt I needed to know about living with a dog. In particular, I've never come across a book that has done this job from a dog's perspective. I should write it, I thought to myself, a few years ago.

Before I could do anything about it, however, fate led me to write another book altogether. Based on my experience assisting owners of dogs with behavioural problems, *The Dog Listener* introduced ideas which I believe can help all owners lead a happier, more fulfilling life with their dogs. To my surprise it connected with dog lovers around the world and set me off down a completely different path. As I travelled down that road, the idea of a comprehensive guide was pushed to the background. For a while I forgot about it. Now, however, I have finally come full circle.

As I found myself sitting down to write this book, my greatest challenge revolved around one question: How could I best sum up a dog's life in a way that would allow its human owners to understand it better? If I was going to tell the story of a human's life, I would divide it up into the usual elements, the traditional Seven Ages of Man – babyhood, infancy, puberty, adolescence, adulthood, middle and old age. On an instinctive level this made perfect sense. Each of us has, I'm sure, intuitively compared our dogs to a naughty teenager, a terrible toddler or a hormonal mother. But do our dogs really experience the equivalent of infancy and puberty, adolescence and adulthood? Do they suffer from insecurity at particular times in their development? And, if they do, what are the basic instincts that drive them through these phases? What are the seven ages of man's best friend?

The solution revealed itself in a familiar place. The ideas I first expounded in *The Dog Listener* were inspired by my observations of the dog's ancient ancestor, the wolf. In recent years, science has begun to link the two species – *Canis lupus* and *Canis familiaris* – more closely than ever. They are, in most important respects, genetically identical. Watching the interaction of the wolf pack – and then seeing it replicated within my own domestic pack of dogs – opened the door to a new way of communicating with our pets. By learning to use the hidden language through which dogs understand each other, I was able to help owners and their pets lead a less stressful and more fulfilling life together.

It was while I was in the company of wolves once more, this time in the flesh during a visit to a sanctuary in Colorado, that I began to see the parallels between these distant relatives might also be useful in explaining a dog's development, both physical and psychological. Through the course of their lives, wolf pups grow from playful infants into eager and energetic apprentices, joining their seniors on the hunt. They mature from challengers for the leadership of the pack into older, wiser, calmer creatures and – in captivity at least – old stagers. And the triggers that mark the transition from one phase to another are rooted in their development as pack members.

On the surface at least, a domestic dog's life is far removed from the elemental one of their ancestor. Our dogs live in a manmade environment that bears next to no resemblance to the wilderness in which the wolf not only survives but thrives. They are cosseted, cared for medically, and treated that way throughout their lives, yet the truth is that they too are hard-wired with the pack instinct. They recognise it as the best way to guarantee their survival and will abide by its rules and follow its leader as long as it does so. So, like the wolf, they too spend their lives developing from naive novices to apprentices and eventually senior members of their own pack – in their cases the domestic, human family with whom they live. And that progression can be summed up in seven distinct phases.

This book is a guide to those seven ages. It is, in effect, a road map. It will explain what is going on in the dog's development and show you what to expect during that development. It will also tell you what to do at different times during your dog's life to maintain its health and welfare. It will help you develop the basic controls essential to keep the dog disciplined, secure, and above all safe within the human world. It will also explain what you need to do if your dog displays behavioural problems.

Of course, no two dogs are identical and no two dogs' lives are going to be exactly the same. In particular, some reach physical and mental maturity earlier than others. Some larger breeds have a significantly shorter life span and reach old age at a point when others are still in their prime. Environmental issues also play their part in a dog's development, in particular the timing of the puppy's removal from its litter. Therefore, I am not saying every dog will pass from one phase to another – say from Playboy to Protégé – at precisely the same time. However, by understanding the dynamics at work throughout an individual dog's life we can successfully manage their transition through each of these phases. And by doing so we can make their lives – as well as our own – that much more relaxing, enjoyable and rewarding.

It is a fresh new way of looking at the life we lead with our dogs. Most of all, I hope it will provide present and future dog owners with the book I've always wished I'd been able to find.

Jan Fennell, Lincolnshire, July 2005

FROM WOLF TO WOLFHOUND: THE EVOLUTION OF THE MODERN DOG

Of all the animals on earth, the dog is by far man's oldest and closest domestic partner. Their friendship dates back some 14,000 years. It was around then, so scientists believe, that wolves were taken in by humans living in early communities. It was a good deal for both sides, each of whom got something out of the new alliance. Wolves provided humans with their superior senses and their extra hunting and tracking abilities. Man provided their new partners with easy access to that precious commodity, food.

As the wolf learned to live in close proximity to humans, so it evolved into a different kind of animal. It no longer had to rely on hunting and downing other animals for its food. It amended its behaviour so as to remain accepted in human society. As its diet changed from raw meat to human leftovers, so its skull and teeth became smaller, relative to the rest of its body. Its brain shrank too. Slowly the wolf became the first species to be domesticated by mankind. The wild animal became a tame one: *Canis lupus* became *Canis familiaris*.

In the thousands of years that have passed since then, selective breeding on the part of man has turned the dog into the most varied species on the planet. If dogs had been left to survive in the natural world, they would have evolved very little. Instead, over the centuries man has crossbred dogs with different traits and talents, creating what are in effect hybrids. And these dogs have reflected the different physical demands, as well as the aesthetic tastes and fashions, of humans through the ages and around the world.

Dogs have been bred to specialise in roles from running down prey to retrieving shot birds, from guarding houses to acting as guides for blind people. Their DNA, and even their basic skeletal structure, remains identical to that of the wolf, but the several hundred different breeds of dog that now exist come in every conceivable shape, size and design. And while some dogs, like the Siberian Husky or Alaskan Malamute, closely resemble the prototype of the species, other breeds bear little resemblance to their forefathers. You certainly wouldn't automatically assume the Miniature Poodle or the Old English Sheepdog are descendants of a common ancestor.

Meet the grandparents: all dogs are descended from their ancient relative, the wolf.

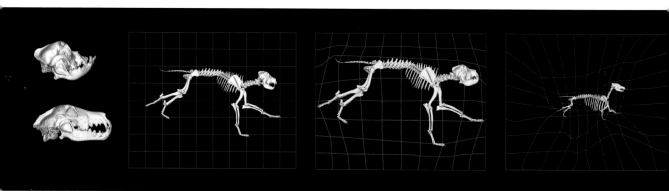

Canine cousins: the graphics, taken from CT Scans of (left to right) a Grey Wolf, Great Dane and Dachshund reveal a skeleton that has remained unchanged in its basic construction. The dog has exactly the same number of bones, arranged to work in exactly the same way, even if – as with the Great Dane and the Daschund – selective breeding has meant that they almost look like different species. The image of the jaw of a bulldog (top left), reveals however, how human selective breeding has altered many of the dog's features, often alarmingly.

Broadly speaking, the following are the seven main groups of dogs and the main breeds within each group:

Gundogs or Sporting Dogs

A large number of dog breeds evolved according to the jobs humans needed them to fulfil. When the invention of the gun provided a new way of hunting, a variety of dogs were bred to perform very specific tasks. Dogs with sensitive noses were bred to locate or 'point' to the hunters' targets. Other breeds were developed to flush out or 'spring' the prey, usually birds. Yet more dogs were bred to retrieve the prey once it was shot. Specific traits were engineered into these dogs. Retrieving dogs, for instance, were bred to have soft mouths that ensured there was no damage to the birds they recovered.

Common breeds within these categories include the Golden Retriever, German Shorthaired Pointer, the Irish, Gordon and English Setters, the Cocker, American Cocker, English Springer and Field Spaniels and the Labrador and Chesapeake Bay Retrievers. The group also includes the Weimaraner and the Hungarian Vizsla.

Working Dogs

The jobs humans have bred dogs to do have been hugely varied over the centuries. Breeds have been produced specifically to rescue people from drowning, guide them through snow-filled mountains, alert them to intruders, sniff out explosives and guide the blind. This diverse collection of dogs includes the Alaskan Malamute and the Bernese Mountain Dog, the St Bernard and the Dobermann, the Boxer and the Bullmastiff. Each of these was bred to excel in specific activities.

Pastoral or Herding Dogs

Among the most useful and intelligent dogs ever bred have been those used for herding. They have been bred to work in different climates and with different animals, from cattle and sheep to reindeer. Because they work in the face of the elements, they have evolved tough, weatherproofed double coats to protect them from even the most severe weather conditions. The most popular breeds of this type are the German Shepherd and the Border Collie, the Old English Sheepdog and the Samoyed. Further breeds also illustrate how they have been bred to do jobs in different parts of the world: from the Australian Shepherd and Cattle Dogs to the Belgian Shepherd Dog, from the Finnish Lapphund to the Norwegian Buhund, and from the Polish Lowland Sheepdog to the Pyrenean Mountain Dog.

Hounds

Some of the earliest breeds developed by man were used as 'sight' or 'gaze' hounds. Such dogs are described in ancient Persian manuscripts and appear in Egyptian tomb paintings. Their special skill was to hunt down prey that humans and their horses, bows and arrows couldn't reach in open country. Often helped by trained falcons, these dogs had the ability to creep up swiftly and silently, running down the prey so that the hunters could close in for the kill. The Saluki and the Afghan are among the oldest examples of this group of dog. More modern versions include the Irish Wolfhound and the Greyhound. Centuries later, Europeans developed 'scent' hound breeds that were able to trail quarry over long distances, eventually exhausting it. Some killed the prey, others kept it cornered while baying to attract the hunters to them. The Elkhound was a typical example of this type of dog. More modern versions include the Bloodhound and the Basset Hound.

It is a measure of how different the demands humans have placed on their dogs that this group contains some of the greatest contrasts within the canine world – from the tallest of breeds, the Irish Wolfhound, to one of the shortest, the Daschund; from the fastest, the Greyhound, to the most silent, the only non-barking breed, the Basenji.

Terriers

The name Terrier comes from the Latin *Terra*, meaning earth. And, as the name suggests, the original terriers were bred to hunt vermin that lived both above and below the ground, such as foxes, badgers, rats and otters. Terriers date back many centuries and are believed to have largely originated in Britain. Popular breeds include the Airedale and the Bull, the Cairn and the Fox, the Irish and the West Highland.

Toy Dogs

Dogs haven't only been bred for working purposes, however. Throughout history, man has also produced dogs that have provided him with nothing more than warmth and companionship, affection and aesthetic pleasure. Lapdogs, for instance, were – as their name suggests – bred specifically to sit on the laps of Tibetan monks. Elsewhere, aristocrats produced breeds that appealed only for the admiring looks they won in and around the Royal Court. Toy breeds include the Maltese and the Pomeranian, the Pekingese and the Cavalier King Charles Spaniel, the Yorkshire Terrier and the Bichon Frise.

Utility or Non-sporting Dogs

Such is the range of breeds man has produced that many don't fit conveniently into any of the main categories in terms of sport or work. Unsurprisingly, those within this group represent huge contrasts. They include such diverse dogs as the Japanese Akita and the Miniature Poodle, the Dalmatian and the Chow Chow, the Mexican Hairless and the Lhasa Apso.

Given their physical differences and the very different environments into which they will be introduced, the lives of modern dogs are more diverse than those of any other species on earth. Some will work, whether as sheepdogs or guide dogs, sniffer dogs or police dogs; some will breed and raise families, while others will simply provide companionship and pleasure. However, whatever breed they are – and whatever life they lead – two things are certain. They each share the same DNA and basic programming as their ancient ancestor, the wolf. And because of this each of their lives will conform to a distinct pattern: the seven ages of man's best friend. What follows is a guide to the dog's journey through those seven ages.

THE FIRST AGE

puppy

0–8 WEEKS

'At first the infant,
Mewling and puking in the nurse's arms'

IN THE WILD

A wolf pup spends the first part of its life, around nine months, within close proximity of the den where it is raised. During these months it passes through the initial distinct phases of its life. For the first three weeks or so, the wolf pup is utterly dependent on its mother. It remains close to her at all times, suckling to her bosom in the den. During this time, the family unit remains undisturbed by the pack. Despite being the leader of the pack, even their father, the alpha male, stays away during this time.

After three weeks or so, however, the puppies will be able to walk and make their first furtive movements away from their mother. At the same time, their father, the alpha, and the rest of the pack begin interacting with them.

A wolf pack is a well-oiled machine, a tightly knit team in which every member knows its place and its job. And from the very beginning every wolf is groomed to take its position in that chain of command. During the pups' first weeks every adult wolf has become 'broody' too, producing a hormone called prolactin. They know the newcomers represent the pack's future survival. They know too that more than half of the new litter will not survive into adulthood. (Disease, starvation and predators claim 60 per cent of young wolves before they reach the age of two.) So, as the pups emerge into the den, the pack begins the job of educating their new members about the day-to-day realities of surviving lupine life.

The messages the pups get during this phase are powerful and formative ones. They see how facial expression and body language convey important signals about status. They learn how their elders also use these signals to avoid confrontations. They see that rank is determined by a combination of experience and personality, with the stronger characters rising to the top of the pack. And by watching the way the grown-up wolves interact, particularly with the alpha, the pups get their first glimpses of how the very top of that hierarchy works.

But the most immediate lessons they learn come from play. As they begin chasing, retrieving and play-fighting with their siblings, they develop not only their physical abilities but also begin to see where their strengths – and ultimately their place in the pack – lie. This is the very beginning of their preparation for fully fledged membership of the pack. In time, the natural herders, stalkers and attackers will begin to emerge.

The domestic dog's first eight weeks echoes those of its ancient ancestor.

Learning fast: at the age of four-and-a-half weeks the wolf on the right already understands its status is subordinate to that of its sibling. The sequence shows the 'junior' pup politely asking its brother permission to sit with him. Throughout, the 'senior' pup stares ahead, impassively.

THE FIRST AGE: OVERVIEW

The first eight weeks of a puppy's life are the equivalent of two-and-a-half human years. So it is not surprising that it spends this time wrestling with a dizzying array of questions. Who am I? What am I? What is my relationship with the dogs and humans around me? How does the world in which I find myself function? And how am I going to survive within it?

During the first days the mother will be entirely responsible for guiding it through this minefield. But, as the dog develops, its human owners will quickly come to the fore, dealing with everything from weaning it off its mother's milk, to toilet training and grooming, worming and starting its vaccination programme.

Most importantly of all, in the absence of the pack, which would teach a dog in its natural wild habitat, humans must take on a key role in helping the newborn's mental and physical development. They must learn to communicate in a language that the puppy will understand. And to be able to do that they must first establish the dog's trust, forging a bond in which the puppy feels safe, secure and happy in their company.

The early hours – birth and beyond

The first few moments of a dog's life are traumatic. The newborn puppy emerges from the warm, safe, dark environment that is the womb into a world filled with new smells and sensations. Often it does so with a bump. I've seen a dog give birth standing up so that its puppies fell out head first, landing on the floor with a plop. It is little wonder the newborn can find it an overwhelming experience. Fortunately its mother will be there to reassure and care for it. And her maternal instincts are by now so intense that she will be fixated on its welfare for the crucial first two to three weeks to come.

The puppy is born encased in a sac filled with amniotic fluid that has been attached to the placenta. Often this is split open during the process of labour, but if not the mother will tear it open herself with her teeth. She will then stimulate the puppy to breathe by vigorously licking at the mucus that covers its face in the wake of the birth.

During these first few moments the puppy is getting used to being outside the womb. The mother will stimulate it until she hears the puppy emitting a sweet, muffled mutting sound and sees it making small movements and nodding its head. She also chews the umbilical cord with her teeth, the ripping movement acting as a stimulant to the puppy.

Unlike a herbivore baby who is up on its feet in minutes, canine puppies are helpless and have no protection at all. Their eyes are closed tight and their ears are pinned back, like little triangles. Their head at this point is disproportionately large compared to the rest of the body. Yet their instincts are already telling them what to do.

Within a very short time the puppy's little head comes up and it begins to sniff the air. It is drawn to the mother's body by her warmth and is soon attaching itself to her teats. It is a wonderful thing to witness a tiny newborn puppy work its way from the rear of its mother into a position to feed. It will push and paddle until it is in the correct position. Within minutes of emerging into the world it will usually have found the teat and started to suckle. It is such a natural action, and it is amazing how strong the suction is.

When they are born, puppies are very lean, so that first input of colostrum (mother's milk) is very important. It is nature's antibiotic, and therefore protection against the world. Even after a couple of hours its effects are clear to see. The puppy loses its gaunt look and begins to look rounder, a sure sign it is getting the nourishment it needs. It is then free to go back to the activity that is going to dominate this first phase of its life – sleeping.

Suckling machines – the first ten days

Because it can't hear or see, the newborn puppy has very little concept of what is happening during the first ten days. In fact it doesn't even know it is a dog at this point. It does not yet have any concept of itself or its siblings. It can do little more than sleep, drag itself onto its mother's teat when it feels the need for food, and whine when it is feeling cold, hungry or in pain.

To say the puppy is totally dependent on its mother is something of an understatement. The mother's role is so all-encompassing during this phase that she also stimulates the puppy to defecate and urinate then eats its faeces and licks up the urine so as to keep the den clean and free from germs. And not only is she the sole source of food but she is also the only means of keeping warm. A newborn pup can't generate or retain heat, so contact with its mother is vital for its survival. If a mother was to leave her pups for half an hour in a normal human home at a temperature of 22°C their body temperatures would plunge by a potentially fatal three degrees, from 38°C to 35°C. Nature has taught the mother this, which is why she hardly strays more than a couple of feet from her newborns during this phase of their young lives.

Yet even at this point the first signs of personality and status are discernible within the litter. The mother's teats are arranged in pairs along the length of her belly, with the best supply of milk available from the middle teats. Already the litter will have begun jostling for access to these prime feeding-stations. Some will have pushed themselves onto the best teats, others will have been forced to feed off the less accessible outer teats. Some may even have been forced away from the teats altogether. The puppies' success – or failure – in getting to those teats will already have begun to have an impact on their personalities.

The first turning point – ten days onwards

The first major turning point in a dog's development comes at about ten days. Around this time the eyes begin to open, ungluing themselves from the inside to the out over a period of three to four days. They then learn to focus. At the same time their hearing is beginning to come into operation as well.

This is a magic moment, both for puppy and carer. One day you'll be able to go in and clatter around the den and there will be no reaction from any of the litter. The next day you will walk in and they'll all look at you and scuttle into the corner of the box. Some even growl at you. It's quite a funny and touching event.

With these senses now functioning, the puppies are more aware of the environment around them. Although they spend a huge proportion of their time sleeping, they are also seeing – to their surprise – that they are not alone, they have siblings. They learn to recognise mum by look and by sound as well as by smell now. They also tend to start sniffing the perimeter of the whelping box as if signalling their readiness to explore the wider world. They will begin getting up on their legs, trying to find their coordination, and making their first tentative steps.

While this is going on, the mother too will be taking her first steps – away from the litter.

The maternal instinct is so strong within the first five days or so that owners often have to lead her away from the whelping box to go to the toilet or eat. But between five and fourteen days she begins to move away for brief periods. This allows the puppy to continue its education and begin to discover who it is by interacting more fully with its siblings.

Their bodies are telling them to rest most of the time, but there is a period between feeding and sleep when they try to barge around and bowl each other over. There is a lot of investigation of what they are capable of – and what others are capable of. The puppies will begin climbing over each other, even trying to gain height advantage over their siblings. They will growl at each other and roll over and fall flat a lot as they learn to balance on their legs. Their wobbliness is due to the top-heaviness of their bodies. There is a lot of sparring and blatting at this point. There are practical lessons to learn too. At this time, for instance, they learn to lap water from a bowl.

All this activity comes in short bursts, however. It is always a maximum of five minutes before they are back asleep. When mum is not there they tend to do this by piling on top of each other and snoozing in one giant heap. This process goes on for between ten days and three weeks.

Three weeks – the extended pack forms

By this point in their development, with their eyes, ears and nose all now functioning, puppies are reacting more to sight, smell and sound. They start to bark and make sounds themselves. They start to wag their tails. They start

Sleeping tight: with playtime over, the litter sleeps in an exhausted heap.

scratching themselves and shaking their heads. And they start play-fighting with their siblings. This is an extension of the interaction that's been going on already, in terms of biting and height-dominance games. They are developing answers to the key questions: Where do I fit into this pack? What am I capable of doing physically? But they are also asking the question, what – and who – is outside the immediate confines of the whelping box? They are ready to claim a little independence for themselves.

In the wild it is now that the pack really comes into its own. While the pups have been suckled by their mother, the alpha female, the excitement has been building among the others. Now, as the mother invites the father and the rest of the extended family to join her, they start to perform their role as surrogate parents. Wolves from all parts of the pack hierarchy will do their bit to educate, assimilate and act as mentors for the new pup. It is how the pup gains the most important information it will need in order to be a properly functioning – and happy – adult member of the pack. The adults will set them their boundaries – gently dragging them back when they wander too far from the den. In short, they are teaching them the rules and the language of the pack.

A domestic dog is living in a very different social organisation – but it is still vital that the dog begins to get the information it will need to function within that group. And it is vital that that knowledge is imparted now, when its most important imprinting is happening. So it is up to us, as humans, to perform the same role as the pack would in the wild.

It's something that can happen naturally and slowly. It's a case of evolution rather than revolution, and around this time there are a few key steps to help ensure this happens with as little stress as possible:

HANDLING THE PUPPY

By three weeks the puppy should be familiar with the sight, smell and sound of humans in the vicinity of the whelping box. They should now be ready for more close interaction with their owners. As we will soon see, this is vitally important for the rest of the puppy's development, so from the outset the aim is for the puppy to associate human contact with warmth, comfort and above all safety. While a little stress is good for the dog's development – as it makes them ask themselves 'What happens now?' – too much stress has to be avoided at all costs. So the dog should be picked up gently and carefully.

STEP BY STEP — HANDLING

- Crouch down to ground level.
- Place your hands underneath the puppy and scoop it up gently but confidently.
- Remaining in the crouched position, raise it up off the ground to eye level.
- Reward the puppy by placing it in your arms, stroking it gently and making calm, reassuring noises.

You are giving them a lot of valuable information during this process that will be helpful in the weeks, months and years to come, so it's important that this is done confidently, so that the puppy feels safe. If it is done correctly a positive association will already have been made; the idea that you are a safe zone will have been implanted in the puppy's mind. When it feels unsafe in the future and begins to ask questions about where it should go, you will already have provided one potential answer.

This, incidentally, is why you should NEVER pick a puppy up by the scruff of its neck, as some people advocate. This habit is based on a misconception on the part of humans, who have seen dogs picking their young up with their teeth. They miss two important points: firstly, the dog clamps its teeth on the pup's back area not the neck; and secondly, it only does so because it doesn't have hands to do the job. If it did, it wouldn't be using its teeth. We do have hands and we should use them. By picking the pup up by the scruff of its neck you are actually inflicting pain on the puppy. This creates a totally negative association, which will be a barrier to you bonding with the dog in the days and weeks to come.

Carers who don't interact with their puppies during this crucial phase of their development are losing valuable time. Indeed, there is strong scientific evidence that a puppy's instinct to investigate and socialise is at its peak during this early five-week period, after which time it begins to fall away. Dogs who haven't been exposed to humans and their environment by the age of 14 weeks find it problematical to do so in later life.

Getting to know you: the first interaction between puppy and owner should pave the way for a lifelong friendship.

Go through this picking-up process twice a day from the age of three weeks onwards. As the puppy gets to trust you more you can extend and develop this interaction. This will allow you to pave the way for its interaction with other humans, vets in particular:

- Place the puppy on a raised surface, like a table. Make sure it is covered and stable, as sudden movement will frighten them.
- Begin a little bit of grooming, running a very soft brush through the puppy's coat.
- Begin placing fingers in their mouths, so as to open the jaw and inspect their mouth.
- Begin holding their head so as to inspect the puppy's ears.
- Teach the puppy to roll on its side in a submissive position. This will achieve two things, preparing the dog for potential visits to the vet, but also underlining the dominance it has already begun to associate with you.
- Get the puppy used to you touching its feet. A lot of dogs don't like having their feet touched, so to get over this hurdle early on is a huge

benefit. This is something that is best done with puppies who are tired as they are easier to work with.

TEACHING RECOGNITION – GIVING A DOG A GOOD NAME

The most important thing you want to instil in your dog during this first eight weeks is the belief that there is nothing threatening in a human voice. When you or anyone else speaks, you want the dog to associate the sound with all things warm and positive. So at this stage it is too soon to start training specific controls, such as the recall and the come. This will change of course. The pup will have to learn some discipline and some self-control quite soon. But for now it is more important it delights in your company and that it makes a positive association with your voice.

However, there is one important step you can make at this point, and that is to get the pup to recognise its name. In doing this you can also do some important groundwork for the time when you do get down to training the dog properly.

The first thing you need to do is choose a name. If you as the breeder have chosen the puppy's name it's a good idea to use that name from the very first time you're picking it up and showing it affection at three weeks. It will be possible to change the dog's name when it moves home, but if the dog is destined for another home and you know the likely owner, it is helpful if they can choose a name that you can begin working with at this early stage.

The next thing to do is to start addressing the puppy within its litter using that name. At this point the dog doesn't see itself as an individual so much as a litter member, so it is possible it may not respond immediately. But if it does, your goal is to get it to stop, look at you and – for the first time – ask, 'Are you talking to me?'

There are a few key points to remember when doing this:

- Eye contact is crucial: when you call one of the puppies they may all look at you, but you must only look at the individual you are addressing.
- Make sure your eyes are soft and inviting, don't glare or look anxious.

- When you call the name, do so in a happy way: the tone should be soft, as should the body language.
- If the dog comes to you on its own, praise it warmly, repeating the name.
- If the whole litter comes, make a point of only praising the one dog: you are also trying to teach the other pups this is NOT their name, and this will help reinforce that.

The beauty of this is that it is something you can now build on. When you are teaching the dog to make a positive association with something, during weaning or toilet training, for instance, repeating the name warmly as you reward it will help.

All this should have a drip effect on the dog. It should soon recognise the distinctive sound of its own name, providing you – and its future owners – with a foundation upon which to work.

THE POWER OF PLAY

Within a domestic litter, just as in the wild, play provides the puppy with some of the most powerful information it will receive during this phase of its life. It will learn what it can and cannot get away with physically with its siblings. It will learn about its status within the litter, and how to recognise the status of others.

Playing with the litter

Far too often you see people squealing and shouting at a litter of puppies. One of the things you must not do is overreact to what may seem like aggression. This is an important part of a puppy's education, so to block play is to block its learning. Only if there is a noticeably weaker puppy in the litter or there is a danger that one puppy is going to harm another should you intervene. In any case, if it is potentially serious, the situation will probably be dealt with by the mother if she is around. She will growl her displeasure soon enough if the litter is misbehaving.

The key is to let things happen naturally. The puppy is learning a new language and – as with any language – it will learn the subtleties when it is older. For now it is dealing in the basics.

Playing with the owner

Play provides an owner with another vital opportunity to establish their relationship with their puppies. It can offer another powerful signal about hierarchy, and it can establish the owner as a fun leader too. Yet it can also set some misleading precedents. This is a relationship that may last for life, so it is vital that play is conducted according to certain rules, essentially three DON'Ts:

DON'T LET THE PUPPY DICTATE PLAYTIME

The sight of a puppy appearing with a ball in its mouth is guaranteed to melt most hearts. But owners must not instinctively and immediately start playing. Responding to this will plant the idea that playtime is something which the puppy instigates. And this, in time, will help instil the idea that the puppy is the leader. It is not, and it must be made apparent that it is not from this early stage.

DON'T ENCOURAGE TUGGING GAMES

This is setting up a problem for later down the line in terms of challenges to leadership. The puppy may get away with it once or twice and begin to develop false ideas about its status. It's also encouraging the puppy to bite harder, which can make matters even worse. What is a funny game with a puppy is not so funny with a fully grown dog, especially if it is a big breed.

DON'T TOLERATE BITING

Anything that encourages a puppy to bite into humans is to be avoided at this point. It will lead to a positive association and may leave the dog thinking it is acceptable behaviour for the rest of its life. This is why dogs whose job it will be to bite – such as police dogs – aren't taught to bite until they are 18 months of age.

The key to this is understanding that it is not an aggressive act on the puppy's part. It is not trying to bite, it is trying to hold on, just as it does when playing with its siblings in the litter. And the key to stopping it is not to make a drama of it. Humans tend to panic when a puppy nips, but this will only make matters worse. The thing to do is to give a little yell as a sibling would do, then immediately walk away. If the puppy chases after you and grabs at your trousers or dress, remove it and put it behind the gate or into another room. Leave it there for a reasonable length of time, up to an hour. Do this without ceremony and don't worry about it being hard on the dog. It's not, in fact it's very positive. As an owner you have stated there is a cut-off point, and the puppy has learned for the first time about the consequences of actions.

CUTTING THE APRON STRINGS – WEANING AND TOILET TRAINING

By the start of the third week the puppy will have begun to make its first moves away from the whelping box. Generally the front of the box is removed around this time, allowing them to explore a few feet away from their sleeping area, to the boundary of the den.

Slowly at first, but then with more and more confidence, they will begin to venture further and further from the spot where they have spent the first formative days of their young lives. They will begin to defecate and urinate on their own. This new independence coincides with the mother's gradual removal of herself from the scene, and it brings with it the first major practical challenges for the owner – weaning and toilet training.

WEANING

Between three and five weeks, the puppies are ready to be weaned off their mother's milk. It will often be the mother herself who provides the signal that it is time to start this process. In the wild, this is the point at which the alpha female will relinquish her duties as the sole provider of sustenance and take a back seat to the rest of the pack. Owners may notice the mother of their puppy behaving in this same instinctive way, standing up to feed rather than lying down, thereby allowing her to move away if she feels she has finished or she is hurt by the puppies' pin-sharp baby teeth or claws.

Owners should be prepared for this new phase. It will take the puppy around three weeks to make the transition off its mother's teat. During that time it may still suckle and feed, but as the demands of the puppies slowly decrease the female's milk will also dry up, so owners will see that feeding times will shorten in length. Indeed, during the early part of weaning the puppy's diet may be divided 50:50 between its mother's milk and other food, but by the end of the sixth week a puppy should be eating independently of its mother. It is vital they get it right.

Off the teat: if properly introduced to food, young dogs should quickly adapt from mother's milk to solid meals soon after they reach three weeks of age.

A Healthy Diet: The Essentials

A healthy, well-balanced diet will be important throughout the dog's life, but during this early, rapid-development phase it is especially vital so as to promote proper growth and stimulation.

Many owners will hand over responsibility for their dog's dietary needs to the dog food companies, whose huge range of carefully planned products are scientifically researched in order to provide the right balance of ingredients for the dog. There is nothing wrong with this, but it is still worth understanding the key basic elements that make up a dog's ideal diet and knowing precisely what role they play in your dog's development.

YOUR DOG IS WHAT YOUR DOG EATS

The old saying goes 'you are what you eat'. This makes perfect sense, of course. The health and condition of our body is dependent on what we put into it. If we maintain a natural, well-balanced diet that reflects the way our body is made we are far less likely to get ill. It is no different for a dog. If we want to maintain our dog's health we need to feed it according to its natural makeup and the elements that make it what it is. So to understand the basic requirements that go to make up a dog's diet we need to know, in simple terms, what a dog is made of and what ingredients help it best live a natural, healthy life.

Water

Just like every other species on earth, the dog relies on water for its existence. Its body is made up of 70 per cent moisture and needs a constant supply of water for all its organs to function properly. Water performs roles from transporting vitamins around the body to cooling the body when it is hot. A dog should never be without a ready supply.

Proteins

Protein is the main component of most of the dog's living tissue, apart from its bones. Its hair, skin, nails and muscles are predominantly made up of protein. Proteins are made up of a variety of amino acids, chemicals that are the essential 'building blocks' of the body. Some amino acids are manufactured naturally in the body, but others have to be provided by the dog's diet. It is vital that a dog gets a plentiful supply of proteins so as to first grow and then maintain its body in a good state of health with good muscle tone. By far the most natural source of protein – in every sense – is meat, although large amounts of protein can also be gained from vegetables, eggs, fish, grains and dairy products.

Fats

Fats provide two key services: they supply energy but they also contain essential fatty acids that play a series of vital roles in looking after the body.

The two main groups of the acids are Omega 3 and Omega 6, both of which – among other things – are associated with helping maintain a healthy coat and skin. They are also important in controlling and preventing a whole range of medical problems from allergies and arthritis to heart disease and cancer. Good sources of these essential fatty acids are found in oils such as evening primrose, fish and linseed oil.

Vitamins

Vitamins play an essential role in building and maintaining a healthy dog. They act as catalysts for chemical reactions and all have specific roles to play. For example, if your dog manages to cut its paw, one vitamin will go into action to staunch the bleeding, another one will go to work repairing the skin. Vitamins come in two forms, those that are soluble in water and those that are soluble in fat. The following are the main vitamins your dog will need.

Vitamin A: This helps to maintain healthy eyesight and skin. Good sources are liver, milk and egg yolks as well as fish oils.

B Vitamins: This group of water-soluble vitamins include B1, thiamine, B2, riboflavin, niacin and others. They each work to regulate the cell-making processes within the body. Normally they are produced naturally, but occasionally – when a dog has been receiving antibiotics, for instance – it may need to have its levels topped up.

Vitamin B12: This helps the development of red blood cells in bone marrow. Good sources are meat such as liver and kidneys, eggs and dairy products. Some breeds, such as Giant Schnauzers, can be born with a condition that prevents them absorbing B12 properly and may need special injections of the vitamin during their lives.

Vitamin C: This acts as an antioxidant against 'free radicals' and also helps the generation of Vitamin E. However, dogs should not be given too much Vitamin C. It can seep into the dog's urine and form into bladder sand or stones.

Vitamin D: By balancing the body's levels of calcium and phosphate, this vitamin helps the formation of healthy bones and teeth. A deficiency of Vitamin D can cause rickets. This is rare, however, because Vitamin D is present in virtually all prepared dog foods.

Vitamin E: This maintains the dog's immune system by reducing the cell-destroying 'free radicals' that can lead to diseases like cancer. It also helps prevent skin diseases, heart and neurological problems.

Minerals

Around four per cent of a dog is made up of minerals, basic chemical elements that either form structures, like the bones and teeth, or influence bodily fluids, in particular the blood. It is essential that dogs have the right levels of each of these if they are to develop into healthy adults, and in particular have good strong teeth and bones.

> **Calcium and Phosphorus:** These two minerals aid the development of strong teeth and bones and influence the nervous system too. Imbalances in one or the other can be a problem. In general, dogs' diets should include marginally more calcium than phosphorus. The ideal ratio is 1.2–1.4: 1.
>
> **Copper and Iron:** These two elements work to transport oxygen around the body in the form of red blood cells.
>
> **Magnesium:** This helps maintain the right balance of calcium and phosphorus, which in turn helps keep the dog's skeleton healthy. It also aids muscle and nerve functions.
>
> **Selenium:** Maintains body tissue like the heart muscles. It can be toxic even in low levels so should only be a very small part of a dog's diet.
>
> **Zinc:** The correct level of zinc in the body ensures healthy skin and an efficient immune system. At the same time it makes sure the taste buds are functioning properly.

OTHER ESSENTIAL INGREDIENTS FOR A HEALTHY DIET

Bones

In the wild the wolf maintains its teeth and gums by ripping and gnawing at the carcasses of its prey. The bones also provide it with all the calcium it needs. However, since it assimilated itself into the human world, feeding in this way hasn't been an option for the dog.

Modern dog foods provide the dog with all the calcium they need. But as the dog gets older and develops its adult teeth it is going to need something that provides those teeth and gums with a good workout. Bones provide the perfect option, especially as they are also tasty, exercise the jaws, and can keep dogs happily occupied for hours on end.

Owners should ensure their dogs only get to chew on the healthier marrow bones. These can be raw or roasted. They should also make sure they are strong, hard bones that do not splinter. Shards of shattered bone can easily get stuck in the throat and choke a dog.

Carbohydrates

Carbohydrates are compounds made up of sugars called monosaccharides. The dog's body is able to convert these to provide almost immediate energy. Carbohydrates also allow the dog to store reserve energy in the form of glycogen. Good sources of carbohydrate include grain, rice, corn and wheat.

Fibre

An essential element of a dog's diet, this stimulates the production of saliva and the gastric juices. It is also a valuable protection against medical problems from constipation and obesity to diabetes and bowel disorders. In the wild the dog gets its fibre from the fur and intestines of its carrion. The domestic dog's best sources of soluble fibre are cooked vegetables and rice, which have the added benefit of being 'sticky' so that they remain in the stomach longer, allowing their goodness to be absorbed for a greater time. Dry fibre comes in the form of bran, commonly found in breakfast cereal. A dog's fibre needs may vary through age. Older dogs in particular may need more fibre in their diets to help their bowels function properly.

Milk

Milk will be a part of the dog's diet during weaning but it may not remain so for long afterwards. A lot of puppies can't digest the sugar or lactose in the milk and suffer stomach problems as a result. This is hardly surprising as they are drinking cows' milk not dogs' milk. If you are not sure whether your puppy can tolerate milk, dilute it half-and-half with water before you offer it to them for the first time.

Feeding Your Dog – The Options

Dogs need a balanced diet that contains the right mix of protein, fat, vitamins and minerals their bodies demand. Precisely how these dietary needs are met, however, is a matter for the owner, who has several options:

HOME-MADE FOOD

Many owners like the idea of cooking for their dog. This is laudable, of course, but they should be aware that it is a complex job. For a balanced diet a dog doesn't just need the right mix of ingredients, it also needs them in the correct proportions to each other.

It is easy, for instance, to imagine that a dog – as the descendant of the wolf – will happily survive on a diet of pure protein in the form of meat. This overlooks, of course, the fact that, in the wild, wolves eat not just the muscle but the bones, internal organs, intestinal contents, skin and hair of their carrion as well. It is in these that they find the other essential nutrients they need. A purely meat diet would be deficient in a range of elements, including vitamins A and D and calcium.

Having said all this, it is perfectly possible to come up with a well-researched diet. Recipes based on a simple mix of chicken, liver, rice, bone meal, salt and sunflower or corn oil can work quite well. A pinch of garlic can also be good for the dog's system. In the age of the Internet there is also a lot of information available.

Any owner contemplating making homemade food must be prepared for a lot of hard work, especially as the dog's needs are going to be changing throughout their life.

PREPARED FOODS

It is no surprise that the vast majority of dog owners place their dog's dietary welfare in the hands of the major food-makers. The big manu-facturers have put huge resources into researching and understanding the complex mechanism that is the dog's body. As a result they have produced a range of foods that satisfy all the owner's main concerns. In the main their foods provide the right balance of protein, fat, vitamins and minerals a dog needs to remain fit and healthy. These foods come in a huge range of recipes, a variety of textures and forms, and are all highly convenient. They also reflect the different needs of dogs at different times in their lives, with puppies in particular very well catered for. In addition, they have guarantees of quality, nutrition and safety. Since the introduction of mandatory nutritional labelling, owners can even monitor precisely what their dogs are eating by looking at the packets.

Prepared foods come in two different categories – **complete** and **complementary**. These should never be mixed, but each has its own merits.

Complete food, as its name suggests, provides an all-in-one balanced diet made up of all the essential nutrients in the right proportions. The dog will not need to eat anything else to maintain good health. Complete foods will be geared for every key stage of the dog's life, from puppyhood and the early growth stages to specially designed foods for pregnant mothers and elderly dogs.

Complementary food is designed to be eaten alongside other foods, such as biscuit mixers or canned meat. The two are combined to give the dog the balanced diet it needs.

Within both these categories there are two types of prepared food: dry and wet. Increasingly popular, dry foods have the advantage of being relatively inexpensive and very convenient. They have basically been cooked under pressure then dried out. They have then had fat and preservatives added to make them tastier to the dog. They can be served dry or softened up by the addition of water. By contrast, wet foods have retained some of the moisture from the ingredients. These foods are served in a soft form, usually in a tin. They too can be complete or complementary, to be eaten in conjunction with other meals.

Which of the two an owner opts for is inevitably a matter of personal choice, but a few factors should be borne in mind:

- Soft or wet food is more easily digestible, but it will place a greater onus on the owner to care for the dog's teeth. Wet food doesn't give the teeth a workout and allows tartar to build. Gum diseases like gingivitis can easily prosper.
- Many of the modern dry foods have been designed specifically to give the teeth a workout as well. The good ones release minerals that become embedded in the plaque of the teeth and block the build-up of tartar.
- Some smaller dogs may well have problems crunching on some of the hard 'kibbles'.

The key thing from an owner's point of view is that you read the instructions of these meals carefully, They usually contain detailed plans for feeding, with precise measures and feeding times. In the main you should stick to what they say.

MAKE-UP OF A TYPICAL DOG FOOD			
NUTRIENT	**FUNCTION**	**AMOUNT CONTAINED WITHIN FOOD AS PERCENTAGE**	
		Average/ small dog	Large dog
Protein	Vital element to build healthy tissues, organs and muscles	28	30
Fat	Supplies energy, essential fatty acids for nerve function and healthy cells	18	11
Carbohydrate	Supplies energy	37	43
Fibre	Encourages and maintains healthy digestive system	2.5	2.7
Moisture	Essential nutrient, 70 per cent of body	7.5	7.5
Calcium	Aids strong teeth and bones, helps nerve function	1.3	1
Phosporous	Helps strong bones and energy production	1	0.8
Sodium	Aids fluid balance and nerve function	0.5	0.5
Potassium	Fluid balance, nerve function and muscle contraction	0.75	0.75
Magnesium	Healthy bones, nerve and enzyme function	0.1	0.1
Omega-3 fatty acids	Aids healthy skin and glossy coat	0.4	0.25
Omega-6 fatty acids	Aids healthy skin and glossy coat	3.4	2.5

This table illustrates how a typical complete dog food reflects the essential ingredients that constitute a dog's makeup. Our dogs literally eat what they are.

Source: Hill's Pet Nutrition
* figures rounded up

NATURE'S NUTRITION: THE BARF DIET

There is a growing body of people who feed their dogs a very different diet, the so-called Bones and Raw Food, or BARF, diet. They believe this is by far the most healthy – and, more importantly, natural – way of eating for the dog. Not everyone agrees with them, but for me, at least, their argument is a persuasive one.

Dog food, at least as we know it today, is a recent invention. It has been around for 100 years or less. So how on earth did dogs not only survive but thrive before this? The answer to that, of course, is by eating what came naturally. For tens of thousands of years dogs lived off food they had hunted or scavenged for themselves. In their very early days they hunted in packs. Their natural prey would be herbivores like rabbits, deer or sheep. At other times they would scavenge the leftovers from bigger animals brought down by bigger hunters, like lions or bears. They would supplement this diet by grazing during the summertime. They were then – as now – opportunistic eaters. They took what they could get, when they could get it.

Yet this diet provided dogs with a whole range of proteins and nutrients. By eating everything from the soft tissue and offal to skin, they helped maintain their condition and warded off sickness too. By eating the carcasses of other animals down to the bones and hair, they also gave their teeth the rigorous workout they needed and supplemented themselves with calcium.

When man first domesticated the dog it was easy for them to maintain this diet. In exchange for their hunting skills, dogs were left to eat everything their human companions didn't want, which, as it happened, was quite a lot. Dogs maintained their natural diet throughout their early days with man. It was another reason why their partnership with man worked so well for them.

It was only when man created the industrialised society that things went awry. Suddenly man and dog were no longer sharing meals together. Man ate everything he wanted, and there were no longer any leftovers. Instead he invented foods that he believed would be of benefit to the dog.

There are many who believe that by returning to their natural foods, dogs receive a much more rounded and healthy diet. For a start they argue that the mere act of cooking or processing food removes up to 70 per cent of its nutritional value. But they also argue that many common diseases – from tooth decay and bad breath to colitis and kidney disease, skin problems and rheumatoid arthritis – are a result of a deficiency in the modern, manmade foods. People who give their dog the BARF diet say their dogs are leaner, fitter, better conditioned and muscled animals. For these reasons they recommend at least partially returning dogs to their natural way of eating.

So what is a natural diet?

The essential ingredients of a raw diet are raw meat, liquidised raw fruit and vegetables and raw bones. Dogs should be fed these according to the following principles:

- Dogs should eat 100–150g of meat for every 10kg of their weight.
- Dogs should be given a variety of meats to benefit from the different nutrients. Pork is the only meat to be avoided. Beef should be avoided if a dog has a skin or bowel problem.
- Offal such as kidney, heart, lung or liver should replace meat once a week.
- Dogs should eat 200–300g of fruit and vegetables for every 10kg of their weight.
- The fruit and vegetable part of the meal can be supplemented by nuts, herbs and cooked beans.
- Feed dogs raw bones at least once a week to exercise teeth.
- Do not feed dogs cereals.

How and When to Introduce a Dog to a Natural Diet

In the wild, puppies are introduced to raw food almost immediately. At first their mother or other pack members will give it to them in the form of regurgitated or chewed food, but they will soon be eating on their own. There is no reason why a domestic dog can't be weaned onto a natural diet just as quickly. The only thing to be careful of is bones. As well as the danger of brittle bones that can splinter and choke a dog, owners should be wary when feeding them poultry such as chicken. Be sure to ensure there aren't too many small, sharp bones as these can also easily get stuck and cause choking.

If you acquire a dog that has not been fed on a natural diet, you should take care to make any transition to BARF gradual. Introduce one or two natural meals a week to begin with. Then, once the dog's system has begun to get used to this, increase the number of natural meals until it accounts for the dog's whole diet.

Hand-feeding a Puppy for the First Time

This represents another very important moment. Because dogs instinctively associate the handing out of food with hierarchy it is a priceless opportunity not just to establish a relationship with the puppy but also to establish your status with it. Hand-feeding is not something that will go on for very long, so it is vital you make the most of this chance to use it effectively.

Many people begin weaning with a cereal, such as porridge mixed with milk. Some opt for tinned puppy food. Others go for kibbles of 'complete food' made up of carefully selected ingredients that constitute an ideal diet. Many people opt for raw meat.

The puppy will by now have a full complement of teeth coming through, but their jaws are still too weak for it to crunch anything and its throat is still too small to swallow food of any size. So it is vital that whatever food you choose to introduce, it is of the right consistency. Porridge with

STEP BY STEP   THE FIRST FEED

- Pick the puppy up gently, as you have learned to do by now.
- Speak to it softly and gently.
- Don't make any sudden movements.
- Make a pad of your thumb and third and fourth fingers.
- Scoop the food onto the pad then put it under the puppy's nose so they can smell it.
- Let them smell it for a moment or two.
- How quickly they accept the food depends on personality – some will only need to smell it and they are digging in, others tend to be unsure and cautious.
- If they are enthusiastic be careful they don't bite; if they are reluctant be patient.
- When the puppy has eaten, stroke it softly with one finger and give it some gentle words of praise.

milk should be made as smooth as possible, while kibbles should be soaked in cold water overnight then mixed in a food processor for better consistency. Tinned food must also be softened so that it is palatable for the puppy. If you go for the raw-meat option, make sure it is minced well.

This is the first time the puppy will have associated you with the providing of food. Therefore, it is vital to make it a good association by taking things slowly and doing all you can to make it as pleasant an experience as possible for the puppy. Time spent getting this right can make the difference between a relationship that works and one that does not. Don't rush it.

Building up a Puppy's Diet

As it grows, a puppy's appetite will increase accordingly. In the first week or so of weaning the puppy should have three feeds a day. By the second week, when it is four weeks old, this should increase to five feeds a day. The key is to feed the puppy a little but often. This way it will not have any digestive problems.

FEEDING BY EYE

Of course, all dogs are different, so no matter how precise the instructions we see on food labels, every owner will have to make judgements on the exact levels of feeding for each individual dog. And this requires owners to be vigilant and to feed by eye as well as by the packet or the tin.

One of the biggest problems with puppies – and indeed all dogs – is overfeeding. If a dog is carrying too much or too little weight it is easy to see. The shoulders are often the most obvious sign. Puppies can often put on weight here so that they seem to have no neck. This is to be avoided, in particular because it can cause diarrhoea and other problems. If a puppy does develop diarrhoea withhold food for 24 hours. It won't starve.

By the same token, underfeeding can result in rapid weight loss. Look out for protruding ribs or thin backs. If this happens simply step up the number of meals rather than the volume of food served. As with all things at this stage of a dog's development, each step must occur gradually.

TOILET TRAINING: WHEN, WHERE AND HOW?

Toilet time: if guided properly, a puppy should quickly learn when, how and where to relieve itself.

When?

In the first weeks of a puppy's life, as previously explained, the mother both stimulates defecation and cleans up afterwards. By three weeks this is no longer the case, so you must be prepared to start training the dog to toilet properly almost immediately it begins to move away from the whelping box.

The first thing to realise is that this is something you are not going to be able to control. A puppy of three to four weeks will urinate 12 or more times a day and will open their bowels five to six times a day. You can't stimulate them to do this, and while they will signal they want to go beforehand by circling around, even with the best will in the world you are not going to spot every occasion this happens.

In other words, no matter how diligent you are, at first you are going to have your fair share of accidents. The good news, however, is that you can anticipate when the bulk of the puppy's movements are going to happen because it will normally defecate after it wakes up and after it eats. This means you can be ready on each of these occasions at the very least.

Where?

At first the puppy is probably going to do its toileting around its den. Dogs are by nature clean creatures so the puppy will try to put as much distance as it can between its sleeping and feeding area and its toilet area. Give it that opportunity. The more you do so the more you are likely to succeed.

You must ensure that you have something in place for the puppies to go to the toilet on. There are plenty of alternatives, newspapers or absorbent padding or perhaps wood shavings. If it is the latter make sure they are dust free.

The puppy isn't going to get to this area every time of course, so during this phase it is vital you also keep the bedding area immaculately clean. You can buy absorbent bedding that takes wetness through to the bottom. A lining of newspaper between this and the floor will provide another layer to take up moisture. This should be changed as often as needs be, perhaps even two or three times a day during the early stage of toilet training.

Dogs prefer to do their toileting in a natural environment so it is good for both you and your dog if you progress the training to the garden or outdoor area as soon as possible. You should start doing this at the age of about four weeks. They should have got the hang of walking now.

Again, you are not going to be able to get it right every time. There are going to be occasions when they catch you out, so be careful to line the dog's route from the sleeping area to the garden with whatever it is you are using to absorb the mess. The ideal thing would be a flap straight from the den to the garden.

STEP BY STEP — TOILET TRAINING

- Accompany the dog to do its toilet first thing in the morning, after meals and when the dog has woken from a sleep.
- Stay with it in the garden or outdoor area.
- When you see it squatting give it food reward and cement the good, positive association with a word or phrase that you will use at all times, for instance 'empty' or 'clean dog'.
- If the dog has an accident en route to the garden or outdoor area, clear it up without a word. Say nothing at all.

How?

You are not going to be supervising the dog while it remains in the den. Your main responsibility during this period is to keep the area clean. If, however, it has accidents away from this area, the important thing is not to chastise the dog. The key to toilet training is to make a good association, so anything negative at this early stage would be most unhelpful for the dog. And when it comes to moving the toilet training outside, this positive reinforcement becomes even more important.

With this positive association being built all the time, it won't take the puppy long to make the connection between wanting to go to the toilet and going outside.

PERSONALITY TESTING

Personality is a hugely important factor in a dog's development – and indeed its life. No matter what else changes, a dog's personality isn't going to alter. So you can predict an awful lot about the way a dog is going to behave generally and in particular situations during its life by looking at the type of character it is.

This will be invaluable later, for all sorts of reasons. If the dog remains with you, then you will be armed with important information that may be crucial in dealing with behavioural and other problems. If it is shy, for instance, you will know it is more likely to display signs of nervousness and anxiety later in life, such as wetting itself when nervous or being destructive around the house. If, on the other hand, it is a more dominant, confident character then it is more likely to see itself as an alpha or leader, with all the problems that come with that.

Equally, if the puppy is going to leave for another home, it is your responsibility as a breeder to know your dog's temperament. You don't want to place an extrovert dog with an owner who is looking for a quiet companion; nor do you want to place a docile, shy dog with someone who intends leading a very active outdoor life with that dog. The consequences of mismatching dogs and their owners can be awful.

Of course, broad personality types are often apparent early on when the litter is first formed. There are the strong characters who dominate

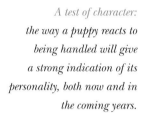

A test of character: the way a puppy reacts to being handled will give a strong indication of its personality, both now and in the coming years.

A contented customer: a puppy that happily allows itself to be cradled is more likely to be a contented and relaxed dog.

the best feeding positions when suckling from the mother's teats. And there are the obvious weaker members, those who have been knocked away from these positions and literally have to fight for their food – and their survival. But personality is a more complex matter than this and requires a little more study. With the first part of their development well underway, the five or six week mark offers the perfect opportunity to conduct a simple personality test that will answer many of your questions.

There are all sorts of theories on how to conduct a personality test – many of them bordering on the barbaric. For instance, some people advocate pinching a dog to see if it retaliates. I can think of nothing worse.

Three simple tests will give you all the information you need – without resorting to violence or cruelty.

1. Testing by Eye

A good breeder should know their litter intimately. They should have spent a lot of time with them, watching them interacting in the early days with their mother, then getting more and more involved beyond the three-week period. By doing this they should already have formed some strong opinions about the different characters in the litter. The evidence will have been there, in front of their eyes.

The first clues come early on. By looking at which puppies get to the teat first you can spot the dominant characters. By identifying those who struggle to get the sustenance they need and perhaps get pushed to the back of the litter you can see the puppy who is going to be the shy, retiring member of the pack. This continues as the puppies emerge from under their mother's wing. As they begin to play and interact with each other you may notice that one takes the toys off the others? Or there is one that sits there watching the others while they play? You can see that this dog is a thinker, one who will always weigh up its options in life before making its move.

There are signals in terms of body language too, with some dogs looking to assert themselves by placing their bodies over pups they already consider to be subordinate. Of course, this isn't going to tell you everything, so there are a couple of physical tests you can conduct to fill in this picture.

2. Testing in the Palm of the Hand

This is designed to test the puppy's reaction to being lifted. It will, of course, be used to this by now, but the way it reacts each time this happens speaks volumes.

STEP BY STEP   **PERSONALITY TEST 1**

- Lift the puppy off the ground.
- Place it in the palm of one hand (or two hands if it is a larger breed) and leave it there for ten seconds or so.
- If they go limp in your hand then they are likely to be a relaxed personality.
- If they start to struggle immediately then that indicates they are more stubborn and more likely to challenge you. It might also be a sign of a nervous dog.
- If they stay there for a little while then start to struggle that indicates a dog who thinks about things first before acting.

3. Testing by Lying the Puppy on its Back

This is designed to test the puppy's reaction to being turned on its back. As with the palm-of-the-hand test, it is not something you should do for long, ten seconds at the absolute maximum.

STEP BY STEP — **PERSONALITY TEST 2**

- Lift the puppy up gently and carefully cradle it in your arms.
- Placing a hand on each side of the puppy, lift it up and turn it on its back.
- Five distinct personality types will reveal themselves:

The Defiant One. Some puppies simply will not have it. The moment you turn them over they will immediately right themselves. And they will repeat the process every time you try. This dog is going to grow into a strong character, an alpha-type. It will take strong, firm and clear leadership to keep it on the straight and narrow.

The Resistance Fighter. This one will fight you at first, but will eventually comply and lie on its back, under protest. This again is a dog that may present a few problems, but one who will respond to the right signals.

The Thinker. Some puppies will initially lie down willingly. They will stay there for a couple of seconds then spring back upright. This indicates a dog that has weighed up the situation, come to a decision – that it doesn't like this – and acted upon it. This is a dog that has got a lot of courage and intelligence.

The Cool Customer. Some pups will present no resistance whatso-ever, they will simply go limp and lie there. This is a chilled-out, laid-back individual. With the right guidance this is going to be a relatively trouble-free dog.

The Bundle of Nerves. Some puppies will curl up in a ball almost foetally. This is a sure sign of nervousness in the dog. A dog that reacts this way is going to be prone to anxiety attacks when they hear loud noises or are faced with strange situations. In the worst cases they may develop problems like wetting themselves. By identifying them as nervous dogs, however, you can factor this personality into your life with the dog and act accordingly, hopefully avoiding problems.

Wellbeing

A HEALTHY START: PROTECTING YOUR PUPPY FROM ILLNESS

No matter how safe, clean and happy an environment they live in, our dogs face a whole range of diseases. They range from infestations – like fleas and worms – to life-threatening diseases like hepatitis and distemper. It's important that owners are aware of these threats and that they know how to protect their dogs from them.

The best way to deal with all the threats our dogs face is by prevention, through early worming, vaccinations, regular treatments, good dental care and grooming. And the best way to avoid serious illness is to begin that prevention programme early, during the initial stages of puppyhood.

INTERNAL PARASITES: WORMING

Two main groups of parasites present a threat – those that live on the outside of the dog, such as ringworm, lice, fleas and ticks, and those which live on the inside, the four types of worms. It is the latter that presents the earliest threat to a puppy's health.

Worms: A Guide to the Main Threats

Worms are an unfortunate fact of life. All dogs will have them at some point and most will have them during puppyhood, when they are most vulnerable to them. It can be a serious matter. Worm infestation can cause weight loss, vomiting, diarrhoea and a painfully swollen abdomen. In the extreme cases they may even cause death. So it is important that dogs are treated – or wormed – from an early age.

There are four main types of worms, each of which live in the dog's intestine and feed on undigested food there.

ROUNDWORMS

Roundworms are the most common in puppies, indeed almost every puppy is born with them present. They look a little like a rubber band

HEALTH +

and can be several inches long. They are spread through the environment and other dogs' faeces. (Yet another reason for owners to practise good hygiene by carrying a poop-scoop or plastic bag to clean up when out and about.) Roundworms mainly infest the small intestine, but they can also affect the large intestine, blood vessels and respiratory tract.

The worms are a real threat to puppies because they can penetrate the wall of the gut and pass via the bloodstream into organs like the liver and lungs. This in turn can lead to pneumonia, hepatitis and fits.

Owners should also be aware that roundworm can infect humans, particularly children, who are most vulnerable.

TAPEWORMS

There are several types of tapeworm that can afflict dogs. The most common lives in the dog's small intestine where it attaches its head to the lining. As it grows new sections are added so that by the time it is visible to the human eye it resembles a string of white grains of rice joined together. They are much rarer in puppies, turning up more commonly in adult dogs and spread by fleas, which act as a host to the larvae in their early development. The most obvious sign of tapeworm infestation is a tickling of the anus region which makes the dog drag or 'scoot' its bottom along the floor. The worms will be easily detectable either in the dog's faeces or protruding from its anus.

HOOKWORMS

Less common than roundworms, these parasites feed on the dog's blood and can cause anaemia. As their name suggests, they hook themselves onto the intestine with six sharp teeth. Hookworms are transmitted via larvae that hatch on moist ground from eggs passed in a dog's faeces. These larvae then infect dogs in one of three ways. They can pick it up directly by ingesting the larvae accidentally from soil or grass. This can then be passed on to puppies through their mother's milk or placenta. Finally, hookworms can infest muscles in other animals and can transfer to dogs this way. Up to a centimetre (half an inch) in length, hookworms can be seen by the naked eye. They can also be detected in the form of hookworm eggs in the dog's faeces.

WHIPWORMS

These thread-like parasites are around five to seven centimetres long and live in the colon and small intestine. They are transmitted via eggs that have infested a dog's faeces and can only be passed on to dogs that ingest them directly. These too are bloodsuckers and, if present in large numbers in a dog, can cause bloody diarrhoea and lead to significant weight loss. In general, however, whipworms do not produce many eggs, which makes them one of the trickier forms of worms to detect, even by a vet.

Other Types of Worms

While most worms live in the intestine, there are a variety of parasites that develop in other organs. The main ones are:

HEARTWORMS

This worm is spread by the mosquito and – as its name suggests – grows in the heart and the pulmonary arteries. It is not that common in the UK, but is a problem in warmer climates, particularly in Australia.

LUNGWORMS

There are two different types of this parasite, one of which is spread when dogs eat earthworms, the other passed on via the mother's saliva. Dogs in North America are also prone to a lung fluke, passed on by eating contaminated crayfish.

KIDNEY WORMS

This worm can grow to a considerable size and may require the removal of the kidney.

When to Worm

Worms can be passed from the mother either before birth or through her milk, so it's crucial you start early, ideally when the puppy is two to three weeks old. After that a dog should be wormed at least three times a year, throughout its life.

HEALTH

How to Worm

The good news is that all worms are relatively easy to eliminate. And thanks to the wide range of modern treatments available at vets' surgeries, owners have a large range of options available. Deworming medicines now come in tablets, granules or liquids, each of which allows the owner to be exact in the dosages they give. The liquid medicines have the advantage of being administrable via a syringe, which can be used to release the medicine into the dog's mouth.

EYE TESTING

Eye defects are common and can occur at different stages of a dog's life. The first formal eye examination should occur at six to seven weeks of age, before the dog leaves the litter. This will look for both congenital and inherited diseases. Problems such as inherited retinal degeneration can occur at around a year, so annual tests are advised from then on. The most common defects are:

Problems of the Eyelid and Eyelash

ENTROPION

Perhaps the most common eyelid abnormality, entropion is an inward rotation of the eyelid so that hair rubs against the surface of the eye. It can cause tremendous irritation and even ulceration. Ultimately it may lead to blindness. It usually becomes evident during the first six weeks of life, but it can develop later as well.

ECTROPION

Here the eyelid turns to expose the mucous membranes and cause inflammation. The cornea may dry out as a result of the poor blinking mechanism. This can lead to severe pain and, if left untreated, blindness.

TRICHIASIS

In this condition the eyelashes grow in the wrong direction, and rub directly against the eyes. This causes pain and can cause severe ulcer problems.

DISTICHIASIS

In this condition extra unwanted hairs grow on the edge of the eyelid and rub against the eye. Irritation and even ulceration can result.

CHERRY EYE

Every dog has a third eyelid, otherwise known as the nictitating membrane. It acts a bit like a windscreen wiper, cleaning and lubricating the eye. In some breeds, like the St Bernard and Bloodhound, it appears naturally, but in other breeds it can be abnormal, with the cartilage being deformed or the rear gland being prolapsed. The telltale sign of these problems is a red lump appearing in the inner corner of the eye. When the gland is prolapsed the lump looks like a cherry, hence 'cherry eye'.

CONJUNCTIVITIS

As with humans, this is an uncomfortable condition that arises due to the conjunctiva becoming inflamed. It can be caused by a variety of factors – from dust and smoke to a scratch or an infection. The most obvious signs of conjunctivitis are redness and discharge, with signs of the dog screwing up its eyes.

KERATOCONJUNCTIVITIS SICCA (KCS) OR 'DRY EYE'

'Dry Eye' is a condition caused by the dog failing to produce the normal amount of tears. Tears clean and lubricate the surface of the eye, the cornea, and play an important role in controlling infection. A lack of them can lead to chronic irritation of the cornea and conjunctiva. Corneal ulcers and even blindness can result.

Dry eye can be caused by viral infections and inflammations, but most of it is inherited. Breeds prone to it include the West Highland Terrier, the Cocker Spaniel and the poppy-eyed breeds. Standard treatment for dry eye is to lubricate the eye regularly, to use stimulants that will produce tears and drugs to control damage to the tear glands.

CATARACTS

Cataracts affect the lens inside the eye, causing it to lose the transparency and become opaque in the afflicted area. The severity of the problem will depend on how much of the lens is affected. A small, non-progressive

HEALTH

cataract will not impair the dog's vision too much. A complete cataract, on the other hand, will make the dog blind in the affected eye.

Again, this is an inherited problem, although non-hereditary cataracts can develop as a result of other diseases as well as trauma. Cataracts can occur in puppies if their mother has been ill or poorly fed during pregnancy. They might also develop as a result of other eye disorders, such as Progressive Retinal Atrophy (PRA) inflammation and glaucoma.

GLAUCOMA

To function properly the eye needs a constant supply of internal fluid. If, however, the eye's drainage outlets become blocked there can be a build-up of this fluid. This leads to an increase in internal pressure and the wall of the eye stretches. Telltale signs of glaucoma are redness, cloudiness, excessive tearing, eyeball swelling, pain and sensitivity to light. Glaucoma can be treated by reducing the amount of fluid produced, improving the drainage, or laser surgery, but the results are usually poor. This is a very serious and problematic disease.

PRA

The dog's retina, like that of the human eye, is the light-sensitive layer at the back of the eye that transforms light into nerve impulses which are then transmitted along the optic nerve to the brain. The most serious disease affecting the retina is Progressive Retinal Atrophy (PRA). In this disease the light-sensitive cells die. An inherited and untreatable problem, it can often be hard to detect in its early stages because it develops gradually. The first sign you may have as an owner is towards the end of the disease's development when the dog loses its vision at night or, worse, becomes totally blind. Needless to say, owners of affected dogs should not breed from such animals. Fortunately, DNA-based tests are being developed to identify those affected before the disease manifests itself, as well as those dogs that carry the genes.

CEA

Some diseases are usually specific to breeds. Such a disease is Collie Eye Anomaly, or CEA, which is almost exclusively confined to Collies and Shetland Sheepdogs. The defect involves the wall of the eye at the back and can lead to haemorrhaging or the retina detaching itself, both of which cause blindness. A degree of CEA is present in a disturbingly large number of Collies, although only one in 20 or so affected lose their sight. Again, breeding from the dogs who are known to have CEA is to be discouraged in the strongest terms, and there are screening schemes in place in an attempt to breed it out of the Collie population. Recently a DNA-based test became available.

RETINAL DYSPLASIA

This is another disease in which the most severe development is retinal detachment and resultant blindness. Most of the affected dogs have no problem with their sight, but sadly breeding from them can result in severely affected puppies.

Eye Tests: Why Take Them?

Some of the most serious eye diseases are those that are inherited, not just because they can afflict a dog early in its life but because an unscrupulous or unthinking owner can spread them still further by breeding. As with other inherited conditions, like hip dysplasia, the responsible authorities – in the case of the UK the Kennel Club and the British Veterinary Association – have introduced eye tests that will identify whether or not a dog is either affected or a carrier of an eye disease. By getting owners to register the results of these tests they hope to reduce or even eradicate the problem. Responsible owners will not breed from dogs liable to pass on any of these diseases.

WHEN AND WHERE TO DO IT?

The first test should be carried out at six to seven weeks of age, and then repeated once a year for the rest of the dog's life. Your vet should have a list of the 30 or so BVA panellists throughout the country who do the work. Once you have made an appointment you will need to take the dog's registration documents with you and you will be issued with the Certificate of Eye Testing immediately following the test.

WHAT IS THE TEST?

Drops are put into the dog's eyes to make the pupils large enough for the examiner to see all the structures within. The dog will be checked for all

HEALTH

inherited and acquired abnormalities within the eyeball and the associated structures, including the eyelids. The dog will then be classified in one of two categories: *clear*, which is self explanatory and *affected*, indicating an eye disorder is present.

The results provide responsible owners and breeders with very simple advice for the future. Dogs that are affected should not be bred from. Only dogs tested as clear should be viewed as potential breeding animals.

Teeth

DENTAL DEVELOPMENT

A dog's dental development is geared to its ancient role as a predator. Like its wolf ancestor, a puppy will first have a set of deciduous or baby teeth that will allow it to educate itself in the ways of the pack. By the age of seven months or so these baby teeth will have been replaced by a full complement of adult teeth. In the wild these teeth arrive in time for the young wolf's first ventures out with the pack and its role as an apprentice hunter.

Typically, the development process will go as follows:

3–4 weeks: The first deciduous or baby teeth arrive, in readiness for the puppy to start interacting and playing with its siblings.

6 weeks: By the end of the sixth week all the deciduous teeth are in place. Normally a puppy has 28 of these baby teeth.

3–5 months: As the dog passes through the next phases of development, the baby teeth are replaced by the permanent incisors, canines (or cuspids) and finally the molars.

5–6 months: The permanent canines break through.

7 months: By the end of the seventh month the last molar in the lower jaw is in place. A properly developed dog should now have 42 teeth, 12 incisors, 4 canines (or cuspids), 16 premolars and 10 molars.

BRUSHING THE PUPPY'S TEETH

The key to good healthy teeth and gums is regular brushing. Chewing on bones and crunchy foods will help do the job, but there is no alternative to using a toothbrush as the ultimate protection.

This, obviously, is something the dog isn't going to be able to do itself, so you are going to have to do this on its behalf. This is another opportunity to build on the bond of trust between dog and owner and should be taken slowly and carefully at first. The key things to remember are:

- Start slowly, using a child's toothbrush and a little specially formulated dog toothpaste.
- At first brush the puppy's teeth only for a few seconds at a time, building this up over a period of days and weeks.

FEET

CLAW CLIPPING

In the wild puppies keep their extremely sharp claws blunt by scratching in the soil. It is nature's way of protecting them – and their mother, who can easily be scratched and cut by the sharp nails. The domestic dog lives in artificial surroundings so this doesn't happen. To avoid puppies digging into their mothers and hurting them, their claws need to be clipped regularly, from the age of three weeks onwards.

Sharp instruments: regular claw clipping should begin early – around three weeks – to avoid the nails becoming sharp and hurting the puppy's mother during feeding.

STEP BY STEP   CLAW CLIPPING

- Place the puppy on a raised surface, and with one arm restraining it around the midriff take each paw in turn.
- Every claw has a vein or 'quick' that will bleed profusely if you cut it so great care must be taken to avoid doing this. When pups are small there is a clear whiteness to the tip of the nail. Using a pair of nail scissors or clippers take a little bit of this off at a time until you see the vein coming through.
- If you allow the claw to grow then the quick will grow longer as well. Regular clipping during grooming will allow you to keep the quick back.
- If your puppy has darker claws it is more difficult to spot the vein. In this case it is advisable to use a nail file to make the end of the claw blunt. Equally, periods of running around on concrete can also help dull the sharpness of the claw.
- Keep a little antiseptic or bandage at hand in case of accidents.

HEALTH +

THE SECOND AGE

pioneer

8–12 WEEKS

*'Then, the whiling schoolboy with his satchel
And shining morning face, creeping like a snail
Unwillingly to school'*

IN THE WILD

By the time it is eight weeks or so old, a wolf pup will be ready to venture a little further afield. It will begin to chase insects, birds or other creatures that gather around the pack. The play rituals it undergoes with its siblings and other members of the pack will intensify. The young wolf will develop its abilities to run and jump, wrestle and bite, skills that it will come to need when it joins the hunters.

Any ideas a young wolf might have of heading off on the hunt will be quickly dispelled, however. At this stage to leave the den would leave it open to attack by predators. So the senior wolves will give them a signal, delivered in clear, unequivocal terms: 'Stay at home, you're not ready to join us yet.' They will also choose one senior wolf to remain with the pups. Once again, the hierarchy of the pack – and the young wolf's place within that structure – is driven home.

Explorer: a wolf pup gets to know the world around it.

THE SECOND AGE: OVERVIEW

The third month is an intense period of growth for a dog. By the time it reaches the end of its twelfth week, the dog will have developed from the equivalent of a two-and-a-half-year-old child to a four-year-old. And like a four-year-old human, its needs are simple. First and foremost it wants to know it is secure and safe. The dog will harbour many fears at this stage so it needs to feel that it is going to be protected from the sometimes bewildering influences at work in the outside world. For many pups this need is especially great because this is the moment at which they leave the litter and join their new homes and human families.

As it explores the world around it further, the dog's other key need is to understand how this exciting new environment works. It needs to know where the boundaries lie, what is and isn't acceptable behaviour. If it has left its mother's side, it also needs to establish a relationship with a new parent or protector figure in the human world.

It is up to the owner to fulfil these two crucial roles. As it turns out, they complement each other perfectly. By correctly performing one, the owner is automatically performing the other.

Feeling at home in the human world – the young dog's needs

The dog's nature has been defined by its first eight weeks within the litter. But, as we know, development is about both nature and nurture. That nurturing has, of course, begun in the litter. But as the dog now moves into the human world it gets underway in earnest.

So what does a dog need so that it can be nurtured into a happy, well-adjusted adult? And what questions is it asking, especially if – as will be the case for the vast majority of eight-week-old dogs – it is now arriving in a new human home.

Practically speaking, the answer is three things. It needs a place where it can sleep, eat, play and defecate. It then needs a human owner who is going to feed, exercise and show it the way things work within their world. Beyond that, however, the puppy's first priority is to satisfy itself that it is safe; that there is nothing about which it needs to feel afraid. So, as it gets used to its new environment it is looking for comfort and peace.

Once it has satisfied itself of this, the dog will also start looking to explore the boundaries of this new world and understand its place within it, where it can and can't go in safety. At this point, that world consists of its immediate home, from where it will not stray until it has had its vaccinations and grown a little more.

In the absence of its mother the dog is also looking for the figure that is going to provide the protection she gave within the litter. So the puppy is asking itself a series of key questions. How far can I go physically and behaviourally without endangering myself? Who rules the roost in this new, extended pack? And where do I stand in the hierarchy of this pack? In the new home the dog is looking for the structure that will make it feel safe again. At first it has no clue where it is going to discover that structure, so it must explore and investigate to find out. In doing so, of course, it will make mistakes.

It is here that the puppy's breeder will help – or hinder – the process. A well-adjusted dog should adapt to its new surroundings relatively easily. It should be familiar with the smells, sounds and sights of the human environment. If it hasn't been raised well, however – if, say, it has been confined to a shed for the first eight weeks of its life – then it is going to find the experience overwhelming. The first time it hears a phone ring or a vacuum cleaner switched on, for instance, it might be thrown into a panic. It might have been fed poorly and behave badly at mealtimes. Its toilet manners may leave something to be desired. Hopefully, however, you have chosen well and the foundations of good behaviour have been laid.

A safe haven – what the dog is looking for in its new den

A dog has no concept of whether it is living in a mud hut or a country mansion. And, even if it did know the difference between the two, it wouldn't matter. What a dog regards as important bears no relation to what humans see as a priority. For the dog, the priorities are these:

THE FIRST 48 HOURS

Leaving its mother and siblings is a traumatic experience for an eight-week-old dog. It is stepping into a world populated by another species, where everyone is speaking an unintelligible language and behaving according to a set of rules about which the dog has no concept. On top of this the place is filled with a host of unfamiliar sights, sounds and smells. It's not hard to see that this would panic any creature. So the most important thing a new owner can do during the first 48 hours or so is to make this as trauma-free as possible. Some dogs settle into a new home immediately. They are running around like a rocket within seconds of coming in through the door. Others, however, do take longer, so you must be prepared for anything.

The settling-in process can begin the moment the dog arrives in the house. Owners should immediately take it outside to do its toileting. When the dog relieves itself as they have asked it to do, they should reward it with a tidbit. This should be accompanied with warm words of encouragement, such as 'good dog', or 'clean dog', and perhaps a stroke of the head or nape of the neck area. The key point here is that the first piece of positive association has been achieved within the first few moments in the home. A good start has been made.

The next stage is to allow the dog to get to know its new environment. Let it explore those areas it is free to roam in. Throughout this, the owner should be giving out gently affectionate signs, smiles and words of reassurance and kindness. At the same time, however, they should not be gushing or over-affectionate with the dog. This will only set a precedent that will be hard to overcome later.

The first night is going to be particularly difficult for the dog. A dark house, with all its odd bumps and creaks, is going to be a really unsettling place. For this reason it is a good idea to let the dog sleep close to you on its first night. Some people go to the extreme of actually having the dog in bed with them. This isn't going to suit everyone, so placing a basket with a warm, soft blanket somewhere near the bed where the dog can smell, hear and see you is the best alternative. If, on the other hand, you don't want your dog in your bedroom, then a night downstairs on the sofa with the puppy close by is another option.

However, this should only happen once – or possibly twice. You cannot let the dog grow used to this.

A SPACE OF ITS OWN

No place like home: a dog needs to feel safe, comfortable and happy in its new environment.

It is important that the dog has its own space, a refuge to which it can retreat when necessary. It doesn't need to be a huge area – as a rule of thumb the dog should be able to lie down on its side with about two inches to spare on either side. There should be a similar amount of space available when it stretches out to full length. What is important is that it is warm, well-insulated and relatively quiet.

There are a variety of options:

- **Cages.** These suit a lot of dogs. They seem to respond well to the enclosed space. They have the advantage of being transportable and can fit into the back of a car easily. They also come in handy if it ever becomes necessary to discipline the dog. If you need to banish the dog for its bad behaviour, the cage can serve as the equivalent of a child's bedroom.
- **Kennels.** A kennel with a run is a great option for owners with the available space. This has the added advantage of giving the dog a natural outdoor area where it can exercise itself independently.
- **Baskets.** There are a wide range of baskets available, ranging from the simple plastic variety to expensive hand-woven 'designer' baskets. The key is not whether the basket looks good to humans, however. It is far more important that the sleeping area it provides is spacious and comfortable enough.
- **Home-made dens.** A dog doesn't need an expensive basket, cage or kennel. A cardboard box, turned on its side and lined with something soft and soothing will do the trick provided it creates a safe, secure space for the dog. A useful tip for making this – or indeed any – dog home comfortable for the dog is to put an item of old clothing worn by a member of the family inside the sleeping area. This will not only keep the dog warm but replicates the aromas of its human companions, to add to its sense of safety and security.

MAKING THE HOME SAFE AND SECURE

If there is a garden, this is clearly going to be an important area for the dog. It is here that it will toilet, do much of its playing and – in time – learn some of the controls it will need before venturing out into the world on walks. As with the home, however, it is important to be certain that the area is secure. Make sure there are no gaps in the gates or walls that a young dog could squeeze through. You can be sure its curiosity will get the better of it. Equally, as with children's gates, try to ensure there are no spaces in the garden gates or fences – or indeed anywhere else – that a dog could get its head stuck. Given that it will be putting that head into every conceivable nook and cranny of the home during its acclimatisation, you can be fairly certain the worst will happen, so it is best to anticipate it.

A PLACE TO PLAY

Nothing will help settle the dog's nerves better than play, so it is important that a young dog has access to a good supply of toys during these early days. Some of these will be permanently available to it; others will remain in the toybox where you, as leader, will exercise control over their appearance and removal.

This doesn't necessarily entail any great expense for the owner. An eight-week-old dog with its immature, malleable teeth will enjoy gnawing away at anything. An old tea-towel or blanket soaked in water with a knot tied in it is one of the most popular playthings in my experience.

'NO GO' ZONES

Inevitably there will be areas of the home where the dog will not be welcome. Bathrooms and toilets, studies and dining rooms, typically, are places humans regard as off-limits to their dogs. The key thing is to decide on where these areas are early on. Every member of the family should then be made aware of what these 'no go' zones are so that everyone can enforce the rules. The best way to ensure a dog doesn't stray into such areas is obviously to keep the doors closed. But if it does find its way into one of these rooms, remove it quietly and quickly with as little fuss as possible.

There are those who advocate that a dog should not be allowed to climb onto your furniture. There is, however, nothing wrong with this. The only point to remember is that the dog must be invited to join you on a chair or sofa. It shouldn't make the decision independently. If it does jump up without your invitation it should be removed, again quietly without any fuss. You can then invite it up. This is another important step towards establishing the first principles of leadership.

It is entirely likely at this stage, of course, that the dog will want to follow you everywhere. And as it settles into the new home, particularly during the first 48 hours or so, it is important it has access to you. For this reason, children's gates are useful devices within the home. They can divide areas like the kitchen and the hallway. It works well both for dog and owner. It allows the owner to keep an eye on the dog at all times, and it gives the dog the comfort of being able to see its new guardian too.

The only word of warning is to watch out for the gaps in the gates. If the bars are wide enough apart for a dog to get its head stuck you can be certain it will do precisely that.

A PLACE TO TOILET

A dog that is happy and confident in its toileting is a dog that is on the way to leading a well-adjusted life. A dog that isn't is heading for trouble.

By this stage the dog may be toilet trained. If it is, it should have a specified spot, preferably outdoors in a place where whatever is deposited can be absorbed naturally into the earth. The key things to remember about allocating this spot are:

- Make it as accessible to the dog as possible. If it is outdoors and the dog needs to be let out, be alert to its toilet habits. Always open the door to let the dog out first thing in the morning, for instance.
- Choose somewhere as far away as possible from the dog's sleeping area. A dog is no different to a human in this respect. Who would like to sleep next to their toilet bowl?
- If it is indoors, make sure the toilet area is cleaned regularly.

If a dog arrives in a new home not toilet trained, this should be tackled immediately. The second you get it home take it outside straightaway to the area you have chosen. Stay with the dog while it does its toileting then praise it with the word you want to use: for example 'empty' or 'clean dog'. As with everything else during this phase, the key thing is to be patient, and never make a drama out of a crisis. If the dog has an accident, simply scoop up after it and say nothing. If, on the other hand, it succeeds in doing its toileting outdoors where you want it, be fulsome in your praise and reward it.

Teach the dog to go first thing in the morning. Don't make a big fuss, simply open the door to the garden or wherever the toilet area has been set up and let the puppy do its business. Then reward them when they have done the necessary.

This should be repeated after each meal. Again, the dog should be encouraged to go outside and rewarded when it does what it should do.

As we have already seen, the stress of moving home may cause stomach upsets and diarrhoea. Puppies can dehydrate and deteriorate very quickly, so if this persists for more than 24 hours or becomes severe you should consult your vet immediately.

DIET

Moving home is a stressful experience, so anything that provides continuity for the young dog is to be welcomed. Food, of course, is the ultimate comfort, so it is important that owners try to keep the dog's diet the same as it was at its previous home, at least until the dog has settled a little.

A reputable breeder should be able to provide a written diet sheet, with details of the type of food the puppy has been used to as well as quantities and feeding times.

Even if you don't like the diet, it is advisable to keep the dog on it for a few days. Young dogs arriving in a new home often show signs of stomach upsets and diarrhoea brought on by the trauma of being separated from their mother and entering a strange environment. Radical changes in diets will only exacerbate this.

If and when you do decide to change the diet, do so when the dog is comfortable in the home. Even then it should be done at a gentle pace. Introduce the changes over a period of three to four days if possible.

CANINE COMPANIONSHIP

Dogs share the human's sense of family values. In general they enjoy company, whether human or canine, in the home. This sociable nature may be rooted in their ancient past, when they were forming the first communities with our ancient ancestors. But it may go deeper than that. Why else would man have chosen the wolf above any other creature to domesticate first? Did they see them as more companionable than any other animal? It is food for thought.

Whatever the explanation for it, this is another factor that should be taken into account when a young dog arrives in the home for the first time. The fact that there is already canine company in the home may help it settle in that much more quickly. Having said this, however, the introduction of a new dog is something that has to be planned with care. Introducing an eight-week-old dog to an existing pack is – in relative terms – a straightforward process. But owners must always bear in mind

*The best of friends: **properly introduced to each other, dogs can provide each other with great companionship.***

that placing a nine-month-old puppy in a home is the equivalent of introducing a hyperactive twelve-year-old to the canine community within the household. Older dogs in particular may not take kindly to their peace and quiet being disturbed.

There are other factors to consider too – mixing breeds, for instance. While a Toy Poodle and an Irish Wolfhound will get along together eventually, because of the huge differences in their physical makeup and consequently their ability to signal to each other, there may be a great deal of friction before they settle into a companionable routine.

For all these reasons it is advisable to introduce the new dog to its prospective pack as soon as possible. The ideal option is to take the existing dogs to the breeder from where the eight-week-old dog is coming. This has several obvious advantages. In territorial terms it is a neutral ground. The new arrival will also be among people who know and can control it in the event of problems. Most importantly of all, if after a few meetings there is clearly a high degree of friction between the old and new dogs, the potential owner will have the chance to think again.

However, if this is not possible, owners should make plans for segregating the dogs during the first few days. Young dogs are, in general, quick to assimilate themselves into environments. In most instances an eight-week-old dog can settle into a new home within 48 hours. Yet there is always potential for confrontations so owners should err on the side of caution. Give both the newcomer and the existing dog or dogs their own distinct space during the early days. Be careful too during mealtimes, when clashes could happen.

The dog's senses – and how to use them to your advantage

By now the dog's senses will be highly developed, and it will be drawing on each of them to help it assimilate to the new world it is exploring. Owners can use this to their advantage to provide the dog with the sense of security it craves.

Typically, humans assume every other species sees and senses the world in the same way as they do. They don't. One of the key differences between dogs and humans is that, unlike us, dogs are led by their senses in a different order. While we tend to use sight first, then sound and finally smell, dogs use their senses in the reverse order. Smell is overwhelmingly the most important sense for them. Then comes sound, then, finally, sight. This is hugely influential in shaping the dog's world.

SMELL

A dog's sense of smell is 100 times stronger than ours. The area of the brain devoted to smell is 14 times as big. It means that, in the wild, a pack can smell its prey from half a mile away. It is little wonder that we humans have harnessed this incredible ability to help us detect everything from drugs and explosives to cancers.

Smell is also the first sense they acquire, so it is no surprise that an eight-week-old puppy is going to be interested in investigating and exploring every smell it encounters in its new world. It will stick its nose everywhere, which is why owners acquiring dogs at this age should be ready and ensure the new environment doesn't have any overwhelming smells. A house that smells powerfully – whether it is of cooking, cleaning fluids, smoke or even flowers – can throw a dog into a real panic. While handling the dog too, it is a good idea to avoid using lots of perfume or aftershave.

Apart from the garden, where there will be familiar smells, the dog may not encounter any smells that are recognisable during its crucial first forty-eight hours or so in the new environment. So, again, owners can help overcome this by bringing familiar items from the kennel where it has been with its litter. A piece of bedding or cloth from the den can act in the same way a security blanket works for a child. It can help make the transition from the old home to the new one a considerably less stressful experience for the puppy.

Similarly, if there are other dogs in the house, you can help prepare the puppy for its meeting with these dogs by bringing items of theirs in the car with you. Again, it will make a good association with that smell in advance.

SOUND

After smell, the most important sense is hearing. Dogs also have a far more acute sense of hearing than we humans do. A dog can hear the howl of an adult up to five miles away. They can hear insects inches underground. So it is little wonder they are so agitated by sound. Equally, it is no wonder dogs see silence as golden: they like a quiet life because that is a life devoid of any strange or threatening noises. Again, this is something that can and should be used to the owner's advantage.

Noise Training – Overcoming the Pioneer's Fear of Noises

Arriving in a new home is a massive culture shock for an eight-week-old dog. The house, if you think about it, is a minefield of strange, inexplicable objects capable of making a range of strange, inexplicable noises. You must do all you can to help the puppy acclimatise to those noises, and you are not going to achieve that by explaining what each object is to the dog, because it will not understand. What it will understand, however, is that if *you* do not fear that object then, provided the puppy trusts you as its new guardian and protector, they have no reason to be afraid of it either.

STEP BY STEP   NOISE TRAINING

- When you are about to vacuum the house, place the dog in the kitchen area behind a baby gate, preferably with another human that it knows and trusts.
- Begin cleaning in the farthest room from the kitchen.
- If the dog reacts to the sound of the vacuum, the person in the kitchen should encourage the dog to come to them and should then hold it. He or she should not be making a huge show of affection here, there should be no stroking or talking to the dog. It should just be held in a reassuring way, very calmly, so as to show there is nothing to fear.
- When the first room is complete switch the vacuum off.
- Then repeat the process by switching it back on again. If the dog reacts, be reassuring once more.
- Carry on in this way until the vacuum is in the same room as the dog.

If a dog has displayed nervousness on first encountering a particular noise or object, for example a vacuum cleaner, then that fear should be tackled head-on. For this work, a baby gate can be a hugely useful asset. It will enable you to keep the dog in a particular area, but at the same time it will allow you to make sure the dog never loses sight of you.

This is not a process that will necessarily work immediately, so you should not rush it. Repetition will get the message across. Usually within a week to ten days the dog's fear should have lifted.

Breeds apart – *what different dogs demand from their owners*

Hundreds of years of selective breeding by humans has produced a bewildering array of different dogs. And, for all their essential similarities, these dogs do bring with them their own set of special needs. Some will need more exercise than others. Some will need much more grooming. Others will have a significantly shorter lifespan and will, therefore, incur the inevitable medical costs associated with old age that much sooner. Size is a factor too. The giant breeds need space in which to move and grow. Anyone considering acquiring a dog should take these into consideration. The demands of the different breeds fall into the following broad categories:

PHYSICAL DEMANDS

Some dogs have been bred to be more athletic and energetic than others. Gundogs or sporting dogs, for instance, will tend to demand high amounts of exercise. These Springers, Pointers and Setters were, after all, bred for the hunt and are able to work and run for long periods during a normal hunting day. They also tend to love water and may retrieve or chase birds, again because of generations of breeding. Similarly, pastoral or herding breeds tend to be attracted to other species of animal and may instinctively try to herd them. Not every owner is going to have a flock of sheep for their Collie or German Shepherd to round up, but they should be prepared to give these dogs a proper outlet for their considerable energies. They need homes that are going to be up to this challenge, and are able to give them plenty of exercise and play time.

At the other end of the scale, the toy-dog group includes many breeds that were designed to provide little more than companionship and warmth, sometimes literally. Toy breeds like the Chihuahua, Pekingese, Pomeranian and Maltese don't need huge amounts of exercise.

SPATIAL DEMANDS

Size is a factor that also needs to be taken into consideration. While toy dogs will not use up much space, large working dogs, for instance, will fill up almost any space they occupy. If they are active dogs as well, this could cause owners problems in a small or restrictive area. Some dogs also enjoy the country life more than others. Everyone, of course, has the right to own the breed of their choice, but allowances should be made for this.

GROOMING DEMANDS

Dogs are naturally clean animals and take a great deal of care about their condition. As a result, some breeds require next to no grooming. Smooth-coated dogs like the Labrador Retriever or the Great Dane, for instance, are low-maintenance compared to other breeds. By contrast, there are some breeds that have been moulded purely for their look and consequently have exceedingly long, high-maintenance coats. Breeds that spring to mind here include Afghan Hounds, Spaniels, Old English Sheepdogs, the Bichon Frise and types of Poodle. Dogs in the terrier group can also require 'hand stripping' to keep their coats looking good.

DIFFERENT BREEDS – DIFFERENT DEMANDS
The different requirements of the most popular breeds

TYPE OF DOG	SIZE	GROOMING	EXERCISE	LIFESPAN
GUNDOGS/SPORTING				
English Setter	L	M	C	B
German Longhaired Pointer	L	M	C	B
German Shorthaired Pointer	L	L	C	B
German Wirehaired Pointer	L	M	C	B
Gordon Setter	L	M	C	B
Hungarian Vizsla	L	L	C	B
Irish Red & White Setter	L	M	C	B
Irish Setter	L	M	C	B
Pointer	L	L	C	B
Retriever (Chesapeake Bay)	L	M	C	B
Retriever (Curly Coated)	L	M	C	B
Retriever (Flat Coated)	L	M	C	B
Retriever (Golden)	L	M	C	B
Retriever (Labrador)	L	L	C	B
Spaniel (American Cocker)	M	C	M	B
Spaniel (Cocker)	M	C	M	B
Spaniel (English Springer)	M	M	C	B
Spaniel (Field)	M	M	C	B
Spaniel (Irish Water)	M	M	C	B
Spaniel (Sussex)	M	M	C	B
Spaniel (Welsh Springer)	M	M	C	B
Spanish Water Dog	M	M	M	B
Weimaraner	L	L	C	B

TYPE OF DOG	SIZE	GROOMING	EXERCISE	LIFESPAN
WORKING				
Alaskan Malamute	L	C	C	B
Bernese Mountain Dog	X	M	M	A
Bouvier Des Flandres	L	C	C	B
Boxer	L	L	C	B
Bullmastiff	L	L	C	B
Canadian Eskimo Dog	L	M	C	B
Doberman	L	L	C	B
German Pinscher	M	L	M	B
Giant Schnauzer	L	C	C	B
Great Dane	X	L	C	A
Mastiff	X	L	M	A
Newfoundland	X	C	C	B
Rottweiler	L	L	C	B
St Bernard	X	C	M	A
Siberian Husky	L	M	C	B
TERRIER				
Airedale	L	C	M	B
Australian	S	M	M	B
Bedlington	M	M	M	B
Border	S	M	M	B
Bull	M	L	M	B
Bull (Miniature)	M	L	M	B
Cairn	S	M	M	B
Fox (Smooth)	M	L	M	B
Fox (Wire)	M	C	M	B
Irish	M	M	M	B

These tables illustrate the different demands of dogs within each of the seven main groups.

TYPE OF DOG	SIZE	GROOMING	EXERCISE	LIFESPAN
Kerry Blue	M	C	M	B
Lakeland	M	C	M	B
Norfolk	S	M	M	B
Parson Russell	M	L	M	B
Scottish	M	C	M	B
Skye	M	M	M	B
Staffordshire Bull	M	L	C	B
Welsh	M	C	M	B
West Highland White	S	C	M	B
HOUNDS				
Afghan	L	C	C	B
Basenji	M	L	M	B
Basset Hound	M	L	C	B
Beagle	M	L	C	B
Bloodhound	L	L	C	A
Borzoi	L	M	C	B
Dachshund (Long or Wire Haired)	M	M	M	B
Dachshund (Miniature Long or Wire Haired)	S	M	M	C
Dachshund (Smooth Haired)	M	L	M	B
Dachshund (Miniature Smooth Haired)	S	L	M	C
Norwegian Elkhound	L	M	C	B
Foxhound	L	L	C	B
Greyhound	L	L	M	B
Irish Wolfhound	X	M	C	A
Pharaoh Hound	L	L	C	B
Rhodesian Ridgeback	L	L	C	B
Saluki	L	M	C	B

TYPE OF DOG	SIZE	GROOMING	EXERCISE	LIFESPAN
Whippet	M	L	C	B
PASTORAL/HERDING				
Anatolian Shepherd	L	M	C	B
Australian Cattle	M	L	M	B
Australian Shepherd	L	M	C	B
Bearded Collie	L	C	M	B
Border Collie	M	M	C	B
Collie (Rough)	L	C	C	B
Collie (Smooth)	L	L	C	B
German Shepherd	L	M	C	B
Old English Sheepdog	L	C	C	B
Pyrenean Mountain Dog	X	C	M	A
Pyrenean Sheepdog	M	M	M	B
Samoyed	L	C	C	B
Shetland Sheepdog	M	C	M	B
Welsh Corgi (Cardigan)	M	L	M	B
Welsh Corgi (Pembroke)	M	L	M	B
TOYS				
Affen Pinscher	S	M	L	B
Australian Silky Terrier	S	M	L	B
Bichon Frise	S	C	L	B
Cavalier King Charles Spaniel	S	M	M	B
Chihuahua (Long Coat)	S	M	L	B
Chihuahua (Smooth Coat)	S	L	L	B
English Toy Terrier (Black and Tan)	S	L	L	B
Maltese	S	C	L	B
Miniature Pinscher	S	L	L	B

KEY

SIZE

S   Small

M   Medium

L   Large

X   Extra large

GROOMING
AND EXERCISE

L   Little needed

M   Moderate needed

C   Considerable needed

LIFESPAN

A   under 9 years
    on average

B   9-15 years
    on average

C   over 15 years
    on average

TYPE OF DOG	SIZE	GROOMING	EXERCISE	LIFESPAN
Papillon	S	M	L	B
Pekingese	S	C	L	B
Pomeranian	S	C	L	B
Pug	S	L	L	B
Yorkshire Terrier	S	C	L	B
UTILITY				
Akita	L	M	C	B
Boston Terrier	S	L	M	B
Bulldog	M	L	M	A
Chow Chow	L	C	M	B
Dalmatian	L	L	C	B
French Bulldog	S	L	M	B
German Spitz (Klein)	S	C	L	B
German Spitz (Mittel)	M	C	L	B
Japanese Shiba Inu	M	M	M	B
Japanese Spitz	M	C	M	B
Lhasa Apso	S	C	L	B
Mexican Hairless	M	L	M	B
Miniature Schnauzer	S	C	M	B
Poodle (Miniature)	M	C	M	C
Poodle (Standard)	L	C	C	C
Poodle (Toy)	S	C	M	C
Schnauzer	M	C	M	B
Shar Pei	M	L	M	B
Shih Tzu	S	C	M	B
Tibetan Spaniel	S	M	M	C
Tibetan Terrier	M	C	M	B

DOGS WITH MEDICAL/LIFESPAN DEMANDS

The average life-expectancy of different breeds varies enormously (see table on pages 273–274). Working breeds tend to be bigger dogs so the majority live shorter lives. Smaller toys, on the other hand, tend to live to more advanced ages.

As a result, those dogs with shorter lifespans are, of necessity, going to make more demands sooner in terms of medical and care needs. Old age tends to be when the owner bears the brunt and visits the vet the most. If the dog isn't going to live much beyond seven years then, inevitably, this period is going to arrive that much sooner. These dogs need owners who are willing to meet this challenge.

Laying down the boundaries – *providing the structure and security a young dog needs*

TRAINING – LAYING THE FOUNDATIONS

As the puppy passes through its second month, it is moving further and further from the first phase of life and its days with its mother and litter. It is beginning to explore the world around it, and starting to interact with humans and maybe other species as well. At this point the puppy will be having a ball. It will be sticking its nose in everywhere, running off with socks, unravelling balls of wool, and generally causing mayhem. It's a fun time for both dog and owner, but there is a thin line between exuberance and over-exuberance. So now is a good time for the dog to learn some self-control – and for its owner to learn the first of their basic controls.

For this to happen, the owner must begin teaching it one of the most important lessons of all – to accept his or her leadership. And to achieve that they need to learn how to communicate with the dog in a language it will understand.

THE ART OF CANINE COMMUNICATION: AN INTRODUCTION

All dogs believe they are part of a social grouping that operates according to the principles of the pack. Even at this early stage, a dog is hard-wired to believe this. So as it moves away from its mother and the litter and begins to interact with the extended pack that is its human family, it needs to find a leader with whom it is comfortable, one it can place its trust in.

In the wild, this information would be provided by means of clear and unambiguous signals from both the alpha pair and the other subordinate pack members. They would leave the young pup in no doubt as to its place in the pecking order. And the alpha pair would make it clear it is they in whom the puppy should place its trust.

As the domestic dog lives in a world designed and run by humans, it is not surprising they can be extremely confused by the pack they find themselves inhabiting. To make matters worse, without realising it, owners are giving out signals that lead their dogs to the wrong conclusions about the hierarchy of their pack. As a result, dogs develop mistaken ideas about their status within the domestic pack, and set themselves up for a whole host of behavioural problems further down the road.

The good news is that there is a simple set of signals that an owner can use to communicate the key messages a dog needs to receive. By learning these signals, owners can not only avoid confusing their dogs, more importantly they can establish themselves as leaders from an early age. And the benefits of this are enormous.

There are four key signals, each of them based on ones used in the wild. To understand them we once more need to understand first how they work in the natural world.

The Four Rituals

In the wild, the alpha pair signal their supremacy in four key areas. A pack is always subtly testing its leaders, asking small questions that require them to show they are still in charge. On a day-to-day basis, the most frequent opportunity the alpha pair get to do this is when the pack reunites after a separation.

The pair have their own personal space, a comfort zone, within which they operate. They effectively say, 'Don't call us, we'll call you.' No other wolf is allowed to encroach on this space unless invited to do so. When the pack assembles, the alpha pair remain in this space until they are ready to receive their junior members. When they are ready – and only when they are ready – subordinates can approach to pay homage.

It is not a point that needs to be made for any great length of time. When they are satisfied the pack has accepted their leadership once more, the alphas will allow the subordinates to approach them. But they will not do so until they are satisfied they are being paid the respect they are due. It is a simple yet hugely powerful way for the alpha pair to re-establish their primacy in the pack, without ever resorting to cruelty, confrontation or violence.

Unsurprisingly, food provides two of the other key methods for underlining their status. The alphas' first opportunity to assert themselves in this way comes during the hunt. This operation requires a combination of organisation, determination, tactics and management skill. It is the alpha's job to provide all these qualities. It is they who search for the hunting grounds and they who lead the chase and direct the 'kill'. It is the job of the subordinates to follow and provide support. Again, any questioning of authority will not be tolerated.

Once the 'kill' has been executed the alphas generally underline their status by getting first refusal on the carrion. Only when they are satisfied and signal their feed is over will the rest of the pack be permitted to eat – and then according to the strict pecking order of the pack, with the senior subordinates feasting first and the juniors last. Back at the camp, the pups and babysitters will be fed by the hunters' regurgitation of their food. Again, this makes perfect sense to the pack. Its survival depends on them remaining in peak physical condition.

The final area in which the alpha pair show their leadership comes during times of perceived danger. Whenever danger threatens it is their role to protect the pack at all costs. The pair does this unblinkingly and with the authority their pack expects of them, reacting in one of three ways: running away, ignoring the threat or defending themselves. (The three Fs: Flight, Freeze or Fight.) Whichever response the alpha pair selects, the pack will again follow their leaders.

The Four Questions an Owner Must Answer

The key to owning a happy and well-adjusted dog is understanding that you – not it – must be the leader. And the key to establishing this early on lies in taking charge of the four key areas through which dogs communicate, and responding to the domestic dog's equivalent of the wolf pack's four rituals. Specifically, the owner must answer the following four questions:

- When the pack reunites after a separation – who is in charge now?
- When the pack faces a perceived danger – who will protect us now?
- When the pack goes on the hunt – who will lead us now?
- When the pack eats – who will eat first?

An owner must ensure that the dog sees him or her as the answer to each of these questions. And they must make sure that the dog reaches these conclusions of their own free will, without any coercion or violence.

Canine Communication – The First Steps

An owner who is able to raise a puppy from birth has a perfect opportunity to introduce the idea that they are the leader slowly, almost subliminally. The initial steps are taken at three weeks during the first interactions, then during weaning and the early grooming sessions. By taking charge of playtime too they underline their status.

Each time this happens, the owner is conveying an important message to his dog: *I am responsible for your welfare, and you can trust me to fulfil that responsibility.* The young dog has already learned the importance of hierarchy and therefore will have elevated the owner to a position above them in the pack.

This leadership will build as the dog grows older. Eventually the dog will be in no doubt that the owner is in charge not just of the four key situations but of the pack to which it belongs. The Pioneer stage offers another opportunity to build up this idea by introducing the first of the basic controls the owner will need in order to keep the dog safe in the wider world.

BASIC CONTROLS – THE COME AND THE SIT

The Come

The life of an eight-week-old dog is remarkably simple. Sleeping, eating and playing dominate its thinking. Owners can capitalise on the latter two of these overriding instincts to introduce the first of the key commands the dog needs to learn – the come. This should be introduced soon after the first 48 hours, when the dog has settled into its new environment.

STEP BY STEP — **THE COME**

- Plan to do this for the first time after the dog has eaten.
- Be prepared with a supply of tidbits, pieces of dried meat or cheese, for example, which you will use as food reward.
- When the dog has finished its meal and begins playing, call it by name.
- When it gives you the telltale 'Are you talking to me?' look, squat or kneel, extend your hand with food reward visible and ask the dog to 'come', doing so in a warm, inviting voice.
- If the dog doesn't move, stretch your hand further to make the food reward more visible – and more recognisable in terms of smell.
- When the dog comes over, reward it and give it quiet praise. Don't be too effusive, just let it know it has done a good job.
- Stroke or ruffle the dog's neck area to underline leadership (touching this vulnerable area is a powerful signal of leadership in the wild).
- If the dog rushes or jumps up, or alternatively rolls over expecting to be tickled, get up and walk away immediately.
- Do the same if the dog does not respond to the invitation after a couple of minutes. Try again a few hours later.
- If the dog fails to come, go away and get on with your day, then try again a few hours later. Remain patient. It will respond eventually, and when it does you will have laid an important foundation stone.

The Sit

The ability to get your dog to sit is going to be a useful tool. You will need it during grooming and when you or your vet is administering medicine, so it is important you introduce this basic control early on. You want the dog to repeat this procedure easily for the rest of its life, but you don't want it to do so because it is frightened or feels somehow threatened. You want it to happen voluntarily, because the dog knows it is a good thing. Dogs are – like humans – essentially selfish creatures. They work on the basis of 'What's in it for me?'. So the only way they will do this of their own free will is if they make a positive association with it from an early stage. Once more, using a food reward is the key to achieving this initially.

STEP BY STEP — THE SIT

- Take a tidbit, show it to the dog then bring it towards and then over its head.
- As you are doing this say the word 'sit' in a kind, warm and unthreatening voice.
- The dog should follow the food with its eyes, and as it does so its natural reflex will be to arch its neck backwards so that its whole body tips back and it ends up sitting down.
- The moment its bottom touches the ground, reward the dog with fulsome praise, stroking it and offering it another piece of food reward.
- Dogs are not mind-readers, so if it does not respond the first time then try again, and again if necessary, remaining calm and patient.

1. 'Sit': to help a dog learn to drop on its bottom, draw a food reward over its head.

2. 'Good dog': when it successfully does what you have asked, reward it with the food so as to create a positive association.

- If, when you pass the food over its head, the dog shuffles backwards rather than tipping over, place it with its back to something solid, such as a door or a wall, so that it can't move backwards.
- If it still refuses to comply, very gently place a hand behind the dog so that you are just touching its bottom, then pass the food over again, using the hand as a stop, just as you would support a baby before it learns to sit on its own.
- When you have successfully got the dog to sit, repeat this process once or twice.
- The three elements – the word sit, the act of tipping over onto its bottom and the food reward – will now be inextricably and positively linked in the dog's mind.

Controlling the Controller

It's worth making the point that you should use the basic controls sparingly at first. You definitely shouldn't ask the dog to sit each time it comes to you. The reasons for this are simple: dogs are highly manipulative creatures and may use the fact they have grasped these principles – as well as your obvious delight at the fact they have done so – to their advantage. It is quite possible your dog may place itself at your feet volunteering to sit on a regular basis at this time. It is crucial you don't respond to this. Remember, one of the key purposes of controls is to underline your status as leader. By allowing the dog to decide when it sits – and gets food reward – you are relinquishing that status. You are letting it control you, the controller. So be careful.

FOOD POWER

Using Food to Instil Discipline

Food is one of the most powerful tools available in terms of signalling. In the wild, every member understands that food is earned. It is not a right. This same message must be inculcated early on in a dog's life. The dog must learn that:

- Food does not just turn up, it has to be earned.
- The person who provides the food is the surrogate protector it is looking for.
- There are certain ways to behave when food is being eaten.

All these points must be reinforced from the outset.

Rules to Remember when Feeding Your Puppy

There are some simple rules when feeding puppies of this age. The four main ones relate to things you definitely should NOT do:

DON'T LET DOGS EAT BETWEEN MEALS

Dogs are opportunistic eaters. If they see a chance to grab a snack they will take it. This, of course, undermines the principle that you are trying to introduce, that you are the sole provider of food, so it can't be allowed. It's important to explain this to other members of the family, and indeed visitors to the house. Simply by slipping your dog a tidbit, a visitor could set your dog's progress back.

DON'T STICK TO SET MEALTIMES

Dogs are also smart, and if you adhere to strict timings on feeding they will quickly work out when to expect a meal. Instead, you should deliberately mix up mealtimes so that they don't anticipate them. This way you will ensure the messages you want to communicate with the dogs – that is, *I am the leader, I choose when we eat* – always come through loud and clear.

DON'T LET THE DOG GET TOO EXCITED

Mealtimes offer an excellent chance to introduce principles of good behaviour, so they must be calm and controlled affairs. Because its sense of smell is so strong, a dog will be drawn to the kitchen or feeding area the minute you start preparing its meal. If it starts leaping around and generally being overexcited, wait. You don't need to speak, just quietly stand with the food on the worktop away from the dog until it calms down. Only then should you continue and serve the meal. When you do so you should walk away, making the point that – as leader – you have decided it is now the dog's turn to eat.

DON'T ALLOW THE DOG TO WALK AWAY FROM ITS FOOD

Your dog must learn that it has no control over mealtimes. So while it is acceptable for it to stand up from its bowl to digest its meal, it is definitely not acceptable for it to walk away. If it does this you MUST remove the bowl immediately. When the dog returns it must not be offered the food again. It needs to learn that mealtime is precisely that – it is not time to go off for a walk or to be distracted by other things. This may seem harsh, but it is a lesson that will be learned very quickly.

Dental workout: chewing-strips provide the young dog's emerging teeth with the exercise they need to grow and remain healthy.

Typical problems

TEETHING TROUBLES: DEALING WITH BITING

There is no more wonderful a sight than an exuberant young dog enjoying itself. Dogs at this age seem to have boundless energy and they use every ounce of it, bouncing around and exploring every nook and cranny of their ever-expanding world. But there is a thin line between exuberance and bad behaviour. And many pioneers will cross that line.

At this age the dog may start to nip or bite people. Or else they may chew at furniture, upholstery or clothing. They, of course, do not know any better. They don't recognise the difference between a dishcloth and an expensive set of curtains: both are potential sources of play. But this is plainly unacceptable behaviour and it must be tackled, otherwise it will escalate into serious misbehaviour when the dog gets older.

You should always bear in mind that the dog is still going through teething. Its milk teeth are slowly being replaced by adult teeth which will also need exercising, so adding some bone to the dog's diet will help enormously. But playtime presents the perfect medium through which to nip these bad habits in the bud.

If the dog is doing something undesirable, whether chewing at a piece of furniture or digging its teeth into a sofa or a pair of curtains, produce the toy box and distract it by throwing a good, chewable toy. You are again making a powerful statement about controlling playtime. Let the dog gnaw away at the toy for long enough to give its teeth a thorough workout. Ten to fifteen minutes should do it. Then, when the dog's interest is waning, reclaim the toy. Make sure not to get into a tugging contest as you do so. If the dog settles down, call it to you and reward it with some food.

If the dog starts chewing at things again, you haven't given it enough time, so reintroduce the chewable toy.

INDEPENDENCE ANXIETY

Being removed from their litter can be a very traumatic experience for an eight-week-old dog. Their every instinct tells them they must stay within the safety of the pack, and – so far, at least – that pack, mother and litter, has been their canine family. So, during its first days and weeks in a new home a pioneer can feel frightened and abandoned. And it can cry a lot. In reality the sound is more like a constant whining, but it is distressing nevertheless. And it must be dealt with decisively and quickly, before the anxiety worsens.

During the first 48 hours you have compensated for the absence of the dog's family by keeping it close to you. But now you have to teach the dog independence. You have to teach it that there will be times in its life when it will be alone. But you must also teach it that it is perfectly safe when that happens.

This can be hard for owners to do, especially if the dog is new to the home. But it is for the dog's own good. The worst possible thing you can do is to treat it as a phase the dog will grow out of. What will happen is the dog will grow into the habit and the result will be serious separation anxiety as it matures.

Teaching a dog independence is something that is done gradually. You must get it used to you being away, at first for short periods, then for longer, more extended times.

The key steps are as follows:

- Engineer a time when you are going to leave the dog for a period by first feeding and toileting it then playing with it for a short time afterwards.
- When you have brought the playtime to a close, leave the room ensuring the dog cannot follow, staying away for ten to thirty minutes. At first remain in the house, using the time to do a household chore, take a bath or mow the lawn.
- Leave a radio on at low level so that the room isn't plunged into complete silence when you go.
- The dog will probably be ready for a sleep.
- When you return, the dog will be overjoyed to see you, but you must not make any fuss or bother. Don't interact with it for five minutes or so, or until the dog has calmed down. Be careful not to make direct eye-contact during this time.
- When that time has elapsed, play with the dog for a good ten minutes, cuddling it and generally making a little more of a fuss of it.
- Repeat this process on a regular basis, slowly extending the period of time that you are separated from the dog.

This exercise will have taught the dog some important lessons. Firstly, it will have begun to learn that lengthy separations are a normal part of life. Secondly, it will have seen that these separations are nothing to be feared. Both lessons are vital if the dog is to be well-adjusted and is going to fit into the daily life of the home.

CRYING AT NIGHT

Dogs often cry at night during this settling-in phase. Again, it is hardly surprising. We go to sleep each night having locked the doors and shut the windows, happy that the house is secure. But what if we were to go to bed with the doors wide open. Would we sleep a wink?

This is the situation the dog faces each night it goes to sleep in this new environment. It has no concept of what a lock is. As far as it is concerned the house is vulnerable to any number of threats. And in the darkness of night its fear of these potential threats is magnified many times over.

So, if your dog cries during the night you need to act decisively to let it know it is safe.

Check first that it does not want to go to the toilet. Do this in a very matter-of-fact way, by offering it the chance to go through the door. If it doesn't want to go, you must signal your displeasure. However, you mustn't do this by scolding or raising your voice. Instead you must issue it with a disapproving look, the sort of stern look your mother used to give you when you were a child.

The puppy will, more than likely, be standing there wagging its tail, looking pleadingly at you. But you must not fall for it. Switch the light off and return to bed.

This may well have to be repeated several times, but you have to remain strong. Eventually the dog will learn that it is not alone and therefore doesn't need to feel anxious about that. It must also learn that it is living by the human rules of the house, and according to those human rules night-time is sleeping time. Most importantly, it will learn that it is safe and that the house's descent into darkness and quiet at night is nothing to be frightened of.

This can be a difficult step to achieve, but it is worth persevering for several reasons. By establishing this precedent early on you will have taught the dog to read your facial expressions. This will lay good groundwork for later. You will also have achieved this without resorting to raising your voice, leaving this option open to you for another time and making it all the more powerful when you do choose to use it.

CANINE RIVALRIES

Many people have problems integrating new dogs into a home that already has one or more dogs living there. It is no surprise. The human members of the domestic 'pack' should be elevated in status relative to the dogs, but below this there will also be a canine pecking order. Sometimes this will establish itself simply, without any confrontation. Equally, dogs can be hugely competitive and the result can be aggressive and potentially violent behaviour.

For this reason it is best if the new dog is introduced to its new housemate or mates beforehand, on neutral territory. In an ideal world, more than one meeting would be beneficial. Reputable breeders should allow for this, and they should also be happy to keep the new dog until it is ready to integrate with its new friends. In the unlikely event that the dogs form a dangerous disliking for each other, they should also agree to keeping their dog without a second thought.

Unfortunately we live in a less than ideal world, so we have to consider how people can best integrate new dogs into all situations. If the existing pack is only going to meet the new dog on the day of its arrival, this

Clash of personalities: the introduction of a new dog can spark confrontations over status if handled incorrectly.

introduction must be the first task of the day. Owners must choose a neutral ground – and here they must be careful to avoid places where the existing pack have strong associations. They will also need the assistance of another calm and experienced handler – someone who will look after either the new dog or the existing pack.

If there is more than one dog in the existing pack, owners should introduce these dogs to the newcomer one at a time. The key thing here is that each time this happens the two dogs must meet on equal status. As the newcomer is going to be on a lead, the existing pack member should also be on a lead. If one is being rewarded with toys or treats, then so should the other. This also helps re-establish your own primacy within the pack.

The dogs should then be allowed to get to know each other. The important thing here is not to panic. The dogs will size each other up, but if they begin to grumble or growl at each other don't be overly concerned. By being relaxed you are also showing qualities of unflappable leadership. Ultimately, dogs enjoy each other's company. Given time and space a friendship can emerge from the least likely pairing.

Once a rapport is established, let the dogs move closer together. Eventually they should come up close enough so that they can play together. This is the most natural thing in the world and you should let it happen as such.

The longer this goes on, the better. In time, however, the dogs will need to head home. When this happens they should travel together. If the existing dog is being reluctant, owners should put the new dog in first. If the situation flares up during the journey, the new dog should be moved to another seat. Once at home, the dogs must remain on equal status, each of them on a lead. They should be released in the garden at the same time. They should be allowed to get to know each other, but always under supervision.

There is every chance, of course, that the two dogs will not get on immediately. Owners will have to exercise common sense and flexibility here. If they get on at once then they can sleep in close proximity to each other. If they are at each other's throats, however, they must be separated. The same applies with other household pets: cats, rabbits or whatever. If they are getting along happily then leave them together. If there is friction, separate them. Always err on the side of caution. And always be patient.

RIVALRIES WITH OTHER ANIMALS

A dog doesn't make any assumptions about what sort of pack it is going to live within. It lives with whatever is sharing its space, whether that is humans, other dogs, or indeed other species. In general it assimilates well into any environment.

However, owners can experience problems in integrating their dog with other animals, and this is an area that needs careful handling. If a dog has difficulty settling into the home with another animal, such as a cat, you should slip a lead on it whenever it is in the same space. If it makes any sort of move towards the other animal you will be able to restrain it. The important thing, however, is that you don't turn this into a huge drama. Don't shout or scold. Just ignore it. After a while the dog's agitation or excitement will ease.

Other smaller animals may present more of a long-term challenge. You should remember that the dog remains a predator. For this reason, a dog should not be left on its own with smaller animals like hamsters or chickens at any time.

'Like cats and dogs': rivalries with other animals, like cats, can be quickly overcome with the right approach.

Wellbeing

VACCINATIONS

It is about now that an owner should begin making arrangements to give the dog its first vaccinations. For the early weeks of their lives, young puppies are protected from diseases by the colostrum in their mother's first milk. This immunity fades quite quickly, however, and vets maintain that the immunity halves every eight days so that by the time a dog is six to twelve weeks old it has faded altogether. This leaves the dog susceptible to the five main diseases that threaten dogs today. Prevention is the best form of cure, and it is important that immunisation occurs at some stage during the first six to ten weeks.

The Five Main Threats

DISTEMPER OR 'HARD PAD'
One of the most dangerous diseases, this is more commonly known as 'hard pad' because of the effect it has on the dog's foot. Over time, the pad becomes hard, thickened and cracked.

The distemper virus affects young dogs in urban and city areas in particular, and is passed on through urine, faeces and saliva. It can even be picked up by a dog inhaling tiny droplets of the virus that have been released into the air by a carrier's breath. Distemper affects the dog's skin, eyes, nose, lungs, stomach and intestines and results in a sore discharge from the eyes and nose. It can also lead to pneumonia, diarrhoea, vomiting and dehydration. Around half of all dogs affected suffer fits.

Any signs of distemper require immediate treatment as it is usually fatal.

HEPATITIS
A disease that initially attacks the liver, this is a particular danger to young dogs, especially those under the age of two. Like distemper it is transmitted via faeces, saliva, urine and droplets breathed in from the air.

Hepatitis spreads to the liver via the bloodstream. It then destroys the liver cells causing the organ to become enlarged and inflamed. The results are jaundice, or yellowing, severe abdominal pain, vomiting and dehydration. The virus can also damage the eyes and kidneys. In severe cases hepatitis can kill a dog within 24 hours. Owners of dogs that contract hepatitis and recover should also be aware that these dogs remain dangerous carriers for up to nine months afterwards and can pass the disease on via their urine.

PARVOVIRUS

Parvovirus arrived in this country in the late 1970s, when it also swept through North America and Australia. It is transmitted mainly through dog-to-dog contact and via faeces. It attacks the stomach and is a particular threat to puppies, who can also suffer inflammation of the heart as a result of contracting parvovirus. It is a menace because it is extremely resistant, surviving in the environment for a year or more and withstanding many disinfectants.

Parvovirus varies in its seriousness. Some dogs will experience vomiting, bloody diarrhoea, high temperature and dehydration, but nothing more severe. Others, however, can suffer depression and collapse physically. Some die, occasionally within 24 hours.

LEPTOSPIROSIS

A bacterial infection that can also cause serious – even fatal – illness in humans, leptospirosis damages the liver, kidneys and blood vessels. It is passed by direct dog-to-dog contact, most commonly through urine, but the disease can also be passed on through cuts and grazes to dog's feet.

Dogs infected by the virus suffer jaundice, haemorrhage, vomiting, black diarrhoea and severe dehydration. If the liver becomes enlarged it causes extreme abdominal pain. Damage to the kidneys can, in the worst cases, precipitate kidney failure. Leptospirosis is not as resilient as parvovirus, however, and can be eliminated by disinfectants.

The seriousness again varies, but in the worst cases death can occur within two days.

KENNEL COUGH

In many senses, kennel cough is similar to human flu. It is highly infectious and is transmitted from dog to dog in highly populated environments like kennels, puppy classes or dog shows. Like the other main diseases, it

HEALTH

is transmitted through the air and breathed in. It then incubates for ten days or so. The first visible symptoms of the illness are sneezing, a dry cough and a loss of appetite. The good news, however, is that – like human flu – it is very rarely fatal. Kennel cough tends to last for a brief period of time, usually two to three weeks. Owners must be vigilant, however, and isolate dogs afterwards because the illness can still be spread for up to ten weeks after the symptoms have cleared.

When to Vaccinate

Opinion differs on when precisely immunity should be topped up through vaccination. Some owners of dogs with high risks of catching the main five diseases vaccinate as early as six or seven weeks. Others wait until ten weeks, although it is pretty much accepted by everyone that the latest they should be given is twelve weeks.

The reality is that it is dependent on what is going to happen to the dog in the coming weeks and months. If it is going to travel with you on holiday, for instance, or if it is going to be crossing areas where other dogs walk freely then the risk of picking up viruses is great and the puppy should be vaccinated early. If, on the other hand, the puppy is remaining at home with you and its litter then the need is not so pressing. As ever, if there is any doubt about the necessity of vaccinations, consult your vet.

Why Vaccinate?

A lot of owners question why there is even a need to vaccinate their dog. The best answer to that is the low incidence of the main life-threatening diseases in this country today. The fact that killer diseases like distemper and parvovirus are so rare is almost entirely down to the vaccination system. The other major point owners need to remember is that, unlike human diseases, the major dog diseases have no specific cures. If your dog contracts one of them, it is, in all probability, going to die. Faced with that stark fact, no responsible owner thinks twice about vaccinating.

Boosters

There is no certainty about how long the immunity that the standard vaccination provides lasts. It is a subject of great debate among current vets. Some vets recommend annual boosters, others recommend they are renewed every three years. Different owners are going to have different views on when – or indeed if – to give their dogs booster injections. It is compulsory, however, that dogs have a current certificate proving they are 'up to date' with their injections before travelling abroad or going into boarding kennels.

GROOMING: THE KEY TO GOOD HEALTH

The importance of grooming cannot be overstated. It is about much more than making sure a dog looks its best at all times. First and foremost it is a vital way of maintaining and monitoring a dog's health. The coat is susceptible to all manner of threats and needs to be continually cared for.

Grooming also provides a chance to perform other routine checks on the dog's welfare.

But in addition it is a perfect way to form a valuable bond of trust between pet and owner early in life. It also allows the owner to underline

Comb control: **to maintain good health, short-haired dogs should have their coats combed through thoroughly on a regular basis.**

HEALTH

the dog's status within the domestic hierarchy. Firstly it lets the owner touch the dog's most vulnerable areas, something that in the wild only an alpha would be able to do. Similarly it allows the owner to take over the cleaning and maintenance work that dogs naturally do themselves, again a signal of superiority within the pecking order. Finally it also puts them in a position of dominance, standing over the dog. For all these reasons, grooming is something that should begin as early as possible within the dog's life, and should be undertaken once a week on average.

The Importance of Maintaining Your Dog's Coat

A dog's coat is the first line of defence against many diseases. It is made up of two kinds of hair – protective 'guard' hair and fine, heat-preserving 'down' hair. Centuries of breeding has, of course, produced dogs with very different mixes of hair. For example, German Shepherds have a coat dominated by 'guard' hair.

In the wild, wolves look after their skin and coat by rolling around in dust or sand. This not only massages the coat but dislodges any accumulated debris and stimulates the skin to produce sebum, an oily substance that naturally protects the skin and hair from infection. Our dogs may occasionally use this method to keep themselves clean, but in general they rely on licking themselves. This isn't enough, particularly given the array of invisible ailments that a dog faces in the human world. So it is up to us to monitor and maintain our dog's coat.

Tools of the Trade

Slicker Brush
Fine-toothed Comb
Wide-toothed Comb
Soft Body Brush
Hound Glove
Bristle Brush
Rubber Gloves
Dematting Comb
Thinning Scissors
Round-ended Scissors

Grooming Different Types of Coat

The principles of grooming are the same regardless of which type of coat your dog has. The object of the exercise is to remove any dead hair and to clean the living hair and the skin, stimulating the oil-producing glands in the skin to lubricate the coat so that it looks sleek and healthy. This should be achieved without hurting or causing the dog any distress, so there are a few guiding principles:

- Don't tug at the dog's hair when grooming.
- If a section of coat is really matted and knotted and can't be teased out with a light brush, cut it away with scissors rather than tugging away at it for minutes on end. There is no need to make the dog suffer.
- When selecting a bristle brush, test it on the back of your hand before using it on the dog. If it hurts your skin then it is going to hurt the dog's, so don't use it.
- When grooming male dogs take care to protect the genital area. Cup the dog's testes in your spare hand while grooming, otherwise you may hurt the dog.

Different types of coats do require specific treatment, and the main brushing should be carried out according to the categories outlined below.

SMOOTH COATS

There are two types of smooth coats; the short fine coats of such dogs as Whippets and Boxers, and the longer, denser coats of Labradors and Corgis. This is the easiest group of dogs to groom in general. The longer coats can be groomed with a comb and a bristle brush, while a 'hound glove' or rubber glove is enough to care for the shorter coats.

Any bits of debris that remain stuck in the coat can be removed by softening them with a little cooking oil. Particular care should also be taken with the undercoat of the longer-coated dogs.

WIRY COATS

Dogs falling into this category include most of the Terrier family and the wire-haired Daschund and Schnauzer. They should be groomed twice a week without fail, much like the coats of Labradors and Corgis, with a

HEALTH

comb and bristle brush. Matting is a particular problem with this type of coat so great care should be taken to remove every gnarled and knotted section. In doing this, however, you should not tug on the coat. If necessary cut away the affected area of the coat with scissors instead.

In addition to this regular grooming, the top coat should be stripped and plucked, preferably by a professional, every 12 weeks or so, and followed by a good bath. If you prefer the dog can be machine-clipped every six to eight weeks; but be aware that by doing this you are dealing with the length rather than the density and this doesn't allow the coat to look after itself as naturally as it should and will cause problems in the long term. These coats also grow around the eyes and ears so care should be taken to clip these with scissors.

LONG COATS

Top to toe: every area of a long-haired dog's body needs careful grooming, including their ears.

These coats are found on Collies, German Shepherds and Old English Sheepdogs among other breeds. Grooming here should start with a general detangling with a slick brush followed by a thorough combing through with a pin brush. Finally the coat should be combed through with a wide-toothed comb. Particular care should be taken to thoroughly comb the dense hair on the legs, chest, tail and hindquarters. These dogs need to be groomed on a daily basis, and trimmed of excess hair once a month at least. Again, bad knotting should be cut out.

CURLY, NON-MOULTING COATS

This type of coat is found on dogs like the Poodle and the Bichon Frise. Unlike every other type of dog, these breeds do not moult, which makes caring for and managing their coats all the more important. They should be brushed through on a daily basis with a specialised 'dematting' comb, with particular attention to the outside of the ears and the feet. The most important thing here is that these coats are clipped every six to eight weeks. This may be best left to a professional groomer. They should also look out for the hair that tends to grow inside the dog's ear canal and can cause problems if not maintained properly.

SILKY COATS

Afghan Hounds, Lhasa Apsos, Spaniels and Yorkshire Terriers are among the diverse group of dogs that have this kind of coat. They require a lot of care and attention for several reasons. First, these coats can quickly become a tangled mess and need regular brushing and bathing to avoid becoming matted. Also, some breeds, such as the Maltese and Yorkshire Terrier, do not have a protective undercoat of 'downy' hair, and as a result have sensitive skin that can easily be cut by rough brushing and combing. So the daily brushing should begin with a gentle teasing out of the tangles with a slicker brush, always remembering to be careful not to touch the skin. Owners should then go on to a bristle brushing and a final thorough comb-through with a wide-toothed comb. Because they can accumulate a lot of dead hair, these dogs should also be trimmed with scissors every three months or so. Electric clipping should be avoided because it fails to take out the dead hair.

HEALTH

Bathing

Opinions differ widely on the best policy towards bathing dogs. Some owners favour regular monthly baths, others don't bath their dogs fully at all. There is no definitive answer. Ultimately it is going to be a matter of personal choice, with the breed and coat-type of the dog itself being an influence on that choice.

It is no surprise that many dogs dislike having a bath intensely. Dogs don't like going against their instincts, and bathing does precisely that.

In the wild, the wolf maintains its coat naturally. Each year they grow a good, warm coat in winter, then lose this during the spring when they moult. They help this shedding process along by rubbing up against stones and rocks, trees and gravel. Anything they can find to scratch it off. They also dive in water more to help rid themselves of the dead hair. During the rest of the year their coat maintains itself thanks to the oil, or sebum, secreted by the body. It is a natural cycle.

The difference with the domestic dog is that we expect it to blend in with our environment and the sanitary standards we live by. We, quite rightly, don't want dogs that smell or are in any way offensive. But, once

Water baby: bath time can be a pleasant experience for dogs if handled correctly.

again, we forget to look at this from the dog's point of view. To the dog its smell is an important way to blend in with its environment. If they smell of the natural world around them they are less conspicuous, and therefore less liable to attack. A dog knows that the more it smells of soap or shampoo the less it blends in. Therefore owners often find that when they finish bathing a dog it immediately goes away and rolls in something disgusting. They don't do this because they like to be dirty. Quite the opposite, in fact, for they are naturally clean animals. The reason they do this is because the smell is not natural. They prefer to smell like their environment.

This can present something of a dilemma when it comes to bathing your dog. In general, you should bear in mind the following principles:

TRY TO USE LOW OR NON-PERFUMED SHAMPOOS

The more pungent the smell the dog's coat carries with it when it dries out, the more likely it is to want to wash that smell away immediately. There are plenty of shampoos on the market that do not carry a heavy aroma. Use them.

DON'T BATHE PUPPIES

During its first weeks the puppy will be kept clean by its mother. After this it should be left alone, barring any major disasters. Among the many lessons it is learning during this phase is how to keep itself clean. Don't interfere with that learning.

How to Give a Dog a Bath

- It might be helpful to have a second pair of hands to hold the dog steady during shampooing.
- Begin by taking off the dog's collar and placing it in the bath.
- With a shower or a pouring jug, wet the dog's back and work the water into its coat on the sides and at the back.
- Apply the shampoo, working it in throughout the body, legs, ears and head.
- Take care not to get soap in the dog's eyes.
- Keep a damp flannel to hand in case this should happen and carefully and gently wipe the eyes.
- Rinse the dog thoroughly from the head backwards.

HEALTH

🐾 In warm weather, give the dog a good run afterwards to dry out. Longer-coated dogs may need towelling first.

🐾 In cold weather, towel the dog down well and let it dry somewhere warm to prevent it catching a cold.

🐾 If you are using a hair dryer, introduce it gently and with care, as the dog may react to the noise.

DON'T OVERBATHE

If you do bathe your dog don't overdo it. The dog's secretion of sebum maintains its coat. By washing too much this natural effect can be disrupted, causing problems.

BATHE BY BREED

Thanks to human intervention, dogs have evolved a long way from their natural model. As a result, we have produced coats that require varying degrees of maintenance.

At one extreme you have breeds like the American Cocker Spaniel. With its hair trailing to the ground it looks like a hovercraft and gathers dirt at a prodigious rate. If you don't bath it on a regular basis you are going to have a lot of problems. At the other end of the scale you have short-coated dogs. This is nature's design, so if you have got a smooth-coated dog you don't need to wash it much at all. If it does roll in something absolutely diabolical then just wash the affected area.

In between these two extremes you have breeds whose bathing requirements are really dictated by their physical nature. Cocker Spaniels, for instance, need their ears washing on a regular basis. Boxers and Pugs need their eyes wiped a lot. A Sharpei with all its wrinkles needs to have these folds wiped out regularly.

THE HOME VET: CHECKING ON YOUR DOG'S HEALTH WHILE GROOMING

Grooming provides a perfect opportunity to check on your dog's general condition. You are not, of course, going to be able to give your dog the thorough examination your vet will provide, but you can look at many of the key areas the medical expert will focus on. And a diligent owner can often pick up illnesses or disorders at a very early stage, thus ensuring they are nipped in the bud.

These are the key areas an owner should look at:

Skin Disorders and Diseases

A dog can be afflicted by a large number of skin diseases, some of which can lead to serious problems. They can be caused by everything from parasites like fleas, mites and ticks, to infections. They can also develop from dietary or hormonal problems, household cleaning products and hereditary conditions.

Invariably, the problem, whatever it is, is made worse by the dog scratching itself. This in turn results in more hair loss and inflammation, which leads to more scratching and so on. It becomes a vicious circle, and can leave the dog permanently scarred.

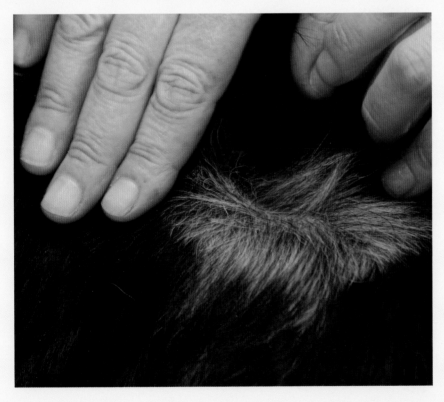

Checking up: grooming allows owners to give their dogs' coats a thorough examination for disorders and diseases.

HEALTH

No owner is going to recognise all of these potential problems, but by looking out for a few of the telltale signs an owner can generally detect that something is amiss and act promptly. Often the best cure is simply to get the dog to stop scratching, either by the use of anti-inflammatory drugs or, if necessary, sedatives. But in some cases the problem is a behavioural one and needs to be treated on a more holistic level.

SIGNS OF POTENTIAL SKIN PROBLEMS

Hair Loss

The key things to look for here are areas of baldness, periods of prolonged moulting and broken hairs on the coat. The causes of this can range from excessive scratching to dietary and hormonal problems. Dietary problems may be treatable at home with multivitamins and a little extra oil in the dog's diet. But if in doubt consult the vet.

Excessive Scratching

This is the most obvious sign of a problem, although given the number of possible causes the solution is usually far less obvious. The first thing to do is to look at the area where the dog is concentrating its attention. If, for instance, it is scratching at sores around the base of its tail, the problem may be impacted anal sacs. Otherwise look for any parasites or spots, sores or inflamed areas of the skin. A particularly nasty condition in puppies is 'juvenile pyoderma' caused by a lack of natural defence against one of the most common mites, demodex. Most dogs carry this mite without any problems, but it can cause a nasty dermatitis around the head and shoulders of puppies which, if infected by bacteria, can lead to pyoderma. Dobermans, Daschunds and Irish Setters are particularly prone to this condition, which can also be spotted by the 'mousy' odour that it produces.

Many parasites can be treated at home with special treatments. However, sores or signs of bacterial infection should be treated by a vet.

Reddening of the Skin

Again there are a myriad explanations for this, from fleas, lice, ringworm and bacterial sores to different forms of dermatitis. If the irritated area is relatively small and localised it can be treated by applying calamine lotion to the reddened area. If it is more widespread it can be alleviated by washing the dog in a lanolin baby shampoo and applying flea spray when it is dry. As ever, though, if the problem persists, consult the vet.

Rashes

Look for itchy red spots on the ears, elbows and hocks. The main cause of this is sarcoptic mange, more commonly known as scabies, a very nasty condition that can affect humans who come into contact with it as well. The condition is caused by sarcoptic mites burrowing into the dog's skin and laying eggs in the resultant tunnels. The scratching caused by this can be very intense and leave the dog badly scarred. Scabies is best treated by insecticidal shampoo. Sedative drugs may also be needed to prevent the dog mutilating itself.

Other signs to look out for here are areas wet from licking, dandruff, matted coats, and dry or scaly skin.

External Parasites

It's a fact of life that your dog will probably be affected by an external parasite at some point in its life. So, even at this early age it is important to look out for the main nuisances: fleas, ticks, lice and mites.

FLEAS

Life Cycle

A flea's life cycle is divided into four stages: egg, larva, pupa and adult. The eggs are laid by the female flea, which like all adult fleas lives in the dog's coat. These eggs then fall off the 'host' dog onto the home environment, perhaps onto the furniture or the carpet. The eggs hatch into larvae, which feed on microscopic scraps such as flea dirt and tapeworm eggs before spinning a cocoon, inside which the pupa develops into an adult.

Fleas are encouraged to hatch by warmth and vibration, either from the 'host' pet or the environment around them. When the flea emerges it jumps back onto a 'host' dog and the cycle begins all over again. The whole process from egg to flea can take as little as two weeks.

An adult flea lives for no more than seven to ten days, but during this time they can cause immense discomfort and irritation to a 'host' dog.

HEALTH

Detecting and Treating Fleas

Often your dog will be your best guide as to whether fleas are present or not. When fleas bite the skin they cause huge irritation and the dog will begin scratching, biting or licking at the area where the itching is concentrated. However, in some cases there will be no obvious indication of fleas being present.

Fleas are hard to spot: they are small and difficult for the naked eye to pick up, and they also move around the body quickly. Fleas do, however, tend to settle in the same region of the dog's body, usually around the base of the tail, the ears, neck and abdomen.

One simple way of checking whether they are present is by combing through the dog's coat and shaking any loose matter onto a small piece of white tissue paper. If there are flecks of red then this is probably flea faeces.

Left untreated, fleas can cause widespread problems such as anaemia. They can also multiply at a terrifying rate and infest an entire household, not to mention all its occupants. So it is important to treat this – and to do so quickly.

There are a variety of flea controls ranging from flea collars and powders to shampoos and sprays. It used to be that you had to dust the dog's entire body, but thanks to modern medicine single 'spot on' treatments can be applied to the back of the neck. The treatment spreads, giving good protection to the whole of the body.

TICKS

Ticks are unpleasant, blood-sucking parasites that can afflict dogs everywhere. The most common varieties are the sheep and hedgehog ticks, which – as their names suggest – originate in other species then cross over to dogs as they roam in grass, woodland or overgrowth.

Ticks are generally less common than fleas, but they can cause abscesses and infections. In some parts of the world they can even transmit potentially lethal diseases like Lyme disease. It is vital, therefore, that they are treated quickly and effectively.

Life Cycle

The life cycle of a tick is thought to last up to three years and begins with the female tick laying thousands of eggs on the ground. When these eggs become larvae they settle onto grass and shrubbery ready to attach themselves onto animals – or indeed humans – as they brush by. Once they are attached to their 'host' they feed until they are ready to fall back off and develop into the next phase, the nymph. This process is then repeated as the nymph reattaches itself to a new host, feeding off it until it develops into a fully grown tick. The tick will then climb onto grass and shrub-land ready to attach itself to a final host. It is now that the real damage is done. The tick finds the point of least resistance in the dog's coat where it fixes itself on by its mouth. Often this is the face of the dog, or the ears or abdomen. It then begins to feed on the dog's blood supply, passing on any infections it is carrying at the same time. Because it bites into the skin it can also cause nasty abscesses. Once the female tick has fed fully it falls off once more, ready to lay eggs and start the cycle all over again.

How to Spot and Treat Ticks

The most obvious sign of ticks is a small grey dot on the dog's skin. It is easy to mistake the dot for a wart or another lump, but this lump will grow larger due to the ingestion of blood, often to the size of a pea.

Removing the tick can be a tricky process because it is attached to the dog's skin by its mouth. It is easy to remove the body but leave the mouth attached, which can lead to more severe problems. If ticks do turn up in your puppy you should see your vet, as they can cause anaemia. Ticks can also transmit infectious diseases to humans, so it is important to act quickly.

You can treat your dogs in advance for ticks. If you live in a rural area and plan to walk your dog in open fields or woodland it is advisable to treat it in advance. If the dog is likely to come into contact with sheep it should also be protected.

FLEAS AND MITES

Dogs can attract a wide range of insects, but in particular they can be a magnet for fleas and mites. These are tiny – almost microscopic – creatures almost always invisible to the human eye. The best way to detect them is by looking out for small specks of grit on the dog's coat during grooming. If, when this is brushed out then dropped onto a white tissue, it leaves a

HEALTH

red mark then it is flea dirt. Fleas are also hosts to tapeworms, so if they are present it is vital that the dog is treated for this as well.

Three types of mite are also a cause of problems:

- **Demodex** – this mite causes demodectic mange which can lead to juvenile pyoderma (see Skin Disorders, page 109).
- **Sarcoptes** – these are the cause of scabies (see Skin Disorders, page 109).
- **Otodectes** – this mite is the only one visible to the naked eye. It causes inflammation of the ear and can be seen in the shape of tiny white moving dots inside the ear canal.

Ear Disorders

Ear infections are relatively common in dogs and take two main types – infections of the external ear canal, known as otitis externa, and infections of the middle ear, or otitis media. Some breeds are more prone than others to infection. Dogs with floppy ears, such as Cocker Spaniels or Basset Hounds, are vulnerable because of the lack of ventilation that gets into the ear canal. This in turn can cause overheating, which can lead to any excess wax inside the ear becoming infected. Dogs with very tight, curly coats, like Poodles and Schnauzers, suffer because they have narrow ear canals, which can result in an accumulation of hair and wax and create a breeding ground for infections. More generally there are three telltale signs of a problem with a dog's ears. The first two should be detectable during your regular inspection of the dog:

DISCHARGES FROM THE EAR

There are three main types of discharge, each indicating an infection of the outer ear (otitis externa):

- **A gritty discharge:** if the discharge is gritty and flecked with dark material the most likely cause is ear mites.
- **A black discharge:** if the discharge is runny and dark this suggests it is caused by a yeast infection.
- **A yellow discharge:** if the discharge is thick and yellow this suggests a bacterial infection.

SWOLLEN OR PAINFUL EARS

If you see your dog shaking its head, twitching or pawing at its ears, or if it registers discomfort or flinching when you touch it around the ear area, there are a number of possible causes:

- If there is a swelling on the inside of the ear flap the most likely cause is a blood clot.
- If the ear looks clean but the dog still seems distressed when it is touched, this may suggest that a foreign object such as a grass seed has become lodged in the ear.

POOR HEARING

It's rare for dogs to go completely deaf, but infections of the ear can temporarily impair their hearing. There are a few telltale signs that a dog has got a problem with its hearing:

- It tilts or scratches at its head.
- It fails to respond as normal when called for its walk or meals.
- There is a discharge from the ear.

CHECKING THE EARS

Look into the ear canal by carefully lifting the ear flap if necessary. Use a torch if necessary. The inside of the canal should be clean, much like the skin on the hairless section of the belly. The main things to look out for are excesses of hair and wax and any disharge. A small amount of wax is not a worry and can be left alone, but if there is a build-up of wax plugging the canal it must be cleaned. Similarly, clogging by dead hairs must also be cleaned. Be careful, however, not to prod around too much, and avoid using cotton buds which can do damage. Instead, put cotton wool on your finger, being careful not to enter the canal. Finish off by applying a general ear-cleaning liquid of the kind available from vets. Place a few drops inside the ear then clean around the outer surface of the ear with cotton wool.

It's also important to smell the ear for unpleasant odours, a good indicator of infections. Any cause for concern should be reported to the vet.

HEALTH

Breeds that are susceptible to ear problems include floppy-eared varieties like Cocker Spaniels and Basset Hounds. Their long, flappy ears reduce ventilation and can cause overheating and excessive wax, which can become infected. Other breeds, like poodles, have narrow ear canals that also make them prone to build-ups of wax.

Eye Problems

CHECKING THE EYES

Your puppy should have had its eyes formally tested at six or seven weeks of age. This will record any permanent conditions or inherited congenital diseases and will be kept on file, primarily so that anyone wanting to breed from the dog is aware of the problems. Before and after this, however, your physical check-up of your dog during grooming should help show up some of the telltale signs of eye problems. In addition, if your dog starts displaying obvious signs of impaired vision, such as bumping into things or walking more slowly and carefully, you should head to the vet immediately.

The most obvious things to look out for are:

Sleepy Eyes

Many dogs get small deposits of 'sleep' or mucus that gathers in the corner of the eye. It is not in itself threatening, but if left to dry can be a magnet for infection and bacteria. Use grooming as an opportunity to either pick out the 'sleep' with a finger, or, if it has begun to dry, use a wet ball of cotton wool to clean the mucus away.

Weeping Eyes

A variety of discharges can indicate eye disorders or diseases. If the discharge is clear it suggests the dog may have, in the worst case, conjunctivitis, or, in less serious instances, a blocked tear-duct. If the discharge is cloudy or discoloured and thick it suggests there is an infection, such as distemper. Both can be avoided by careful clipping of the hair around the eyes, although it is best to leave this to someone with experience. In the short term each can be alleviated by irrigating the eye with cold weak tea. In the long term, however, you should consult your vet.

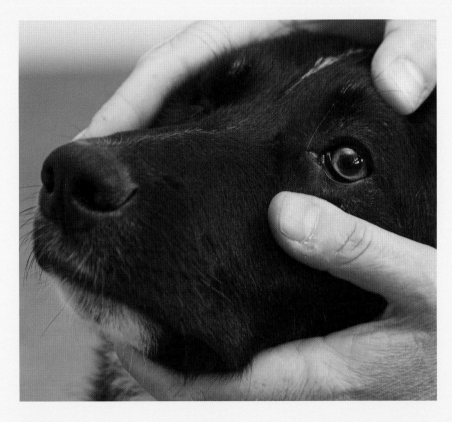

First start: **regular inspections of the eyes should reveal early signs of diseases.**

Caring For Your Dog's Teeth

In the wild, it is not overstating things to say that strong and healthy teeth are the most vital weapon a wolf can possess. Its survival depends on them. It is with its teeth that a wolf captures its prey. It is with its teeth that it kills, dismembers and divides up its food.

Yet these functions also maintain the wolf's dental health. By ripping, gnawing and chewing at carcasses – often for long periods of time – the wolf simultaneously maintains the sharpness of its teeth, massages its gums and releases increased amounts of healthy saliva into its mouth. The extensive workout it gives its teeth on an almost daily basis prevents the build-up of damaging tartar and also staves off gum diseases.

Of course, these natural processes are not available to our domestic animals. The sometimes woeful state of our dogs' teeth is underlined by recent statistics which indicate some 85 per cent of dogs suffer from

HEALTH

dental problems. By far the most common complaints are excessive build-ups of tartar, and gum diseases, specifically gingivitis. Our dogs' dental health is one of those areas that is often relegated to the bottom of the owners' list of tasks to take care of, yet it is one of the most vital aspects of all. And the earlier we get into the habit of checking and maintaining our dogs' teeth the better.

Thankfully, the better dog-food manufacturers have come up with special tooth-friendly foods that help prevent the build up of plaque and tartar. They make these foods in the form of a crunchy kibble, which gives the dog something substantial to chew on. They are not quite the equivalent of a wolf working its way through its prey – often it does not give the incisors or canines at the front of the mouth the stimulation they need, so the dog's teeth will still need to be brushed as well. As the dog gets older we can also give them bones to gnaw at and use during playtime. Be careful to use the harder marrow bones and to avoid bones taken from a cooked piece of meat like lamb or pork. These bones are too soft and can easily splinter, blocking or tearing the dog's digestive system.

Mouth and Teeth Disorders

Maintaining a good, healthy set of teeth and gums is vital. Yellow sticky plaque can build up on the surface of the teeth, and if this accumulates it can form into a cement-like mineralised deposit called tartar. This in turn becomes a breeding ground for gum diseases that can, if left unchecked, cause serious illness. Dogs are prone to getting foreign objects stuck in their mouth, and there are also a number of conditions that can affect the exterior of the dog's mouth. So it is important that grooming includes a thorough cleaning and checking of these areas.

CHECKING THE DOG'S MOUTH

It is important this is done gently and carefully. Again, it is something that should be done once the bond of trust is established.

- Sit the dog on a raised surface so that you can see its mouth from every angle.
- Firmly hold the lower jaw with one hand, then with the other hand draw down the lower lip and raise the upper lip to reveal the teeth and gums.

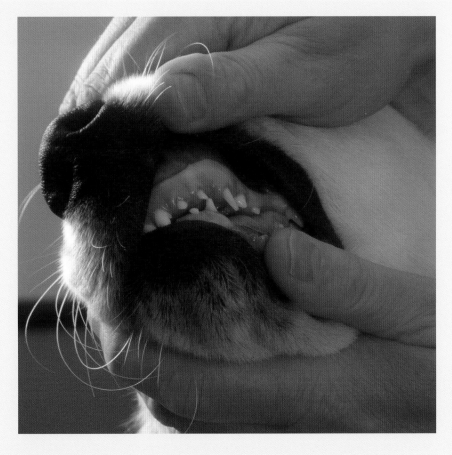

The root of the problem: regular checks of the dog's mouth can help spot dental diseases at an early stage.

🐾 Firstly examine the outside of the teeth, looking for discolouration or a lack of the usual translucence a healthy tooth has. If there is a discolouration it may indicate dead tooth pulp.

🐾 Look for obvious build-ups of mineral-like tartar, the forerunner to gum disease.

🐾 Examine the gums for any signs of inflammation or discolouration.

🐾 Do this on both sides of the jaw.

🐾 Examine the upper jaw by using your thumb and forefinger to open the mouth further.

🐾 Inspect not just the inner teeth and gums but also the hard palate and the tongue.

🐾 Finally, smell the dog's breath. If it smells unpleasant consult your vet.

HEALTH

The main dental disorders are:

Halitosis

Bad breath is usually caused by one of three things: bacteria developing in the debris trapped between the teeth, tartar, or a gum infection. For this reason any hint of it should be reported to the vet.

Gum Diseases

There are two main gum conditions, both relating to the tissue surrounding the teeth. Gingivitis is an inflammation that develops in the gums, or gingiva, when bacteria accumulates. Periodontal disease occurs in the periodontal ligament, the deeper structure around the tooth.

This is very common in dogs, indeed almost every dog will develop it at some period in their life. It is why dental problems are the most common causes of visits to the vet. However, both can be minimalised by good dental care. There are specially formulated toothpastes and antiseptic mouthwashes that can help combat infections at an early stage too.

Retained Baby Teeth

At around the five-month mark the baby teeth are replaced by the adult teeth. At this point the deciduous teeth normally fall out, but in some cases a few baby teeth remain in place. When the adult teeth come up alongside them they are pushed out of their normal alignment. This can lead to severe problems for the dog and needs to be dealt with early. When the dog reaches the age when its adult teeth are coming through, the dog's jaw should be checked for signs of double sets of teeth. The baby teeth then need to be extracted.

Malocclusions

The 'perfect' canine bite, or occlusion, occurs when the jaw closes and the upper incisors just overlap with the lower ones. Jaws that deviate from this norm are known as malocclusions. A jaw in which the lower jaw is shorter than the upper jaw is known as an overshot jaw. The reverse, in which the lower jaw is longer than the upper one is known as an undershot jaw. Because of selective breeding, these conditions are now common to around 20 per cent of dogs. The Boxer, for instance, has been bred specifically to have an undershot bite.

This condition can occur unnaturally, however. Dogs that develop a malocclusion can be treated, but they should never be used for breeding.

Broken Teeth

Young dogs will put absolutely anything into their mouths. As they test their new teeth out they will chew away at rocks, pieces of wood, metal, rope – anything. The upshot of this, unfortunately, is that many dogs crack or even break their teeth. This can be a painful experience for the dog. It may be possible to fix it with root-canal work but extraction may also be necessary in severe cases.

MOUTH PROBLEMS

Lip Inflammation

Mouth infections can also affect a dog's lips. The corners can become very dry as well as flaky and chapped. The lips can also be inflamed by the dog chewing rough objects. These conditions can heal themselves, but there are good softening creams that can be effective.

Lip Fold Inflammation or 'Cocker Mouth'

Some sporting breeds have been bred with a 'fle' or fold of skin in the lower lip. Food and saliva can collect here and this, in turn, can develop bacteria. This can lead to an inflammation of the folds which, as well as leading to potential disease, produces an unpleasant odour. One of the breeds most likely to develop this is the Cocker Spaniel, hence the condition's popular name 'Cocker Mouth'. For this reason the area needs to be cleaned regularly with Epsom salts and water.

Feet

Some breeds, like Spaniels, grow a lot of hair between their toes. This can easily become matted and – in the case of country-based dogs – accumulate grass seeds, dirt and other bits of detritus. If left unattended the seeds in particular can penetrate the skin, leading to an infection and the formation of a cyst. It is therefore important to check this area regularly, clipping away any excess or matted hair and removing any debris.

HEALTH

THE DEW CLAW

Dogs are born with an equivalent of a thumb on the side of their front legs and very occasionally on their back ones too. This is known as a dew claw. It's a product of evolution, a part of the dog's anatomy that has – over generations – become obsolete. In some instances it may need to be removed, particularly if it is likely to grow inward and cause pain or, in the case of working dogs, it is likely to get caught in undergrowth. In some breeds their removal is a matter of tradition. If it is required a vet should do the job, preferably during the dog's first few days.

If the dew claws are to remain, however, they should be checked along with the rest of the foot during grooming. Any accumulation of hair, dirt or grease should be removed. The claw should also be trimmed like the rest to avoid it growing inwards.

Anal Sacs

Probably the least pleasant chore a dog owner has to perform is checking its dog's anal sacs. These are two cavities about 5mm in width which are located either side of the dog's anus, at the 4 o'clock and 8 o'clock positions. They are lined with cells that regularly secrete a very pungent discharge. In the wild the secretions are used to mark territory, but in the domestic dog they have little use apart from getting them attention from other dogs who (for reasons humans find impossible to comprehend) find it attractive.

All dogs need to empty these sacs on a regular basis and often do so while defecating. In some cases, however, they can get blocked and become impacted, a very painful condition.

A dog suffering from this often demonstrates obvious signs of distress. It may 'scoot' its bottom along the ground or lick at the painful area. If it does this you should consult a vet as blocked sacs can become infected and even – in rare cases – cancerous. To make sure things don't get this far you should check the area regularly during grooming by feeling around the side of the anus.

Sacs that are full feel like a bunch of hard grapes. It may also be that the dog reacts as if in pain when you touch. It is important the problem is dealt with quickly. You can stimulate the dog to empty them by either inserting a finger behind the blockages and removing them, or by using a piece of cotton wool to squeeze the sac externally. Neither is a pleasant experience for either the dog or the owner, so it is best to get a vet to perform it, at least on the first occasion.

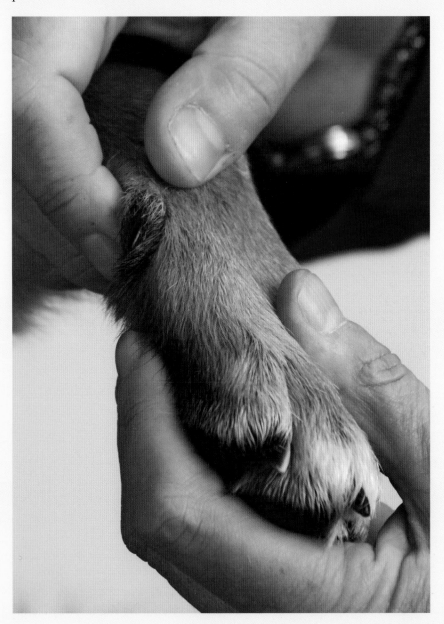

Surplus to requirement: evolution has made the dew claws obsolete but they still need careful checking to avoid potential infection.

HEALTH

THE THIRD AGE

playboy

3–9 MONTHS

*'And then the lover,
Sighing like a furnace, with a woeful ballad
Madew to his mistress' eyebrow'*

IN THE WILD

The wolf is developing quickly now, both physically and mentally. Inside the den and around its perimeter, the building blocks are continuing to be laid for its emergence – eighteen months or so down the line – as a mature adult wolf. Interaction and socialisation with its fellow pack members continues to be the focus.

At this stage the wolf is also becoming more aware of its sexual identity. Between the ages of six and nine months puberty will begin, but it will not be an instinct that a young wolf will be allowed to follow without the permission of the pack. In the main it is a principle of pack life that no wolves are allowed to mate outside the alpha pair. Otherwise the process of natural selection of the fittest will be compromised and the pack will be placed in danger. And no pack member is ever going to do that.

This, of course, is the one aspect of the young dog's development during this phase that will not precisely echo that of its ancient ancestor. All dogs are, in theory, able to mate and reproduce. Yet a responsible owner should – like the hierarchy within a wolf pack – do all they can to ensure natural selection does its job too.

Playtime: vigorous tugging games allow young wolves to learn about their place within the pack's hierarchy

THE THIRD AGE: OVERVIEW

This next six-month period is crucial in the dog's development. It will be during this phase that the dog will do most of its physical growing. By the time it is nine months it will have put on between 80 to 100 per cent of its full adult weight. All the adult teeth will be in place.

Yet mentally it is still very much in its youth. And as that youth continues, so the dog continues to ask itself questions about its status within the pack. Where do I fit in? During this phase too, the dog will begin to venture a little further into the world, developing its physical skills and going on short controlled walks. And as it does so it will encounter other dogs. This too will raise a series of questions. Am I safe in their company? How do I communicate with them? So that they can deal with these situations, the dog will need to learn the basics of walking to heel and on a lead during this phase.

Physically, however, by far the most important development during this phase is sexual. By the age of five months male dogs will be able to produce sperm. By the age of six months a female may be ready to have her first season. Puberty has arrived. With the dog interacting more and more with other breeds, this brings yet more questions – this time for the owner. To neuter, or not to neuter?

Growing up fast – the physical change

The dog's first year is a steep upward curve of development throughout. Even allowing for this, however, the six months that make up the Playboy phase will see the dog passing through its most intense growing spell yet.

At three months, depending on their size and breed, dogs will weigh somewhere between 20 and 30 per cent of their adult weight. By the time they reach nine months they will have grown to such an extent that they will now weigh well over 80 per cent of their full maturity weight, reached at around two-and-a-half years old.

The rates of growth vary widely. Small breeds, unsurprisingly, grow quicker than large breeds, so that some dogs have reached well over 90 per cent of their adult weight by the time they reach nine months. For the large and giant breeds of dogs, the real growth spurt comes between three and five months. They still continue to put on weight after this, but the rate slows and becomes more steady as they head towards maturity.

The dog's dietary demands during this phase will be great. But so too will the risk of it becoming overweight.

WATCHING YOUR DOG'S WEIGHT

As with humans, weight problems can happen all too easily. All a dog has to do is eat too much and do too little exercise. The calories that aren't burned off on the daily run or walk will be stored in the body in the form of fat.

In some cases it is down to the metabolic makeup of the dog, but mostly it is down to the owner failing to be responsible about food and/or the dog's exercise regime. The most common mistakes owners make are:

- Feeding the dog poor-quality leftovers from their own meals.
- Giving them regular snacks or treats, particularly human ones such as chocolate.
- Overusing food reward in training, thereby encouraging the dog to be constantly on the lookout for tidbits.
- Failing to give the dog sufficient exercise.

Between 40 and 50 per cent of our dogs are overweight. As with humans, it is becoming an epidemic that could have disastrous consequences. Dogs that are carrying too many pounds tend to live shorter and less healthy lives than those who are at the ideal weight. The extra pounds place an increased burden on bones and joints as well as the heart. The dog may also be less well equipped to resist infections. And once a dog does go overweight, a downward spiral can set in. They can become lethargic and lose interest in playing or taking any form of exercise. This in turn will lead to a further deterioration in their health.

According to some vets, weight problems can be genetic. Among those breeds predisposed to being overweight are the Beagle, Bassett Hound, Cairn Terrier, Cavalier King Charles Spaniel, Daschund, Labrador and Retriever. If left unchecked, weight problems can lead to a whole host of diseases and conditions. These include:

- diabetes
- liver diseases
- strains on the heart
- heat intolerance
- a deterioration of coat and skin condition
- reduced resistance to infectious diseases
- respiratory problems
- arthritis
- hip and elbow dysplasia
- spinal disc problems
- ruptured joint ligaments

Given this, it is vital that you monitor your dog's weight during this period. The simplest way to do this is at the vets, where a visit to the scales should be part of the regular visit. You can then compare its weight with breed standards, to make sure it is on target. But it is also important you body score your dog.

BODY SCORING: HOW TO MONITOR YOUR DOG'S WEIGHT AND CONDITION

With dogs prone not just to obesity but to so many other related diseases and disorders, it's vital that you maintain a close eye on their physical condition throughout their life; but this is particularly important during this crucial six-month phase of their development. It is not just obesity that owners should be concerned about, of course. A dog that is seriously underweight can also develop problems that will at best handicap it later in life, or at worst shorten its life considerably. Keeping a close monitor on your dog's condition means much more than running an eye over them every now and again. It demands a regular evaluation of their weight and condition so as to give you a body score.

How to Score

One of the benefits of having developed a good relationship with your dog early on is that it will allow you to touch it. This will be invaluable here, as to thoroughly examine your dog requires you feeling its body all over.

The main checks are on the ribs and the tail-base. Run your fingers over them and assess how easy it is to make out the bones. The other key thing to look for is the shape of the abdomen. The best way to assess this is by standing over the dog so you are looking directly down at it.

There are five categories of body condition:

1. EMACIATED

A score of one represents a dog that is thin to a dangerously unhealthy degree. Its ribs are easily felt and have no fat covering. Its other bony points are also easily found. Its tail-base is prominent and has no tissue between the skin and bone. From above it is easy to see a pronounced and severe tuck in the abdomen.

2. UNDERWEIGHT

This represents a dog whose ribs are still easy to feel and that has only minimal fat cover. The tailbase is raised and bony and has little tissue between the skin and the bone. In a puppy over six months there will also be a tuck in the abdomen when it is viewed from the side. When looked at from above it will have a distinct hourglass shape.

3. IDEAL

Here, the ribs are easily felt with a thin belt of fat between the skin and bone. The bony points are also easily felt with a healthy amount of fat. With dogs over six months there is a well-proportioned waist visible from above, while there is a tuck in the abdomen when viewed from the side.

4. OVERWEIGHT

A dog scoring four is defined as being overweight. Its ribs are hard to feel underneath a significant layering of fat. The tail-base is thickish and lies beneath a similar amount of tissue between the skin and bone. It is still relatively easy to feel the bony parts of the body, but they too are covered by layers of fat. In animals over six months there is no tuck in the waist when viewed from the side, and the back is wider when looked at from above.

5. OBESE

A dog that is obese is categorised by a score of five. Its ribs will be very hard to feel under a thick covering of fat, as will its tail-base. When viewed from the side, older dogs will have no waist as such, instead there will be a bulging and slightly pendulous belly. When inspected from above, the dog's back will be significantly broader than normal.

DEALING WITH WEIGHT PROBLEMS

Dealing with dogs that are marginally under- or overweight is a relatively straightforward matter. A reduction in the amount of food they eat and a corresponding increase in the amount of exercise they get should do the

Piling on the pounds: with the wrong diet and exercise regime a dog can quickly become overweight, threatening its health in the process.

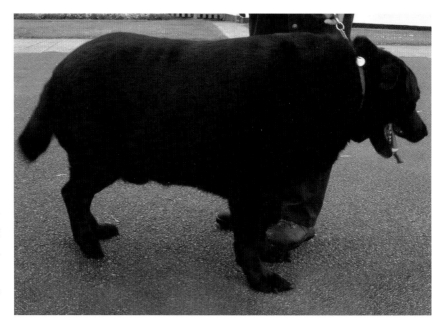

trick. The only caveat is that the transition should be made gradually, over a period of a week or so. Otherwise you risk delivering a shock to the dog's system. In addition to this, owners must cut out snacks, stop feeding leftovers and get the dog out of the habit of demanding tidbits constantly.

Treating a dog that is seriously over- or underweight is another matter, however. This is something that should be done in conjunction with a vet. They will be able to advise you on the best way to tackle the problem, and in particular they will be able to recommend the most appropriate diet.

Veterinary science has made such advances in recent years that there are now dozens of very specific diets geared to particular needs. These include low-calorie diets for weight loss, and high-energy/high-calorie diets for weight gain. Work with your vet to find the right one for your dog.

Pushing the boundaries

Until now the dog has been confined to its home environment. This has been necessary for several reasons. Primarily the dog hasn't yet developed enough to be able to cope with a long walk. It would get tired easily and may do harm to its still-developing feet and bones. More importantly it has been completing its vaccinations. Without proper protection from the multitude of threats the outside world presents it can't go out.

Now, however, it is ready to take its first steps into the wider world, and in doing so to give its body the greater workout it needs to develop physically. It will still not go far. Small breeds are simply not up to long marches yet. And big breeds, with their vulnerable bones, can do severe damage if they are allowed to push themselves too hard physically at this age. So walks should not take the dog further than a mile or so radius of home.

Before any of this can happen, however, the dog needs to learn the all-important rules that will dictate the walk. And they are that they must walk on a lead and accept some more important instructions from their owners.

Of course, this is not all they must be prepared for. The dog's world is not going to expand much, but it is once more going to bring it into contact with myriad new experiences – all of which it will have to assimilate.

Here the owner needs to be prepared to help the dog deal with this by understanding its body language.

HEEL WORK AND PREPARING FOR THE WALK

By the age of 14 weeks the dog should be comfortable with its human environment. The fears of a few weeks earlier should have been allayed. It should be familiar with the sights, smells and sounds in its home. It should also be fully vaccinated and ready to interact with dogs outside the home.

The next natural step will be for the dog to push the boundaries of this environment and to go out on a walk of a few hundred yards or so. Before this can happen, however, it needs to learn the skills it will require to survive in the wider world.

Heel Work

It is in both the dog and the owner's interests that it learns to walk to heel at the end of a lead.

From the owner's point of view, no one wants to go for a walk with a dog that is constantly straining at the lead. It defeats the object of what is meant to be a pleasant, enjoyable and above all fun exercise.

From the dog's point of view, it wants to explore the wider world as freely and enjoyably as possible. If it is constantly being yanked by the neck, or if its owner is repeatedly cutting short its walks, that is simply not going to happen.

If, on the other hand, it learns to walk in harmony with its owner, speeding up and slowing down, stopping, starting and turning at the same time as its guardian, then this really is going to be the highlight of every day.

Two words of caution, however. As with so many areas of dog training, the best results will be achieved through a structured, disciplined approach, and this is not something that should be rushed. Invariably, if you allow one hour it will take fifteen minutes to get something right. And if you allow only fifteen minutes it will take an hour to achieve your goal. So allow plenty of time.

The other thing to be careful of is the use of food reward. You are going to be using a lot of it during this training process. Be careful about the amounts and the frequency. The idea of exercise is to improve the dog's health – not damage it.

STEP BY STEP — HEEL WORK

1. CHOOSE YOUR SIDE

- You must first choose the side you are going to want the dog to walk. For most people this is their left side. (This is something that has developed from the gundog or sporting-dog world where most people are right-handed and want to carry their broken gun under this arm while out hunting. It is easier, and safer, for them to keep their dog to their left.) There is, however, nothing wrong with training the dog to walk on the right. What is important is that once a decision has been made you adhere to it.

- The guide that follows assumes that the owner has their dog on their left. If you want to train your dog to walk to the right, simply reverse the instructions where applicable.

2. BRINGING THE DOG TO HEEL

- Working somewhere there is enough space for dog and owner to walk a dozen or so paces, begin by arming yourself with a piece of food reward. Place this in your left hand then turn your back on the dog. Bring your left hand down along the side of your left leg until it is being held at the dog's nose level. As you do this, call the dog's name and ask it to 'heel'.

- If the dog appears at your side as you've requested, give it the food reward as well as warm praise.

- If it doesn't appear, don't try again immediately. Leave it an hour or so before retrying. Again, patience is a virtue.

3. WALKING SIDE BY SIDE

- Once the dog has successfully responded to your request to come to heel, you are ready to begin walking slowly. The aim of the ▶

exercise here is that the dog remains close to your left leg as you move along, and that the lead remains loose in your hand.

- Begin by calling the dog to heel once more. Then take a couple of steps, encouraging it to accompany you with the food reward. It is important to remember here that the dog is not a mind-reader, and walking to heel is not something that it would do naturally in the wild. If it strays away from you, encourage it to return to your side with a positive association and give it some more food reward. Remind it to stay where it is by repeating the word 'heel' as you go. When the dog gets it right and walks at your side for the full distance you want to go, reward him warmly with praise and with one final piece of food reward.
- As ever, the main thing to remember is to stay calm and unflappable. No matter how frustrated or cross you might feel at your dog's lack of response, you mustn't show it. The dog will pick up on your anxiety, and it will also lose some of that precious trust you have built up. If this happens it will want to get away from you, which is the last thing you want. Simply allow things to calm down and start again later.

4. VARY THE EXERCISE

- Once the dog has got the knack of walking alongside you, start varying the direction and duration of your practice. Stop and start every now and again. Get the dog ready for the reality of the outside world, where it is going to be travelling on a variety of different routes.

Walking on the Lead

The lead is the most important piece of equipment your dog is going to wear. It is its safety line, its link to the guardian who is going to protect it from the many terrors it is going to face in the outside world. In extreme cases, it might save its life. So it must get used not just to wearing it, but walking properly and responding to the lead well in advance of its first walk.

STEP BY STEP — USING THE LEAD

1. SLIPPING ON THE LEAD

- Bring the dog to heel as usual. Lean over and carefully place the loop of the lead over its head. Make sure it fits comfortably. It shouldn't be so tight that it might choke or chafe the dog. Equally it shouldn't be so loose that it might slip off if pulled on vigorously by the dog. If this happened the dog might well flee.
- Place the lead on gently and without any fuss. When it is safely on for the first time give the dog some warm praise.

2. WALKING ON THE LEAD

- Repeat the usual walking-to-heel exercise, encouraging the dog to stay at your side as normal. If it starts to tug or yank at the lead, stop and calmly stand your ground. The dog needs to learn from the very beginning that tugging matches are simply not going to happen. Resume the walk by once more getting the dog to come to heel. Once it is back in position, carry on. When the dog reaches the end of the walk without having once pulled on the lead, praise it and give it some food reward. It deserves it.

a. *b.* *c.*

3. LEARNING TO TURN

- No walk is ever going to head in a straight line. The dog is going to have to turn and must learn to do so under your control.

a. Gently does it: a lead must be introduced carefully and calmly so as not to upset or frighten the young dog. Begin with the lead hanging very loose and open on the dog's neck.

b. A new sensation: feeling a lead on its neck will feel odd for the dog. Let it get used to the weight.

c. Taking it slowly: keep the lead loose while asking the dog to walk attached to the line for the first time. Do things nice and slowly, being sure not to put too much pressure on the line at this stage.

These manoeuvres again should be practised at home long before the first walk is attempted. (Remember, I am assuming here that most people will walk with their dog to the left. If, however, it is the right, simply reverse the instructions.)

To Turn Right

- Even if it is obvious to you that a turn is required, a dog isn't going to know it unless you make it obvious. And the best way to do that is to use the sort of body language it understands best. To turn right you should first pivot around, leading with your right leg. Don't lead with the left, it will cause confusion and problems: the dog will be blocked from turning right and both dog and owner run the risk of tripping up over each other.
- As you are pivoting use a distinctive word, something that the dog will always associate with this manoeuvre (a traditional choice is 'close'). As you turn your body, the dog's head will move with the lead and its body should angle around to the right as well.

To Turn Left

- This is a little more complicated. Begin by gathering up the lead so that there is no slack. This will have the effect of bringing the dog to your side. Now extend the left leg out as far as you can. At this point the leg should be touching the dog's shoulder and neck. Once more choose a distinctive word that you are going to stick to from now on. (The traditional one is 'back', for the simple reason that the dog is being asked to drop back.)
- As you pivot to the left, the dog should naturally drop back. And because your body is now gently applying pressure to the dog's body it should naturally turn to the left as well. The key here – as always – is that there is nothing sudden or violent about this. It should happen smoothly, seamlessly and calmly. The dog should be reacting naturally to the movements of the owner's legs.

4. STOPPING – TEACHING THE 'WAIT'

- Inside the home you are working in a safe and predictable environment. Outside the world is going to be anything but safe or predictable, so you must be able to bring the dog to an instant halt. It might be the control that saves the dog's life.
- Introducing the 'wait' instruction into heel work is straightforward. As you develop heel work throw in an occasional sudden stop. Accompany it with a short, sharp – but not too intimidating – instruction to 'wait'.
- If the dog does so, reward it. This is something that needs a positive association. Then carry on with the walk. Introduce stops like this at regular intervals from now on.

5. SIMULATING THE REAL WALK

- With all the elements in place you can now make use of whatever space is available to extend the length of the walk. Now is the time to begin simulating the demands of what will be the real walk. Throw in all the different elements – the turns, the wait – mixing them up so that the dog doesn't know what is coming next. Keep it guessing and thinking all the time. Work towards a situation where there is no tension on the dog's lead at all. Aim for such a well-coordinated relationship between you and your dog that someone watching you would conclude that you must be joined by an invisible line.
- When you have achieved this, you are ready to head out into the world.

FIRST STEPS: GOING OUT ON THE WALK

It is always worth spending a moment to think about things from a dog's perspective. And this is certainly the case when it comes to the first walk.

The dog sees itself as a member of a functioning pack. So when it steps out into the world with that pack, it equates that with its ancient ancestor the wolf going out on the hunt.

This is another of the key moments when the leader, the alpha male, again stamps its authority on its subordinates. The alpha decides when the pack goes out on the hunt. Before the pack leaves, it checks to see whether it is safe to leave the den. And when it decides the coast is clear, it is the alpha who leads the way out into the world – and then chooses the direction in which they are to head.

The domestic dog attaches the same importance to its walk, and for that reason it is vital that the owner takes charge of each aspect of that walk, just as the alpha within the wolf pack does.

By now the fundamental foundations should have been laid. The dog should have formed a close bond of trust with its owner. It should also have learned to walk to heel. So it should be ready to follow into the wider world, secure in the knowledge it will be safe as it does so.

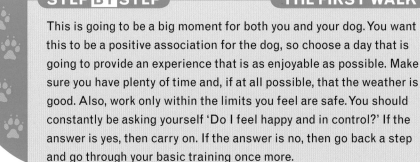

STEP BY STEP — THE FIRST WALK

This is going to be a big moment for both you and your dog. You want this to be a positive association for the dog, so choose a day that is going to provide an experience that is as enjoyable as possible. Make sure you have plenty of time and, if at all possible, that the weather is good. Also, work only within the limits you feel are safe. You should constantly be asking yourself 'Do I feel happy and in control?' If the answer is yes, then carry on. If the answer is no, then go back a step and go through your basic training once more.

When the moment does come for the first walk, be sure to adhere to the following principles closely:

1. PREPARING TO LEAVE HOME

- The key thing to remember here is that you must lead from the front. You must be the first person across the threshold and you must be the person who decides the length, duration and direction of the walk. Have this at the forefront of your mind throughout.
- Call the dog to heel as normal and slip on the lead. Start heading towards the door.
- Dogs are smart and will quickly pick up on the fact there is something different about today's routine. If it suddenly gets agitated or tries pushing in front of you, stop. As usual, this should be done calmly,

without any histrionics or raised voices. Once things have calmed down, bring the dog to heel once more and try again.

2. THROUGH THE DOOR

- Make sure you are the first to cross the threshold. Again, if the dog tries to force its way past you, stop. Return to the house, bring the dog to heel and start again. This principle is important, so it must be learned by the dog from the outset.
- Once you have got through the door properly, however, you can relax a little. This is, after all, a thrilling moment for your dog. You can let them enjoy it.
- The dog should begin walking to heel. Don't worry too much if it gets a few steps ahead. That is the point of having a lead with a length of leather or rope on it. Only act if there is any significant tension on the lead. If there is, simply call the dog to heel. When it does this reward it warmly with praise. Complying to your request when there is so much excitement going on around makes the dog worthy of it.

3. TAKING DIRECTION

- The dog must learn at this early juncture that it is not in charge of any aspect of the walk. So the next crucial moment comes at the boundary of the home, where dog and owner are suddenly faced with the option of heading in one of several directions.
- If the dog begins heading off in one direction, execute a smart about-turn and start walking the other way. If the dog starts veering off again, change direction again. Keep repeating this until the dog has understood that it is not in charge of the walk. Once again, your aim is to keep the dog thinking. In this case it is going to be asking: 'Where are we going?' By taking control you will assist it in reaching the conclusion it needs to reach – 'It's not for me to decide' – and you will have helped it to start exercising self-control. As with all good teaching, a student must be allowed to make the right decisions for themselves.

4. BUILD IT INTO AN ENJOYABLE EXPERIENCE

- The first walk should be a gentle introduction for both dog and owner, and it should continue this way for the next few days.
- Owners should build up their confidence with the controls they have developed so far. The dog should become used to the idea that when it steps out into the world with its guardian it always returns safely home. At this point the dog should not be let off the lead. This step has to be planned carefully too, and if rushed could have dire consequences. Literally, the dog must learn to walk before it can run.
- An owner can derive immense pride and joy from leading a dog that is light on its feet and responding well to its requests. You only have to look at the way a young dog walks along wagging its tail and happily exploring the exciting new world opening up around it to understand that it is having even more fun than you.

Understanding Your Dog's Body Language

Controls are vitally important for going out on a walk, but owners need to know when to use them. They need to know when to help their dogs deal with the outside world.

The most obvious times owners will be needed are when walking near roads or other potentially dangerous spots. But the dog will face subtler terrors too, ones that the owner may not appreciate. While a dog will not be able to verbalise the fears it is feeling, it will, however, be signalling its discomfort.

To help the dog's transition into the wider world, it is therefore important to understand how a dog communicates its feelings.

READING YOUR DOG

Our dogs may not be able to communicate with us in our own language, but they are certainly able to give us a range of powerful signals using their own, highly developed body language.

It is a language all dogs will learn during their early development. With a movement of their ears or tail, or with a change in body position, the young dog will learn how to send a message that another dog will be able to read immediately.

As the young dog matures it's important that we learn to recognise these signals too.

SIGNALS

Dogs use an array of tools to deliver their body-language messages. We only have to look at two extremes to see this. If we look at a dog that is signalling fear, for instance, we will see anxiety in its eyes, its ears pinned right back, there will be tension around the mouth and the body will be slouched backwards in a defensive posture. Finally, its tail will be between its legs.

Equally, if a dog is standing upright with an inquisitive, happy look in its eyes, no signs of tension in the body and its tail wagging, it is a clear signal that the dog is happy. But between these two extremes there are subtleties that owners need to understand. And to do that we need to understand how the dog uses different aspects of its physicality to express itself.

Sending a message: dogs use their stance, body position, eyes, ears and tail to send powerful signals about their authority.

Ears

In the wild, the wolf uses its ears as a major part of its defence – and attack – system. They are able to twist them so as to pick up sounds, whether those of potential attackers or prey. The ears also allow wolves to interact as a hierarchy. If a wolf's ears are pricked it is signalling that its interest is aroused in something. A relaxed state of mind is signalled by the ears being turned to the side while still slightly pricked.

Our dogs use their ears in a similar way. The key positions are:

- Ears pricked forward – alert, interested
- Ears slightly pricked to the side – relaxed
- Ears held back – respect
- Ears pinned right back – fear, submission

Early warning system: a dog's ear position gives out a strong signal about the way it feels. In this sequence of three photos, the dog's ears are: a. pricked to show it is alert and happy, b. cocked back to indicate respect and c. dropped down to convey anxiety.

Eyes

They say that eyes are the mirror of the soul and this is certainly true with dogs. You can see a whole range of emotions by looking into a dog's eyes, everything from strength and confidence to fear and pain. And you can always be certain that what you see is what the dog is feeling. Dogs, unlike humans, don't lie.

Generally speaking, the main signals are:

- Wide, bulbous eyes – stress, fear
- Fixed gaze – strength, confidence
- Glare – threat, aggression
- Soft eyes – relaxed

Teeth

In the wild, teeth are the ultimate weapon in the wolf's armoury. They know they can kill with them, so it is not surprising that they are used as a powerful signal.

The amount of teeth shown varies according to the amount of information the wolf wants to convey. If it wants to issue a general warning it will lift its lip just enough to show a tiny percentage of its teeth. If this message doesn't get through it will show slightly more teeth. This will continue until it has rolled back its lip to reveal a whole set of teeth and gums. In conjunction with a glare of the eyes, this conveys a message that is unmistakable. Then, at the opposite end of the emotional spectrum, the teeth can also be used to demonstrate contentment.

A domestic dog taps into this same vocabulary to signal its feelings:

The Commissar

The lower jaw works in conjunction with the teeth to provide extra subtleties of signalling. The more forward the commissar the more aggressive the expression is. If it is pulled back it is more defensive.

Stance

As a well-designed running machine, the wolf has a very balanced frame. It uses this to send subtle signals, pushing it forward to show potential aggression, pulling it back to show submission, in particular towards its superiors within the pack. Our dogs do this too.

Foreface

The foreface is the area around the nose and mouth. By manipulating this area, the dog is able to deliver a range of expressions from a smile to a crunched-up face that is a sign of aggression.

Hackles

The dog's ability to make its hairs stand on end is essentially a mechanism for making itself look bigger. Again, it is something acquired from the wolf and its instinct to avoid confrontation wherever possible. The wolf's thick coat allows it to add inches all over to make itself look more intimidating. Yet, equally, raising the hair can signal joy.

Tail

This is the ultimate signal for a dog, and one that is unique to its species. The tail tells you a great deal about the dog's personality, its confidence level, its status and its mood. It will also tell you a great deal about its reaction to the world around it.

There are four key positions:

- Normal: When a dog is in a relaxed and happy state its tail should hang at a downward angle, without any obvious tension in it. This indicates the dog is comfortable with the world.
- Tucked: If the tail is tucked beneath the dog's tummy it is a sure sign it has been frightened by something.
- Level Carriage: This is the position adopted when a dog is out on a walk. The tail comes out from the dog's rear horizontally.
- Upper Positions: The higher the tail carriage goes the higher the dog's confidence and its perceived status. In the wild an alpha wolf will carry its tail almost at right angles to its back.

The tension – or lack of it – in a dog's tail is also a strong signal. In the normal position the dog's tail hangs limp, like a flag at half mast. But if that tail is high, say at ninety degrees to its back, and rigid as well, then it is a pretty clear indication of aggression.

In the wild, dogs need to be agile and quick-witted to survive. For this reason the wolf is fast and very flexible in its movements. Thousands of years of breeding have removed this asset from a large number of breeds. And we have to be aware of this as owners.

Breeding and Signalling – Being Aware of Your Dog's Limitations in Communicating with Other Dogs

The original dogs, wolves, were perfectly equipped to communicate with each other. Their physical makeup was designed to give them the ability to get the message across to their peers quickly and efficiently. They had an evenly spread skull, pricked ears and uniformly shaped forefaces, for instance. They all looked alike so there was little room for misinterpretation or confusion.

After 14,000 years of human breeding, however, the dog has evolved in a multitude of different directions. There are now thousands of diverse breeds, many of them moulded to meet the tastes and practical requirements of human society rather than those of the canine world. The upshot of this, however, is that dogs cannot read each other as well as they used to. And this can cause problems, especially when dogs that are unknown to each other interact.

So as owners prepare to guide their dogs through this important phase it is essential to spare a few moments to understand some of the limitations their pets may face. Some breeds have restrictions in terms of what they can and cannot signal. Their physical structure may limit them. As our dogs go out into the wider world and interact with each other, this is potentially a problematic area. And it is important that we as owners are aware of this. Like us, dogs view the unfamiliar with suspicion, and it is important that we as owners are aware of this.

EARS

Never off duty: with its cropped ears, a Boston Terrier seems to be signalling it is constantly on the alert.

In trying to understand why some dogs attack other dogs, it's worth thinking about how they see each other. For instance, if a dog is showing another dog what it perceives to be a lack of respect by not dropping its ears, this may act as an antagonistic signal. But what if the offending dog simply cannot drop its ears? A Springer Spaniel, for instance, cannot drop and raise its ears like other breeds so your dog needs to learn that there are subtleties to their species, that not all dogs look like those they have been used to in the litter and at home.

In some countries it is common to crop a dog's ears so that they are fixed in a permanently pricked position. To other dogs this is signalling a state of permanent alert, which is always going to leave them on their guard.

EYES

Wolves have eyes that are proportional to the face and allow them the whole range of expressions. Breeding has removed some of these options from certain dogs, however.

Dogs need to be able to see frowns and grimaces, for instance, but breeds like the Sharpei have developed so many layers of folds on their faces that other breeds are going to find it very difficult to spot these subtleties.

For dogs, eyes are for seeing and to be seen with. However, dogs with very small eyes can also have difficulty communicating with other breeds. Furthermore, through breeding, some breeds like pugs, boxers, chihuahuas, Cavalier King Charles spaniels and bull breeds have very wide and bulbous eyes. To another dog this may give the impression that the dog is stressed or aggressive, and it may mean it won't want to play with it in a social situation.

FOREFACE

The foreface is one of the most expressive areas of a dog's face. It is the area between the eyes, down along the nasal passage to the snout and along the side of the jaw, and it provides dogs with a range of signalling options. A tiny movement here can allow them to bare their teeth, or wrinkle their nose, or even to smile. Because of the number of muscles at play here, it is immensely flexible. But again, if breeding has produced a dog that cannot manipulate its foreface, then problems and misunder-standings arise – for both the signaller and the recipient. King Charles spaniels and boxers, for instance, have had their nostril area bred shorter and shorter. This means they are now denied the array of signals available with a full face.

If a dog is slightly upset, it can signal this with a slight, almost imperceptible curl of the lip. If it is more angry it will show more teeth. If it is really angry it will show a full set of teeth. If the foreface can't do this, then none of these signals are available.

THE COMMISSAR

As mentioned, the more forward the commissar the more aggressive the expression is, and vice versa. The more it is pulled back the more defensive the message. Yet some dogs have been bred deliberately with a severely undershot jaw (the lower jaw protrudes out so that it cannot connect with the upper jaw). Examples include boxers, bulldogs and pugs. This has the unfortunate effect of leaving them unable to use the jaw to signal submission or respect. Quite the opposite, in fact, they are always presenting a picture of aggression, regardless of their true intent. This has led to dogs like Staffordshire bull terriers, for instance, getting a reputation for aggressiveness that very often is more deserved by their thoughtless owners than it is by the breed.

STANCE

Dogs with very broad chests, such as boxers, are not nature's norm. Their overdeveloped chests and broad shoulders make them look like the canine equivalent of Arnold Schwarzenegger: top heavy. As a result they also appear threatening to other dogs. Their back end is lighter, making them look as if they are leaning forward, which adds to this effect: as if they are pressing forward.

Breeds like the Pekingese, on the other hand, are confusing. With their long coats and short legs it's hard to see where the body begins and ends. You don't know whether they are standing up or lying down. Their flat faces only add to the uncertainty other dogs will feel when meeting this type of breed. They won't know whether to play with it or eat it! Again, owners should bear this in mind when they begin introducing their dogs to other breeds.

The Terminators: with their broad shoulders and chests and their forward-leaning stance, bulldogs look like the canine equivalent of the top-heavy Arnold Schwarzenegger. This conveys a threatening message to other dogs.

HACKLES

People often see the raising of fur along a dog's back as being associated with aggression; but it can be signalling an entirely different emotion – joy. So if you have a dog whose fur is standing up all the time – such as a Pomeranian – be aware that this can confuse other dogs. Equally, dogs like dalmatians or Chinese crested, with smooth or furless coats, don't have the option of raising their hackles – again, something that limits their ability to communicate with other breeds.

TAIL

The tail is a feature that has been changed a lot by generations of human breeding, and as a result it can be the cause of a great deal of confusion and misunderstanding among dogs. In particular, owners should be aware of the following tail types:

Long Tails

Some breeds, such as Bassett Hounds and Dachshunds, have been bred with such short legs that their tails look disproportionately long. The natural position for other breeds is to carry the tail slightly below the horizontal, but if these dogs did this they would be trailing their tails along the ground. So, to be comfortable, they carry their tails slightly higher. You and your dog know this is normal, that the dog is compensating for what is in effect its disability. But other breeds will see something different. They could easily misinterpret this as a challenge.

Raising the alarm: a Basset Hound naturally carries its tail high, sending a confusing signal when it first encounters other breeds.

Curled Tails

Some breeds have been altered so as to have very curved tails. Examples include the Elkhound, the Banzeji and the Pomeranian. It is easy to see how this will be confusing to another breed encountering one of these dogs for the first time. They will wonder whether it is signalling it is relaxed or making a threat.

Docked Tails

Docking is very common among many breeds. While dogs that have been docked are still able to use their stumps to a degree, they are nowhere

A kitchen mop: on seeing an Old English Sheepdog for the first time, another breed will be deeply confused by the seeming absence of eyes, ears, a tail or a foreface. They won't know whether it's a dog, let alone what it is trying to signal.

near as efficient or as easily understood as a full tail, especially from a distance. Another dog may get completely the wrong end of the stick when it first sees a docked dog. By the time it gets up close and sees the reality of what it is signalling, it may be too late. In breeds where other features are limited as well, such as Spaniels with their floppy ears, a docked tail only adds to their disadvantaged status.

Some dogs, of course, are handicapped by a combination of all these factors. Consider the poor Old English Sheepdog, for instance. Another dog coming into contact with this breed for the first time will encounter what looks like a giant kitchen mop. They can't see eyes, ears or a foreface. They can't see a tail. All they see is a broad-chested animal covered in fur.

It isn't even clear that it is a dog, so it is no surprise that other dogs often misread this breed in particular.

Moving into the wider world – *typical problems*

The dog's journey into the big, wide world outside the home is full of excitement, but it holds its share of potential problems and pitfalls as well. Owners must be ready to help their dogs deal with each of these.

CANINE CONFRONTATIONS

Socialising and interacting with other dogs – and, more to the point, other 'packs' – is an unnatural act. In the wild, packs instinctively avoid each other and mark out their territory specifically to ensure this happens.

In the human world, of course, this isn't possible or desirable. Dogs need to exercise and – unless you are lucky enough to live in a particularly isolated corner of our overpopulated planet – this will inevitably result in them meeting other dogs and their owners.

As we have seen, dogs can send out confusing and dangerous signals to each other when they meet on their own. But when they meet with their owners there is an additional ingredient that can inflame the situation. The dog will react to this, possibly aggressively, so it is important that you are prepared to deal with this potential problem.

The key is to practise 'cross-packing' – that is, getting your dog used to encountering other dogs and their owners while providing calm and consistent leadership. When you approach another dog and its owner do the following:

- Keep walking with your dog on its lead, trying to give the other dog as wide a berth as possible.
- Don't acknowledge or look at the other dog and its owner as you walk past.
- If your dog walks past without acknowledging or confronting the other dog, when you reach a reasonable distance reward your dog with food.

As ever, it is all about making a positive association. And the more often you do this, the sooner it will cease to be a problem. Of course, you are not the only element in the equation here and it is quite possible, indeed likely, that the other owner has less control and understanding of their dog than you do. So, unfortunately, you do have to be prepared for the possibility that another dog may act aggressively towards you. The key to dealing with this situation is, again, to remain calm. But in addition you should remember the following:

- Remove your dog from the situation as quickly and quietly as possible.
- Do not make a huge fuss or engage in a shouting match with the other dog and its owner – this will only inflame the situation and panic your dog further.
- If it is small, do not pick up your dog. Obviously there may be circumstances where the danger is too great, but even if you have to do this try to remain calm. The way you deal with the situation sends out important information, both to your dog and the dog causing the problem. Don't become part of the problem. Your dog will not see you as weak for removing yourself from this situation. The need to survive overrides all others.
- If your dog removes itself without overreacting, again, reward its behaviour with a small treat.

FEAR OF NOISES ON THE WALK

The outside world is full of strange, surprising and sometimes very loud noises. They are shocking for humans, let alone dogs. However, we can at least rationalise what they are and where they are coming from. Dogs cannot.

At home we can teach our dogs to ignore such sounds by exuding calm and a lack of panic. But as the dog begins to venture further and further away from the home this isn't always going to be enough. Everything from cars and motorbikes to alarms and aeroplanes can upset a dog. In the most extreme cases the experience can leave them nervous and anxious for a long period, even for life, so it is important to tackle this head-on.

A dog is never going to understand what an alarm or a fire engine is, or tell the difference between the sound of a firework or a backfiring car. All it can know is that the sound isn't threatening its safety. And the only person who can tell it this is you, its owner.

When you reach the road, wait there. When the dog reacts to the first car or lorry passing by the key thing is that you don't mirror its panic. Simply let the vehicle pass and the sound fade, then reassure the dog simply with a 'good dog' and a piece of food reward. However, don't make a fuss over it. This process should then be repeated. You should wait for the next vehicle, let it pass and again reward the dog afterwards. Slowly it will get the message that you aren't worried by what is going on here. And nor should it be...

INTRODUCING DOGS TO OTHER BREEDS

Because dogs are such intelligent creatures they will do everything possible to survive in this world. They want to avoid confrontation and will do what they can to achieve this. So, for instance, when it is growing up, a Basset Hound puppy will quickly learn that a high tail-carriage is not necessarily a signal of dominance within their breed. Given their short legs and long tails, to drop the tail to the normal, slightly drooped position would leave it dragging uncomfortably along the floor. When they meet other dogs, of course, they will encounter animals who don't see things the same way. And so problems may set in.

This is not to say two breeds can't play together, but they must have time to overcome their confusion. Dogs operate according to an old saying, 'beware instant friends', so when they go out into the world patience must be the byword.

Because dogs of different breeds will confuse each other with their different signalling, it is often helpful if dogs of this age are given the chance to get to know a wider range of other dogs. We have altered the physicality of our dogs so much that they need this time to assimilate with each other. One way to do this is via good-quality socialisation or puppy classes, where puppies can meet each other and learn to be comfortable in each other's presence. Yet, even here, owners must be aware that things aren't necessarily going to work out immediately. Don't rush things, give the dog time.

TRAVELLING: GETTING USED TO THE CAR

With the dog now fully immunised, it is more likely that you will want to travel further afield as well. You may, for instance, want to go on a family holiday. To be able to achieve this with your dog you will need it to be comfortable with travelling in your car. And, again, this is something that should be tackled with care and planning.

Dogs can easily form phobias about travelling in cars. Their reactions can vary from shivering and generally cowering in the car to completely over-the-top panic, leaping around and barking. Neither is good for the dog or the owner, who has to drive while all this is going on around them. So for the sake of both – and for the safety of other road users who could be affected – the dog needs to get used to travelling around.

The puppy's first experience of travelling in a car will probably have come at eight weeks when it moved home. It may not need to travel again until it goes for its vaccinations a few weeks later. Yet it is important that it becomes used to the environment inside the car – and to travelling short- to medium-range distances in it – before that point.

As with so many other areas, the key is making a positive association, and this is something that can be done as an extension of the familiarisation process that's already going on.

As the dog begins to explore the outside world around the house you should encourage it to spend time around the car. Once it gets used to this something can be done.

Getting Ready for the Journey

The first thing an owner must ask themselves is: Is the dog ready? The car is an extension of the house, and if the dog is not assimilating to the home fully then clearly it is not ready to assimilate to the car. If, on the other hand, it is well-adjusted and responds positively to you, then it should be ready to take this step.

Your first trips with the dog should be relatively short affairs, perhaps just a drive around the local area without stopping anywhere. Make the trip after meal-time and after the dog has had a good play and is relaxed. Have some newspaper, a towel, a blanket and some wet wipes to hand in case the experience proves too much for the dog. Car or motion sickness is very common among dogs, particularly young ones. You should also have something comforting, perhaps a blanket or a toy that makes the association a happy one.

If you have another dog who is a good traveller, it might be a welcome addition too. If you have a dog that is not a good traveller, however, it shouldn't be brought along. Bad habits rub off on each other. Finally, you should also have someone to accompany you, preferably someone whom the dog knows and is comfortable with.

There are several options for housing the dog. The important thing is that it is comfortable and secure. It should never be put in the passenger seat alongside the driver. You can opt for:

- a harness in the back seat
- a cage at the back of the car
- a cardboard box if it is a small puppy
- if necessary, put the dog in the foot-well of the passenger seat.

It isn't hard to imagine what an overwhelming experience this is going to be for a young dog. It has been familiarising itself slowly with unfamiliar sights and sounds for a few weeks now, but the journey it is about to take is going to be a sensory overload, filled with innumerable new sights, sounds and smells. So be prepared for its reaction to be strong.

If the dog becomes distressed when you start the engine and move off, the passenger should offer a reassuring stroke of the hand. It shouldn't be overly dramatic, just a comforting presence. Equally, if there is a physical reaction – if the dog is sick or soils the car – there should be no response from you. The mess should be cleared up and you should head home. Wait a few days before trying again.

If, however, all goes well, when you arrive home immediately take the dog to the garden or toilet area where it will probably need to go. Praise it warmly when it does this, laying the seeds for a good association.

If the dog suffers persistently from motion sickness you should consult your vet about travel-sickness tablets, which are highly effective. If you don't do this the dog's bad association with the car is simply going to get worse, and the problems will become self-perpetuating.

Wellbeing

GROOMING/HEALTHCARE

Retained Baby Teeth

Between the ages of three and five months the dog should be losing its deciduous or baby teeth and growing its adult teeth. The incisors, canines and cuspids will come first, followed by the molars. As this happens the baby teeth should fall out and be reabsorbed by the dog. It is important during this phase to monitor your dog's teeth to ensure this process is happening as it should.

The main problem to watch out for are retained baby teeth. In some instances they aren't ejected. The adult teeth that erupt beneath them are then pushed out of their proper alignment, and this will lead to problems. If during grooming you see your dog has two sets of teeth in the same place you should consult your vet as soon as possible. If spotted early enough, the problem is easily rectified by extracting the baby teeth. The dog's adult teeth will then develop in the normal healthy way.

Puberty

HOW TO TELL WHETHER YOUR DOG HAS ENTERED PUBERTY

Male

The male dog's testes are made up of a mass of coiled tubes which are stored in the scrotum. When puberty arrives they will begin to produce sperm, and will continue to do so throughout a dog's life, although in smaller quantities as the dog gets older.

The testes develop in the puppy, fixed to the scrotum by a ligament. As this ligament contracts, the testes drop through into the scrotum. The testes should be descended within the first few weeks of the puppy's life and can often be felt, but as the dog grows the fat around the scrotum they can be less easy to find until the onset of puberty at around four months.

As the dog reaches this age it's important to check it has two descended testes, although owners shouldn't panic if only one drops to begin with. Cases of retained testicles are not uncommon, with the second testicle dropping as late as 18 months. As usual, however, if there is any doubt, consult a vet.

A male dog reaches puberty at a young age. In theory this means that it could start fathering puppies from the age of five or six months old, but it is not a good idea to let young males breed. First and foremost, of course, letting your dog roam free impregnating every in-season female it encounters is going to fill the world with even more unwanted dogs. But there is a behavioural aspect to this as well. A young dog that is allowed to mate freely can develop aggressive and dominant tendencies. This, once more, goes back to the wild, where only the alpha male is allowed to mate. A dog that is allowed to mate when and where it wants will naturally assume it is a leader, which will have major behavioural repercussions. So, at this early stage in life, owners should be vigilant in keeping their males under control at all times.

Female

Females tend to enter puberty within a month or so of developing fully physically. For this reason, smaller breeds – who reach their adult size that much quicker – will have their first season much earlier than larger breeds. A dog from a small breed can have its first season as early as five months old. Giant breeds, on the other hand, may not reach puberty until as late as two years of age.

THE REPRODUCTIVE CYCLE

A female dog will usually come into season twice a year. Each six months it passes through a reproductive cycle that is made up of four phases.

HEALTH

- **Pro-oestrus.** The first part of the dog's 'season'. During this phase the dog's vulva begins to swell and there is a discharge, which can result in spotting or more obvious signs of blood on the coat or around the rear. Dogs also become fastidiously clean. This can last between 8 and 13 days.
- **Oestrus.** By this stage the bleeding has normally stopped and the discharge is clear or straw-coloured. The female is now ready to ovulate and breed. This period lasts for around a week and it is generally reckoned that the second day is the optimum time for mating. Obviously, the more matings that take place during this time, the more chance there is of conception.
- **Metoestrus.** There are no signs of activity at this point but the female's body is still hyperactive, this time preparing the uterus for a long, quiet spell. The dog's hormones can be so active that a female can believe she is pregnant. Such false pregnancies can be so convincing the dog makes a nest and comes into milk. If this happens consult a vet.
- **Anoestrus.** This is the quiet period in the female's reproductive cycle and lasts typically for about four months.

CHECKING YOUR FEMALE

Owners should check female dogs from the age of six months onwards. Often the dogs themselves will offer telltale signals. For instance, the dog might start showing more interest in its hygiene, cleaning and licking itself. Nature is telling her that she is vulnerable and needs to look after herself.

The surest way to check is by examining the vulva. Using a white tissue, touch round the vulva area. If there is any pinking or any red discharge then you can be pretty certain she is coming into season and the pro-oestrus and oestrus stages are underway. She will remain this way for three weeks.

SAFETY

A female is extremely vulnerable during this period, not just to unwanted conceptions but also to diseases like Pyometra, infections of the uterus. So as well as keeping the female dog isolated from males and other dogs in general, it is vital that she is kept clean and clear from infection.

NEUTERING

Deciding whether to castrate a male or spay a female dog is a big decision, but one that many owners make. I have no objection to it, in particular when one of the following situations exists:

1. The dog is going to be an 'assistance dog', that is a guide dog or other kind of human help. If the dog is a female in particular, the possibility that the dog will be unavailable to its disabled owner for long periods while it carries and raises pups has to be removed.

2. Rescue dogs. Many rescue organisations insist on neutering dogs that arrive with them. Again, this is understandable. In almost every case the organisation will know next to nothing about the dog's background.

3. Dogs with clear hereditary problems.

4. Dogs whose responsible owners have made a firm decision they are not going to breed.

WHEN NOT TO NEUTER

Equally, there are also some circumstances when neutering is not recommended.

1. For behavioural reasons. This is the WORST thing you can do. Behavioural problems are essentially psychological, to do with the dog's inability to carry out its perceived role as leader of its domestic pack. These problems should be treated by relieving the dog of its status as leader not by creating an even more wounded animal. Neutering – particularly castration which lowers the dog's testosterone levels – only creates an even more insecure dog and can make it even more panic-stricken and aggressive.

2. If an owner intends showing a dog. Kennel Club requirements may stipulate that a dog must be 'entire' or that it is able to reproduce.

3. If you are uncertain whether you want to breed or not. It's not reversible so you have to be sure.

HEALTH

SINGLE-LITTER MOTHERS

Many people believe that a female should be allowed to have one litter before being spayed. The argument is that it is somehow better for the dog, that she feels somehow 'more complete' as a dog having fulfilled her natural instincts to breed. This is wrong, for several reasons.

In the wild, only the alpha female breeds. Other female wolves are perfectly at ease with the fact they will never be mothers. Secondly, a female isn't going to miss something she has never experienced. Finally, breeding simply so that a female can then be spayed is irresponsible. You are not bringing puppies into the world for the right reasons.

OVERHEATED HORMONES: DEALING WITH AN OVER-AMOROUS DOG

Dogs can become over-amorous during this phase. Their hormones are flying around all over the place and they may try to simulate sex with each other. It is not just confined to males either. Bitches too can climb on top

Over-excited dogs can become highly amorous during puberty, mounting everything they encounter.

of each other or onto toys or pieces of furniture, even their blankets. It is, of course, perfectly natural, but because it doesn't fit in with what we expect to see in our human world and so embarrasses owners, it is to be discouraged.

Rather than rushing to have the dog neutered, however, there is a straightforward way to deal with this. The dog must simply be taught that it is not acceptable:

- Take hold of the dog's collar gently but firmly without saying anything.
- Remove them from the other dog or object.
- Hold them while they remain excited, again making sure to be firm and never aggressive. Do not speak as you do so, or you will block their learning.
- When the dog's body has relaxed let it go.
- If it returns to the dog or the object of its attention repeat the process.

HEALTH

THE FOURTH AGE

protégé

9–18 MONTHS

'Then a soldier,
Full of strange oaths, and bearded like the pard,
Jealous in honour, sudden, and quick in quarrel'

IN THE WILD

The wolf's childhood is a long one. It has to be, for it has a great deal to learn during its first nine months. The events of these early phases have all been leading to the moment when – around this time – the young wolf is now allowed to take its first steps into the wider world by joining the hunt. The physical and survival skills learned during the early phases of its life, within the den and the security of the pack, will now be put into practice. It will become an apprentice hunter.

This marks a hugely significant turning point in the wolf's life. But, as ever, it is one that is underpinned by its pack instincts and its place within the hierarchy. Both keep the apprentice within invisible boundaries.

As it begins to venture out into a dangerous new world, the young wolf takes its place at the back of the pack. From here it will observe and learn the ropes. It will spend more time watching its fellow pack members than the prey it is hunting. By doing this it will learn about the practical realities of hunting. By watching its seniors in action it will learn how to sniff prey, and how to stalk and get herds of animals moving. It will learn where to position itself and how to bring down an animal. This process will continue for around nine months, until the wolf is around 18 months old. Only then will its apprenticeship draw to a close. Only then will the wolf be ready for the final step towards maturity.

Leading the way: an older wolf leads two new apprentices on the hunt.

THE FOURTH AGE: OVERVIEW

In human terms the dog is now entering the equivalent of adolescence, the hugely formative period between 12 and 20. It is beginning to think of itself as an independent creature, something that will be encouraged out in the world where its horizons will be expanding.

During this phase the dog's walks will become more extended and it will be allowed to run free off the lead for the first time. But with freedom comes responsibility, and the dog will have to learn more rules about the way it behaves as it enjoys its liberty. The stay and the recall will have to become second nature.

With such potentially conflicting developments going on it is not surprising that this is the age where many dogs begin displaying serious behavioural problems. Dealing with them will require the owner to understand and apply the principles of pack leadership. And to do that they too need to learn a set of rules.

The apprentice

Just as the nine-month-old wolf is venturing out into the wider world as a junior member of the hunting pack, so the domestic dog is about to widen its horizons by going off the leash.

Even the best-behaved dog can rebel at this point. Looking at it from the dog's perspective it is easy to see how it may jump to the wrong conclusions. The boundaries previously laid down seem to have been loosened. It is venturing further and further from home. So, as it sees an opportunity to expand its physical horizons, it also sees a chance to push its behavioural boundaries as well. The walk is going to be a perfect outlet for this rebellion and many problems occur here. For this reason, the dog must begin this phase of its development by learning the rudimentary skills it will need to be a disciplined member of its own 'hunt'.

The stay and recall

The dog will soon be let loose in a world full of threats and potentially dangerous situations. In the wild it will have older, wiser heads around to protect it. In the human world it will have you, its leader. So it is important at this stage that the dog learns two vital new skills that will enable you to protect it better: the stay and the recall. By responding to the first it will learn to freeze in its tracks. By responding to the second it will also learn to return to its owner's side when requested to do so.

The two disciplines build on the work that has already been done and can be learned as one.

STEP BY STEP — **STAY AND RECALL**

The stay and the recall are effectively an extension of the sit and the come commands that the dog learned to recognise during its early days as a pioneer. In this case, however, they can be learned together. Again, food reward is an important tool in helping the dog to assimilate the information here, but be sensible in rationing the amount of tidbits the dog is given as you practise these skills.

1. The Stay

- Ask the dog to come and then sit.
- Position yourself so that the dog is now facing you.
- Take one step back, and as the weight is transferred to your back leg, extend an arm and place the flat of a hand in front of the dog's face. At the same time say 'stay'. Do so in a firm, authoritative voice, but without raising the volume or tone of your voice. You do not want to panic the dog.
- Finish the transfer of weight onto your back leg so that there is now one stride separating you from the dog.
- If the dog comes towards you, close the gap by transferring your weight back onto the front foot.
- Ask the dog to sit again on the original spot where you began.

- If necessary place a gentle hand on its chest to get it into the right position.
- Repeat the withdrawal movement, again transferring your weight onto your back leg and asking the dog to 'stay'.
- The dog will soon realise you are not leaving it and remain fixed to the spot.
- Stand for a few seconds with your two feet together then return to the dog, rewarding it with praise only.

Teaching the recall: begin teaching the stay and the recall by stepping back one stride then asking the dog to come to you. Reward it with warm praise when it gets it right.

2. The Recall

- Repeat the above process so that this time you end up standing two strides away from the dog.
- Once again, if the dog moves towards you, fidgeting or even raising its bottom, tell it to sit.

- When you are successfully standing two strides away, invite the dog to come to you.
- At this point reward it with food. This is a big step forward for the dog. The sit and come routine has successfully evolved into the stay and recall.

3. Putting Distance Between You and the Dog

- Build on the stay by extending the amount of time you ask the dog to stay to 30 seconds.
- Add to this by moving further and further away.
- Develop the control by turning your back on the dog while it sits.
- If the dog tries to follow you, repeat the 'stay' instruction.
- Keep building on this until you can move 20 yards or more away from the dog without it moving from the sit position.

Off the leash – letting your dog run free on the walk

The moment when your dog is let off the leash for the first time is another very significant landmark in its life. However, it is also a moment fraught with potential problems. In particular, an owner can never be entirely sure what is going to happen.

The big problem, of course, is that you cannot have a trial run. With the best will in the world, you are never going to be able to replicate in your garden the open spaces the dog is going to encounter in the outside world. Nor will you ever be able to try out the conditions your dog is going to face there in terms of other dogs, strange noises and the sheer excitement of being out in the open. So you can never know precisely how it is going to react. If a dog is not ready, its release off lead can be a disaster. It can bolt off, heading into no end of trouble.

So for this reason, this is a step that must not be taken a minute too soon. The dog must be ready before it is given its freedom.

Fortunately, there are a few ways to prepare for the situation. Firstly, the dog's general behaviour should be a good indicator. Before being allowed off-leash, in general, the dog should have progressed to the point where:

- It behaves well at feeding time.
- It responds well to all instructions while walking on the lead.
- It behaves well when visitors arrive at the home.
- It is generally a relaxed and happy dog.

You can also test its probable response to being let off the lead in the garden by working with it at the end of a long line attached to its collar. If in this situation the dog comes back to heel when asked, there is every chance it will do the same when it is let off the lead outside. Retrieval games are another useful way of preparing for the outside world. Again, if a dog comes back to you when a toy is chased, there is a good chance it will do the same thing in the local park.

Freedom – first time off the lead

There is no finer sight than that of a dog being let off the leash, free to express its personality, athleticism and natural exuberance. It is here that it is truly in its element. However, this moment has to be planned carefully.

STEP BY STEP · OFF THE LEAD

- Choose a place that is quiet, then, when it is clear there are no major distractions such as other dogs, large groups of people or other animals, it is time to let the dog loose.
- Bring the walk to a stop by asking the dog to 'wait'.
- Lean down and carefully remove the lead from its collar.
- Now ask the dog to walk to heel with you for a short distance, say twenty paces.
- Release the dog with a new request, perhaps 'go play'. It is probably the only instruction that will never need repeating.
- Let the dog run free for a few minutes, ensuring of course that it is not getting itself into trouble. Also, don't let it stray too far so that you are out of visual or vocal range. The main aim of this first exercise is to build short-range control.
- With the dog at a distance of about ten yards away from you, call its name then ask it to 'come'. Use food reward. The incentive is going to need to be strong.
- If the dog comes, reward it effusively and give it a tidbit.
- Build this up by increasing the distances by ten yards or so at a time. Get the dog to answer to the recall from 20, 30 and then 40 yards away from you. Don't stray any further than this. Beyond this distance there is a loss of control.
- Be watchful of potential threats. If, for instance, you approach a bend or a spot where you may not be able to see what lies ahead, bring the dog to you for safety. Keep it close until you know the coast is clear.
- Be careful not to over-exercise a dog of this age. Don't let it jump from any heights as this can do permanent damage to the still-maturing skeleton.

ACCIDENTS WILL HAPPEN

Of one thing you can be certain. Your dog will use its newfound freedom to explore every corner of its new world. This, of course, is a joyous thing to behold. But you should also be aware that the dog is going to stick its nose, paws, claws – and indeed every other part of its anatomy – into places it shouldn't place them. And accidents may well be the result.

Hopefully, of course, you will not need to treat your dog for an injury. But it is always better to be prepared than to be caught off-guard. For this reason it is a good idea that owners always have a small first-aid pack either in the car or at home when they are out on a walk. This should include:

- bandage
- gauze
- eyepads
- scissors
- antiseptic
- a sheath of some kind in case of injuries to the tail
- wound powder
- Sellotape.

What follows is a brief guide to some of the most common problems a dog encounters once it is out and about, along with suggestions on how to treat them. As always, if you are in any doubt about the seriousness of the problem, consult your vet.

DIAGNOSING THE PROBLEM

Because the dog is no longer in sight all the time you are together, the chances are you are not going to see it if it has an accident. This, allied to the fact that dogs are resilient creatures, hard-wired to override pain and get on with their lives, means it is sometimes hard to spot that they are injured at all – even when they are badly hurt. However, there are some telltale signs:

Licking or Pawing at an Area
This may indicate:

- cut paw pads
- grass seeds, thorns or other foreign objects stuck in its toes or ears
- bites or infections.

Limping/Lameness

This is indicative of:

- sprains and strains
- torn ligaments
- fractures and dislocations.

Swellings

Possible causes include:

- abscess caused by a grass seed or foreign object in toes
- bite wounds
- sprains and strains
- fractures and dislocations.

SPECIFIC INJURIES

Injuries to Feet

Dogs walk around with no protection on their paws. So, given the amount of detritus sitting around in our parks and open spaces, it is hardly surprising they suffer a lot from feet injuries. They often cut themselves on sharp objects and are also prone to getting grass seeds and other bits of natural material wedged between their toes. If during or after your walk you see your dog licking at its paw, check it for foreign objects.

If you find something follow these general principles:

- Remove objects carefully, always using a pair of tweezers sterilised with a flame or antiseptic.
- Clean the wound with antiseptic.
- Objects like thorns may be only partially visible. If so, use a sterilised needle to draw back a small section of skin then pull the object out with the tweezers.
- If the object is under the skin and not extractable, bathe the foot in salt water until the object emerges to the surface of the skin.
- If the object is embedded too far under the skin consult a vet.

Bleeding Nails

Dogs can easily rip off nails from their feet. The stump that is left bleeds heavily, and although the condition isn't serious it does need treating.

With a piece of absorbent material apply pressure to the wound for a couple of minutes. Alternatively, apply a 'styptic pencil', a treatment of silver nitrate, to the wound. If the nail is hanging on loosely remove it.

Bites and Cuts

Dogs can pick up cuts, abrasions and bites in all sorts of places. They can scrape themselves in bramble bushes or get bitten by other animals, dogs included.

BLEEDING

If you do spot your dog bleeding the key thing is to stop the flow of blood.

Place an absorbent pad over the wound and apply pressure so as to control the bleeding. Then wrap the wound in a bandage. If the wound is to the tail, sheath it in something like a bit of tubing or an old syringe case. Then strap the tail to the dog's side to prevent it shaking the sheath loose when wagging. Visit your local surgery as soon as possible so the vet can apply a proper dressing. They will also advise you on any antiseptics or other treatments you may need to apply.

BITES FROM OTHER DOGS OR ANIMALS

If your dog is unfortunate enough to be bitten by another animal, you must take it to the vet as soon as possible. Aside from the wound, the biggest worry in these circumstances is that the dog might have been infected and the disease transmitted could be a zoonotic one.

In simple terms, zoonotic diseases are those that are passed on from one species to another, including humans. They are rare, but they can be extremely serious and threaten the owner and their family as well. And the most worrying one is rabies.

Large sections of the world are now, thankfully, free of rabies. The UK and most of Europe are clear, as are countries like Australia, New Zealand and Japan. But in regions where it is still prevalent, the disease is generally fatal. The virus travels via the nerves to the brain, where it results in inflammation known as encephalitis. The dog then becomes slowly paralysed or, in some cases, highly aggressive and irrational. The biggest worry, however, is that the rabies may be passed on to humans via the dog's saliva. Anyone who suspects their dog has been in contact with a rabid animal should see their doctor immediately.

There are a variety of other zoonotic diseases, some of which are transmitted by parasites such as hookworms, tapeworms and ringworm. One of the most serious conditions transmitted in this way is Lyme disease. This jumps between species via a tick that can be carried by a variety of animals, including mice and deer. Infected dogs can suffer severe fever and can pass it on to humans, where it is believed it can lead to joint disorders.

Impalements
Very occasionally dogs accidentally impale themselves on sharp objects like sticks, pieces of metal or glass. The key thing to remember here is not to push or pull the object out. If it has penetrated to any depth, it could be compressing a main artery. Support the impaled object so that it doesn't move and cause any more damage and get to a vet as quickly as possible. This can be difficult with a dog that is excitable or in immense pain, so take great care.

Sprains and Strains
All dogs are prone to sprains and strains, but they are a particular threat to the more active dogs. A sprain happens when a dog overstretches a ligament. A strain occurs when the dog damages a muscle or a tendon. Both can be caused by a sudden trauma, but they can also be triggered by the dog being over-enthusiastic or making a mistake when running or jumping.

The less energetic dogs are not immune from such problems, however. A torn ligament can happen even when the dog is taking gentle exercise. By far the most common injury of this type is to the anterior cruciate (or knee) ligament. This can afflict overweight dogs, particularly as they reach the later years of their lives.

Each of these injuries is hard to detect with the naked eye. Swelling around a joint can be relieved by applying ice packs (or packets of frozen food), but it may require an x-ray for the vet to confirm the details. In each case, however, the cure is much the same. The dog must be rested.

The vet will guide you as to the length of time the dog will have to be kept in the home, but it is important to realise that returning to physical activity too soon can transform what was a relatively minor problem into a major one that may remain with the dog for the rest of its life.

Fractures and Dislocations

Dislocated bones are fairly common among dogs. Knees and elbow joints in particular are prone to separation. Breeds with long spines in relation to the rest of their body, like the Dachshund and the Basset Hound, suffer a lot from slipped discs. Again, these can be difficult to detect and may need an x-ray examination to confirm. Treatment is to rest.

Fractures or breakages of the bones are far more serious. The amount of force needed to break a bone is such that they tend only to happen in road accidents or other traumatic situations, perhaps if a dog falls from a height. The most commonly broken bones are the femur, jaw, spine and pelvis.

There are a variety of different fractures. The most serious are compound breaks in which the bone sticks through the skin, while others might be just tiny cracks in the bone that are hard to see. All, however, need careful treatment.

DEALING WITH A BROKEN BONE

If your dog suffers a compound break, in which it is clear there is a bone sticking out from a wound, you need to act decisively. Dirt can gather in the wound leading to infection and the threat of amputation or worse.

You should immediately take the following steps:

- Keep the dog warm. Dogs often go into shock after suffering a trauma.
- Check for any bleeding and staunch it by applying clean absorbent material and holding it under pressure for a couple of minutes.
- Using the cleanest dressing you can find, wrap up the area around the broken bone and its wound.
- Don't try to straighten or interfere with the bone in any way.
- If you are within easy range of a vet, wrap the dog up in a blanket or coat and transport it there, taking great care not to shake it around too much.
- If you are not within range of a vet, improvise a splint using pens, pencils,

lengths of umbrellas or broom handles, or even rolled-up magazines or newspapers. Put one on each side of the broken bone and bind them together with the dressing or using adhesive tape.

Choking

Dogs should be discouraged from putting small objects in their mouths from an early age. It is something that can be tackled during training at home. They can be dissuaded from playing with small objects by having their toys removed when they do so, thus forming a negative association. As they get older, they should also be discouraged from retrieving foreign objects like sticks. It is amazing how many owners still consider this a suitable form of play with their dogs. All it needs is for the stick to break to damage the mouth or throat, and the dog could choke.

The telltale signs of choking are obvious and include:

- distress and choking sounds
- gagging
- agitation
- bulging eyes
- pawing at the mouth
- rubbing the face on the ground.

If you encounter any of these do the following:

- Try to stay calm.
- Restrain the dog so that you can examine inside its mouth.
- If you have another pair of hands available, enlist the other person's help. Dogs can lash out and bite when distressed.
- Hold the upper jaw in one hand and press the upper lip over the upper teeth.
- Using the other hand, pull down the lower jaw.
- Use an object like a pen, small spoon or tweezers, pry the offending object out of the mouth.
- Be careful not to do more harm than good. If, for instance, you see string or fishing line in the mouth, don't pull at it as it may well be attached to a hook, in turn fixed to something inside the throat or stomach.

🐾 If you are unsuccessful in removing the obstruction head immediately for your vet.

USEFUL TIP: PLAYING IN THE SNOW: HOW TO AVOID ICE BALLS

Dogs – just like humans – adore playing in the snow. There's nothing more rewarding than seeing a dog running excitedly through a white field. The only drawback is the way that – particularly in countries like the

The Icedog cometh: a simple application of vegetable oil can prevent dogs from ending up in this condition.

UK where snow tends to be wetter – the snow forms itself into ice balls that get impacted and attach themselves to the dog's coat. For dogs with longer coats this can be a real problem. The ice balls can be an absolute nightmare to eliminate as they take ages to dilute and evaporate. However, there is a handy and easy way of avoiding them. Before your dog heads out into the snow lather a small amount of vegetable oil into your hands and rub it into the lower areas of the dog where snow may build up. It will save you – and your dog – a lot of hassle.

Dogs behaving badly – how to deal with 'difficult' dogs

Dogs can misbehave in many different ways – from barking and biting to bedwetting and bicycle chasing. And they can do so at any time in their life. However, there are phases in a dog's development when particular problems are more likely to crop up. Older dogs can be snappier and more aggressive towards other dogs, for instance. Similarly, young dogs of ten weeks can become an over-exuberant nightmare if they are over-indulged at playtime.

In general, behavioural problems are most prevalent during the three 'teenage' phases that begin with the protégé. This is hardly surprising, given that this marks the time when the dog is making the difficult transition to adulthood. The range of strange and disruptive behaviour they can manifest is less understandable, however. I have seen dogs display the most curious characteristics during this phase, from chewing their feet to eating their own faeces.

Unfortunately, this is one of the main explanations for the fact that many dogs are passed on or back to their breeders at this point. (In the US, 40 per cent of dogs change hands in their first year.) They are no longer cute puppies, but challenging dogs. And some people don't feel up to that challenge.

That is, for the owner at least, the bad news. The good news is that regardless of where, when and how this misbehaviour occurs, it can be treated in almost exactly the same way. By practising four key elements of

*'Problem child':
the challenging and
aggressive behaviour dogs
often display as they enter
adolescence can take
all forms.*

canine communication and displaying a range of signals that the dog cannot fail to understand, all behavioural problems can be relieved.

When you encounter what you see as a 'problem' with your dog, you should understand a few key points. Firstly, this isn't a problem but a challenge. You have an otherwise lovely animal that is in trouble. It needs your help. Secondly, this behaviour hasn't got anything to do with some of the causes to which many people ascribe problems. It is not to do with its breed or health, for instance. And the third and most important thing to understand is that whatever it is doing, *it isn't the dog's fault.*

When you look at it from a dog's perspective it is no wonder some have what their owners refer to as behavioural problems. When we take on a dog we do so expecting it to fit into our world and its conventions. We expect it to behave in ways that don't offend or upset us, our family or our neighbours. So we train it to go to the toilet in the same spot, to accept a lead when it is out on a walk and to come to us when we ask. We train it not to get too excited or aggressive when it senses danger, to behave around other dogs and to generally demonstrate good manners at all times. This is a lot to ask, especially when you consider that unless we know otherwise we make all these demands in a language that the dog does not understand in any way, shape or form. Can anyone be surprised our dogs get it wrong at times?

As if this is not bad enough, we make the situation even worse by using signals that convey completely the wrong messages. Given that it is inhabiting a human world, a dog needs its owner to take charge and to lead it through that world. Yet the signals owners generally give out tell the dog that, in fact, it is in charge of the extended pack that is the family. So it is hardly any surprise that a dog gets itself into such a state at times. Think of it from the dog's point of view. It sees a stranger approaching the door of the home. To the dog this is a sign of danger, and as leader it is their job to deal with it. No wonder it barks and gets excited. A member of the family – its pack – leaves the home without it. Because it doesn't speak human language it can't ask them where they are going or when they will return. No wonder it may sometimes behave obsessively until that person is back home safe. Wouldn't you?

Once we appreciate this fact, we can begin to see that no matter what form the bad behaviour takes, its root cause is essentially the same.

Because an owner has given the dog the wrong signals it has come to the conclusion that it – not its owner – is the leader of its domestic pack. Hopelessly unequipped to perform this role in a world made by another species, it reacts in all sorts of different ways, most commonly by becoming stressed, aggressive, obsessive or overprotective.

It stands to reason then that the only way to treat a dog in this situation is by first relieving it of this central misapprehension and stripping it of the job of leader. At the same time we place ourselves, as owners, in the dog's former role, as the freely appointed and unchallenged head of the household. Once this has been successfully done, almost any behavioural problem can be tackled.

TAKING CHARGE OF THE FOUR KEY AREAS

The key to taking the reins of power within the domestic pack lies in communicating your leadership in the four fundamental areas of day-to-day life. In doing so you are answering the four questions at their root:

- When the pack reunites after a separation – who is in charge now?
- When the pack faces a perceived danger – who will protect us now?
- When the pack goes on the hunt – who will lead us now?
- When the pack eats – who will take charge of mealtimes?

As we have seen, elements of these four areas can be handled naturally and organically if an owner has been with the dog from birth or it arrives in the home well-adjusted. A good owner will have control of mealtimes, will take charge of play periods and – crucially – lead the walk.

However, if a dog arrives in a home badly adjusted, or develops real problems, these key areas must be tackled in a more formal and emphatic way so that the dog's perception of its role is readjusted.

This section outlines how owners can take control in these areas.

Who Is In Charge Now? – Reuniting After Separations

IN THE WILD

In the wild, the leader of the wolf pack, the alpha male, along with his partner, the alpha female, re-establishes his leadership every time he returns from a hunt or has been absent from the den. He has to do this because of the dynamics of the pack. It is always testing him, always checking his leadership credentials. It has to – the pack's survival depends on it. The alpha gets its message across through a subtle series of rituals. Primarily it ignores the other wolves until it is ready to interact with them. They recognise this and stay away until summoned to pay homage. When they do so their body language reflects their status. They will keep their bodies below the alpha or allow it to lick them. It is not something that takes more than a few seconds to communicate, yet it is powerful nevertheless.

WHAT YOU NEED TO DO

To take charge of this situation effectively you must once more see things from the dog's perspective. It believes you are a member of a pack of humans and canines. That pack has been temporarily separated. As it reunites, one member of the pack must assert itself as the leader. If the dog senses any weakness on the part of you as the human, it will try to push itself forward for the job. You must usurp its power, however, by taking the role for yourself.

WHAT IS A SEPARATION IN THE HOME?

It is important to understand what constitutes a separation. Obviously, when the dog remains at home while a member of the family leaves the house to go to work or school for the day, or heads off to the supermarket for a couple of hours, separation has occurred. But what if someone pops into the garden or the toilet? Or is called away to the telephone? Does that constitute a separation?

The best definition is to see a separation as any movement when a member of the household leaves the dog's physical space and then erects a physical barrier between them so that it is impossible for the two to communicate or connect directly. So when someone moves from one room to another within a house while leaving the doors open, a separation has not happened. The dog can still follow that person and place itself physically in their proximity. If there is a barrier between them, such as a closed door, however, the dog can't see or follow.

If this happens, the reunification happens when the person returns to the dog's space, whether by opening the closed door or re-entering the room some other way. It is at this moment that the dog will look to see who is in charge. And it is at this point that you, as the owner, must establish your leadership.

HOW TO ESTABLISH LEADERSHIP WHEN REUNITING: STEP BY STEP

1. WHEN AND WHERE?

The object of the exercise is practical. It is not simply about achieving dominance over the dog for its own sake. You want the dog to fit as naturally into the home as every other human member. And you want it to be used to the natural rhythms and routines of the household, and so comfortable that it doesn't react to members of the household coming and going to school or work. It should be happy with the idea that everyone gets on with their busy life. And it should be at ease with the idea that the owners will interact and play with it when they have time.

Owners shouldn't worry about this being somehow uncaring or negligent, in fact it is quite the opposite. By organising their lives so that they interact with the dog when they are ready and able to do so they are improving the quality of life for both themselves and their pet. They will be able to shower their dogs with all the love and affection they want; they will simply be doing so on their own terms, and at times that suit them – not the dog.

So, given all this, it is important that the process of establishing leadership in this situation takes place in as normal an environment as possible. It should be practised during the daily routine and treated with respect, not as a piece of fun. The dog regards it as a serious ritual, and so should you. By doing all of these things you will reap benefits when the dog has accepted your leadership.

2. FIRST SEPARATION AND THE REPERTOIRE

The less artificial these first separations are the better for everyone. Within the first few hours of the day, the moment is inevitably going to come when someone in the household goes to the toilet or steps outside into the garden. As you do so, prepare yourself for the moment when you return to the dog. The moment you re-enter the dog's space it is going to react. How it does this will depend on its personality. It may ignore you altogether. More likely, it will begin going through a routine that is probably familiar to you. It may start barking or jumping up, pacing the room or dragging its favourite toys around. Whatever it does, its behaviour should be recognised for what it is – the dog's attempt to clarify who is the leader of the pack. For this reason you have to act decisively – and behave like a leader.

In the wild, an alpha does not interact or acknowledge its subordinates until it is ready to do so – and you must do the same. Regardless of how dramatic or hyperactive the dog's repertoire, it must be ignored. You must not acknowledge or interact with the dog in any way, shape or form. Even by making eye contact, touching or even simply shouting 'stop it' you will be sending a fatal signal that the dog will interpret as an acknowledgment of its primacy.

It may take some time, but the repertoire will begin to peter out. The dog will wander off or lie down on the floor, as if to signal it has accepted the situation. Asking how long it will take for this to happen, however, is like asking how long is a piece of string. It is completely unpredictable. On average it takes a dog around ten minutes to assimilate the message, but I have seen dogs succumb in seconds – and I have seen one dog going through its histrionic repertoire for three and a half hours. This presents a real challenge for an owner. It can become a battle of wills. But throughout you must be calm, consistent and, above all, convincing in what you do.

If, for example, the dog is still behaving in a completely over the top manner ten or fifteen minutes after you begin, you should isolate it. Take it by the collar and lead it into another room. If its behaviour makes this impossible, remove yourself from the room. It will see this as decisive action and – slowly but surely – begin to get the message.

The great consolation for owners who face such battles, however, is that the first time is by far the worst. Once the principle has been established, it will become easier and easier to re-establish leadership. It is in the dog's DNA to accept a good leader. In time, what has taken ten minutes will take ten seconds, or even less.

3. THE FIVE MINUTE RULE

The key thing now is that the dog is given plenty of time to fully assimilate what is happening. The minimum time necessary the first few times you use the technique is five minutes. As the dog accepts your leadership more and more this time will be reduced. By the time the dog is fully adjusted it could take five seconds. But it is crucial that at this stage things are not rushed. Apart from everything else, this period allows a dog that has not felt calm before to appreciate how good a feeling it is. And once they have done that they are more likely to want to feel this way again. They will have taken an important step towards exercising self-control.

4. USING THE COME

An important piece of information has been relayed to the dog. It has sensed a new order is in place. Now it is important to build on this breakthrough by underlining the fact that you, the owner, and not the dog, are in charge. And the best way to do this is by proceeding to use the 'come' to confirm the pecking order.

STEP BY STEP — THE COME

- Make sure the dog has stopped going through its repertoire.
- Wait five minutes, as outlined above.
- Prepare yourself by having food reward available in the form of tidbits.
- Squat or kneel, then, addressing the dog by name, ask it to come to you.
- Do so in a warm, inviting, non-threatening voice.
- If the dog is reluctant stretch out a hand with the food reward clearly visible.
- When the dog comes over reward it and give it quiet praise.
- Stroke or ruffle the dog's neck area, to underline leadership (touching this vulnerable area is a powerful signal of leadership in the wild).
- If the dog rushes or jumps up, perhaps responding to the smell of the food, or alternatively rolls over expecting to be tickled, get up and walk away immediately.

- Do the same if the dog does not respond to the invitation at all.
- In both these cases remain separated from the dog for an hour before repeating the process.
- Continue until it does respond.

This can be a difficult thing to do. Many owners feel that by withholding affection in this way they are somehow being cold or cruel to the dog. This is simply not the case.

This is not going to change the loving, trustful nature of the relationship between you and your dog. It can only improve and strengthen it. You will still give it plenty of affection – only in a different and more appropriate direction.

More importantly, the dog has learned two important things here. First that its actions have consequences; and secondly to accept you not just as its owner but its leader. It has also seen that one of the leader's privileges is deciding how, when and where affection is given out.

YOU'VE GOT MY VOTE – THE TELLTALE SIGNS THAT SHOW A DOG HAS ACCEPTED YOUR LEADERSHIP

The aim of the previous exercise is to go from hyperactive to happy as quickly as possible. Different personalities will, of course, respond in different ways. In the most extreme cases docile, compliant dogs will acquiesce quite quickly, while, at the other end of the scale, the really defiant dogs will take an age before they finally, reluctantly, give up the ghost. Most dogs will be somewhere in between.

There will be some dogs, however, who will indulge in a little bit of kidology. They will pretend they have given up, then – the moment you acknowledge them – snap back into their repertoire. For this reason, therefore, it is important that you recognise the telltale signs that indicate when a dog has – and hasn't – ended its repertoire:

Look For a Softening of the Eyes

The eyes are a big clue to the dog's state. If they are wide or bulging then it is clear the dog is still agitated and anxious. It has not come to terms with what you are asking of it. If, however, the eyes are soft, then it has relaxed and accepted what is happening. In monitoring the dog's eyes, be careful not to engage in any direct eye-contact. Do it with a sideways glance instead.

Watch the Dog's Body Language

If a dog drops back on its hind legs, Sphinx-like with its ears pricked, it hasn't finished. It is sitting coiled like a spring, ready to bound back into action at a moment's notice. The protest is far from over. If, on the other hand, the dog starts going through a stretching routine, arching its back and splaying out its legs in front of it, then it is relaxing.

Look at the Dog's Mouth and Lips

Rather like humans when they are deep in concentration, dogs have a habit of licking their lips when they are thinking hard about something. If you see your dog doing this it is a good, positive sign. It means the dog is processing the information it is being given. In time it will arrive at the right conclusion.

Listen out for the Dog Sighing

In humans, a sigh can be taken in one of two ways – as a sign of pleasure or of frustration. In a dog, however, it is only ever the former. So if you hear your dog releasing a long, deep sigh you can be sure it is happy with the situation in front of it. And that is a very positive sign indeed.

Toileting

In extreme cases, where a dog has been stressed out by its role as leader of the household pack, the relief of being released from this burden can be immense. If your dog suddenly wets itself or defecates it is a sign that it has crossed an important bridge mentally.

Watch to See How the Dog Reacts to You Moving

If the dog is relaxed it will not react to this. If it has still not accepted the change that is occurring within the status quo it will move as well. If it does so, you know you have to give the situation more time.

SECOND NATURE

This is an important step towards ridding the dog of its undesirable behaviour. But the key thing to understand is that this is not a quick fix. From now on you must always behave this way around your dog. It must become second nature to you – and the dog.

Each day must start the same way, with you letting the dog out of the door to do its toileting without acknowledging it. Then, when the dog has finished and you are first reunited with it, your initial contact and interaction with the dog must be on your terms and when the dog is calm.

If you slip and start acknowledging the dog or allowing it to get excited while you greet it when you reunite, you will soon be back at square one. The dog will have begun to suspect the leadership does not rest with you. And this simply can't be allowed to happen.

This may seem daunting. The good news here, however, is that within a short period three things will happen. Firstly, the routine will become second nature. Secondly, the dog's attention-seeking repertoire will reduce until finally it almost fades away. Finally, as a result of this, the owner will be able to drastically reduce the period of time they need to wait before calling the dog to them. The five minutes will gradually become five seconds.

Who Will Protect Us Now? Dealing with Times of Perceived Danger

Some of the most extreme behaviour dogs demonstrate occurs in situations when something out of the ordinary happens within the household, such as visitors arriving or someone knocking on the front door. Depending on their personalities, dogs can get extremely aggressive – sometimes dangerously so – in these situations.

Once again, however, it is not hard to understand why this is, particularly when you look at it from the dog's perspective. If it believes it is leader – which it will unless it is given the correct information by its owner – the dog will regard the protection and security of that den as one of its absolute priorities. As leader, the buck stops with them.

Therefore, the sound of the doorbell or the front knocker sets alarm bells ringing for the dog. And unless the person at the door is able to explain precisely who they are, why they are there and what they intend to do in the house, and do so in canine language, the dog is going to assume the worst. And as a result it is not going to be terribly well-disposed to the visitor.

Similarly, even the arrival of the morning post is a threat. How is a dog to know the strange paper objects being thrust through the letterbox aren't some sort of danger to it and the household? So is it any wonder it may attack the hand that is delivering this unknown menace into the house?

Protecting the den: anxiety over perceived threats to the home can lead dogs to extreme behaviour.

To add to the confusion, the dog feels at times that owners can also exacerbate the situation. When they see their dog barking or leaping around manically at the sound of someone at the front door, it is all too easy for an owner to become embarrassed or angry and castigate the dog. In the worst cases owners can become physically abusive towards the dog. This doesn't make any sense to the dog, who thinks it is fulfilling its role as the guardian of the household. It would expect the humans to congratulate it, not shout and remonstrate.

Given all this it is vital that, as they establish their relationship with their dog, owners learn to relieve their pet of the responsibility of dealing with these situations as soon as possible.

HOW TO DEAL WITH TIMES OF PERCEIVED DANGER

The domestic home is a minefield of sights and sounds that could easily be construed as being potentially dangerous. Outside there is the sound of cars, lorries, aeroplanes and passers-by. Inside there are the assorted sounds of daily life – from washing machines and telephones to the bumps and bangs of young children crashing around in their rooms. Dogs who believe they are in charge of the domestic pack can perceive all of these as a potential attack on the den and react accordingly.

The key to successfully managing perceived threats lies in displaying firm, decisive leadership. The dog must first be reminded of its status as a subordinate. It must then be reminded that this role does not require it to deal with the situation at hand. If it believes wholeheartedly in your ability to lead, your dog will trust you no matter what the perceived danger.

A SIMPLE 'THANK YOU'

Whenever something happens that could be perceived as a threat by your dog you must instantly establish that you are going to deal with the situation. When the doorbell goes, for instance, head for the door, ensuring the dog is between you and the entrance.

If the dog barks or growls say simply 'thank you'. You are conveying three messages here. As leader you are acknowledging:

- that you heard and have acknowledged its warning
- that you are grateful for its contribution
- that you will now deal with the matter.

This will be a phrase that should become familiar.

If the visitor comes into the house and the dog carries on its undesirable behaviour you have two choices. Either you can hold the dog close to you by its collar without speaking until it stops, or you can remove it to another room.

The important thing to remember is that you always do this calmly and quickly. And no matter how irritating the dog may be, you must not chastise or shout at it. You must never make something out of nothing and dramatise the situation. By remaining calm you are displaying all the credentials of a leader.

You should repeat the same process if the dog becomes excited when a visitor is leaving. Again, thank it for its contribution, and then deal with the matter yourself. By taking charge of the comings and goings in the house like this, you will help the dog feel good about itself.

Remember, even after it is demoted from the role of leader, the dog's instincts are geared towards integrating itself into a happy and successful domestic pack. It wants to feel useful, that it is contributing. By listening to the dog's views, then telling it that it has contributed to defending the den, you are reassuring the dog about its importance as a pack member. The dog will appreciate this.

STRONG PERSONALITIES

Of course, all dogs have different personalities, and some may react to perceived danger in more aggressive ways. For this reason, if the dog does have a history or tendency towards being aggressive, it should be fitted with a collar during the early days of tackling its errant behaviour. If a dog does leap up at or attacks a visitor, you must act decisively. The dog should be led by the collar or, if necessary, a lead, away from the visitor. The owner should then guide the visitor into the house, and away from the dog. If the dog's behaviour is so aggressive that it fails to remain out of the way, the owner must remove it from the scene. It must learn the consequences of its actions.

Who Will Take Charge of Mealtimes? Gesture Eating and Using Mealtimes as a Means to Establish Leadership

Raising a dog from puppyhood provides a perfect opportunity to leave no doubts about who controls mealtimes – and therefore who is leader within the household. Whether you are hand-rearing or weaning, using food reward as a means of positive reinforcement or introducing the young dog's diet, the signals are unmistakable.

However, for the many owners who will be acquiring a dog at this – or any other – more advanced stage, there is every chance the groundwork will not have been laid. So when a dog that has been raised in another environment joins your house, you may have to make up for this.

The dog may have formed a deep-rooted misapprehension about its role by this point. It may be used to being given food whenever it wants it. At the other end of the scale, it may be a rescue dog that has been used to scavenging independently for every scrap of food it can find. Whichever, the remedy required to rid it of such ideas needs to be a strong one. Fortunately, a technique called 'gesture eating' provides precisely the powerful message needed in this circumstance.

In the wild, food provides the alpha pair with the most potent means of underlining their status. In general they are the first to feed on any carrion caught during the hunt. The rest of the pack understand the

Food power: a dog knows it should respect the authority of whoever provides its meals.

importance of this – after all, their survival depends on the survival of the alpha pair. It is very simple for owners to replicate this simple signal during mealtimes. As with every element of training a dog with behavioural difficulties, the key is to be consistent. So it is important this technique is used at every mealtime until the dog's behaviour improves. It can also be re-introduced if the dog's behaviour reoccurs at a later date.

STEP BY STEP   MEALTIME 1

- Ensure the dog is in the kitchen or eating area while you are preparing its meal, and that it can see you as you get its food ready. Before giving the dog its food, place a plate containing a small snack, maybe some biscuits or crackers, on the worktop alongside the dog's food and again in full view of it.
- If other members of the family are present, it is helpful if they join you.
- With the dog watching, each member of the family should now take a bite from the snack. No one should make eye contact with the dog or acknowledge its presence in any way. The object of the exercise is to establish that each member of the human pack ranks higher in the household hierarchy than the dog.
- Only when everyone has eaten and returned an empty plate to the table or worktop should the dog's food be placed in front of it. Once more there should be no fanfare or fuss.
- When the dog has eaten, its bowl should be removed instantaneously. The signal is unmistakable: you as leader provide the food and you also decide when feeding time is finished.
- For this same reason, if the dog walks away from its meal while any food remains, the bowl must still be removed immediately. You must retain the power inherent in food, and by leaving the dog free to eat at times of its choosing you are relinquishing that power.

Taking Charge of the Walk

In the wild the alpha wolf takes complete charge of the hunt. As our dogs go out on their own equivalent version of the hunt, you as the owner must exercise precisely the same amount of control. And you must do so from the very beginning to the very end of the walk.

The key things to remember are:

- You must decide when the walk takes place. Don't be bullied into going out by your dog standing next to the door or appearing with its lead in its mouth. If you go out at the same time every day, be sure you are the first to instigate things. If the dog anticipates things before you start getting ready, delay things.
- Lead from the front. Each and every time you step out of the door you must do so as the unchallenged leader. So if the dog gets overly excited about heading out, underline your leadership by letting it calm down then calling it to you. When you leave, be sure to go through the threshold of the house first. Make sure you decide which direction you are heading when you reach the boundary of your property. Never, ever be pulled in a certain direction by your dog. If necessary, head in a completely different direction to begin with, simply to underline your primacy.
- Behave like a leader throughout the walk. You must deal with any moments of perceived danger in the outside world, whether it is another dog or a noise that the dog may not recognise. And you must not tolerate any challenges to your leadership while you are out on the walk. Dissent should be dealt with swiftly and symbolically. The walk must be brought to an end.
- Always control the duration of the walk. When you say it is time to head home, make sure it happens. Don't allow your dog to avoid coming to you immediately.

As with every other element of training, if you don't feel happy and in control at any point, you should go back a step to a place where you do feel that way.

HOW TO BE AN EFFECTIVE LEADER

Every second you are with your dog you are giving it information. So tackling bad behaviour requires all four of these elements to be working together in unison. They act together cumulatively to effectively blitz the dog with signals.

As it passes through these important middle stages of its development, this is the only way it is going to be relieved of its mistaken belief that it is in charge of the domestic pack.

The common thing in applying each of these key signals is that you present a picture of calm, commanding leadership. Not everyone, of course, is a natural leader. Some people are shy, physically frail or simply not used to issuing instructions to others. There are a few key attributes to a successful leader, and they are worth bearing in mind when you apply these principles:

Projection

A great deal of leadership is down to projection. Body language is a means of communication dogs understand all too well, and they will pick up on anyone who seems tentative or weak immediately. At the same time, they will respond just as quickly to anyone who displays obvious signs of authority.

As we all know, first impressions are lasting impressions, so it is vital that owners present the right image from the very first minute of the first day. Walk with an upright, confident posture. Keep the head high, and the eyeline above that of the dog. Avoid any eye contact until you are ready to interact.

Decisiveness

A leader's actions should be firm, final, and immediate. The dog will test this from the start, so it is vital that owners are not thrown by their behaviour. They must not be tempted to react to gesturing or barking. They must continue to ignore the dog until they are ready to acknowledge its presence. And if a dog comes to an owner uninvited, it must be met with an immediate rebuff. This is vital, because even letting it rest against the owner's leg for a few seconds allows the dog to believe it has some authority. From the outset, owners must establish the principle that they – not the dog – decide what goes on in the house. Yet this decisiveness must never be violent or aggressive in nature. You must always be firm in your head but kind in your hand.

Tone of Voice

Talking incessantly to a dog is counter-productive. The constant noise becomes nothing more than a background drone. Dogs – much like humans – respond much better to people who speak only when they have got something important to say.

When the time comes to talk to the dog, it is vital that the tone of voice is consistent with the body language being displayed. So you should speak clearly and decisively, yet non-threateningly and without shouting. Short phrases or words are best – *come, sit, stay* – all convey powerful yet simple messages. They take on even more power when they are delivered in conjunction with the dog's name, which should always happen when a request is made.

When the dog responds correctly, deliver praise with a smile and an extra softness to the voice. Again, be brief – use phrases like 'good dog', 'good, clean dog' or 'clever dog'.

Wellbeing

HIP AND ELBOW SCORING

With the dog now physically almost fully developed and exercising more and more, its body is going to be placed under new strains. Exercise is, of course, in general a good thing for a dog. Nevertheless, the dog's bones, joints and muscles can come under greater strain, leading to a variety of problems. Some of these are going to be cumulative, but others will be the result of inherited conditions. As the dog reaches its first birthday, it needs to be tested for two specific kinds of inherited joint diseases: hip and elbow dysplasia.

Testing for Hip and Elbow Dysplasia

As veterinary science has improved, we have learned more and more about our dogs and the physical problems they may face. Years ago, dogs with walking or movement difficulties were simply marked down as being lame. Now we know that lameness can be caused by a range of conditions, many of which develop within the dog's first year. Two of the most common – and fast-growing – are hip and elbow dysplasia.

In the days before the wolf became domesticated by man, survival depended on fitness. Life was very simple. If a wolf wasn't fast, supple and

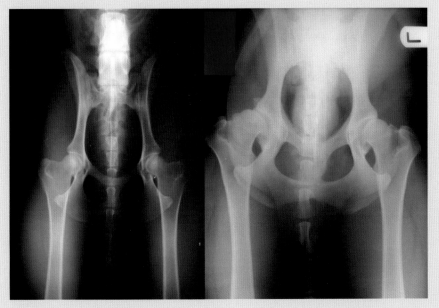

Positives and negatives: two x-rays illustrate how severe hip dysplasia deforms the dog's pelvic area. The picture on the left is of a normal set of hips, the one on the right is of dysplasia affected hips. The disease has created new bone formations, which have deformed the ball and socket on each side.

springy enough to outrun and outjump its prey then it would starve. Thanks to its overwhelming instinct for survival, the wolf remained in peak physical condition.

When the wolf joined forces with man, however, these skills, although still important, weren't such a matter of life and death. Its new life allowed the wolf to occasionally rely on their human companions' abilities, not to mention their weapons, to provide food. The seeds of decline had been sown. In the thousands of years since, the domestic dog has become an increasingly unfit creature. It has paid a price for domestication, and two of the most serious penalties it has paid are hip and elbow dysplasia. As the dog approaches its first birthday its physical development will be almost complete, and it is time to assess its vulnerability to these potentially damaging conditions.

Hip Dysplasia

THE HIP JOINT
The dog's hip joint – in common with that of many other land animals – is a 'ball and socket' mechanism, held together by a network of ligaments,

HEALTH

tendons and muscles. It is a beautiful piece of natural engineering that allows the dog to move with a blend of power, speed and agility. In a healthy dog, the ball and socket fit together closely, their surfaces protected by large areas of cartilage and lubricated by joint fluid. If the mechanism is working well then the dog is able to move and run freely. If the mechanism is malformed or becomes damaged or inflamed in any way, however, serious problems can occur.

ROOT CAUSES

Hip dysplasia is a malformation of the hip joint that leads to a steady degrading of the joint, so that, for instance, additional bone develops inside the socket or the cartilage becomes worn down, meaning the ball element fits less well and begins to rub against the socket. The hip joint becomes damaged and doesn't work properly, causing considerable pain to the dog and eventually resulting in lameness. In the most serious cases a dog may become effectively crippled, unable to move without excruciating pain. The problem is most common among larger breeds, such as German Sheperds and Labradors. There is a strong genetic component to this condition which is why dogs need to be monitored early in life.

HIP SCORING

Thirty or so years ago the British Kennel Club and the British Veterinary Association came up with a system for 'scoring' hip joints. The idea, quite rightly, was to identify dogs predisposed to hip problems, primarily so that owners would not breed from them. The system has gone on to become a standard that all owners use.

The hip score is calculated by x-raying the dog then awarding points for each of nine features within the hip joint. The lower the score the less dysplasia is within the joint. The score can vary between a minimum of zero and a maximum of 106 (53 for each joint). After thirty years of measuring the scores for every breed, the BVA and Kennel Club have come up with 'breed mean scores' that show what level of dysplasia is average within the breed. As a rule, dogs with hip scores well below the breed mean score are considered good breeding candidates. Those with scores above the breed mean score are not.

This system is slowly but surely helping to limit the amount of dysplasia present in dogs. At the moment, however, it is no guarantee. Even if a dog has a good score there is no certainty that dysplasia will not develop in its puppy.

WHEN TO HIP SCORE

The youngest a dog can be hip-scored is twelve months. By this age the physical development of its body will be well-established. Your vet will arrange for the x-ray to be done and an official record will be lodged with the Kennel Club and the BVA.

DIAGNOSIS AND TREATMENT

Dysplasia can be hard to detect because dogs are generally good at dealing with pain. Your dog may be suffering each time it walks but it will not necessarily yelp or grumble. So it is important, again, to monitor your dog. Any sign of limping or dragging of the feet should be checked out thoroughly. You should also watch out for dogs suddenly losing interest in exercise.

If a dog is suffering from dysplasia it can be treated in a number of ways. Painkillers and heat treatments can significantly ease the pain. Often the best cure is a carefully planned exercise programme that restricts the damage being done to the hip joint. In severe cases, however, surgery may be the only answer.

Elbow Dysplasia

Elbow dysplasia is another condition identified relatively recently. Like hip dysplasia it is on the increase worldwide and much work is being done to limit its spread by monitoring and identifying dogs prone to the problem so that they do not breed. A number of breeds, mostly larger ones, have been identified as having a greater incidence of elbow dysplasia. These breeds are the Basset Hound, Bernese Mountain Dog, English Mastiff, German Shepherd Dog, Golden Retriever, Great Dane, Irish Wolfhound, Labrador Retriever, Newfoundland and Rottweiler.

WHAT IS ELBOW DYSPLASIA?

ED is an abnormal development of the elbow joint. As with hip dysplasia, cartilage or the structure around the joint develops abnormally.

HEALTH

These abnormalities – or primary lesions – then have a knock-on effect. There are three main types of lesions:

OCD – Osteochondritis Dissecans, common in Rottweilers
and St Bernards
FCP – Fragmented or Ununited Coronoid Process
UAP – Ununited Anconeal Process

The elbow joint is made up of bones and cartilage which form a complex jigsaw that fits closely together. All it needs is for one of these parts to change in shape and problems will develop. In many ways the joint is like a hinge. If a piece of grit gets into that hinge it will not function properly. So it is with the elbow. If an abnormality develops then the dog's gait will be affected, exacerbating the problem.

As with hip dysplasia, one of the great problems with elbow dysplasia is spotting dogs that are suffering from it. Many dogs have lesions in their elbows that do not result in lameness. The chances of them passing on a more serious version of the condition to any puppies they may produce is high, however, so dogs should be x-rayed for this as well.

THE ED GRADING SYSTEM
Once again, the BVA and the Kennel Club have teamed up to produce a screening scheme. Three different views of the joint will be taken, two from either side and one from the front. The dog will then be graded according to the number of primary and secondary lesions present. The grading system is simple, with four grades of ED:

GRADE	DESCRIPTION
0	Normal
1	Mild ED
2	Moderate ED or primaray lesion
3	Severe ED

Owners thinking of breeding are advised that only dogs with a score of 0 or 1 should be chosen as potential parents.

TREATMENT

While dogs who have mild or even moderate ED may never show signs of lameness or pain, those who suffer from severe ED are likely to begin displaying the condition between the ages of six and twelve months. As with hip dysplasia, treatment ranges from limiting exercise and losing weight to ease the strain on the joints, to pain-relieving drugs. In the worst cases surgery may be necessary to remove bits of cartilage or bone that have become loose within the joint. In most cases, however, the dog will be able to lead a reasonably normal and active life.

HEALTH

THE FIFTH AGE

pretender

18–28 MONTHS

'And then, the justice
In fair round belly, with good capon lin'd,
With eyes severe, and beard of formal cut,
Full of wise saws, and modern instances'

IN THE WILD

As an apprentice hunter, the wolf has been continually asking itself questions. How do I track and select prey? How do I corner it; how do I bring it down? Where should I be within the pack? Now, as it approaches maturity it begins to have the confidence to ask itself a much bigger question: What is my position in the pack? And if its personality is strong, it may well be asking itself the biggest question of all. Should I be a member of an alpha pair?

Not all wolves will see themselves as leaders. But even if they are not that ambitious, it is now that they will reach an accommodation with themselves about their position within the pack. By the end of this period the wolf will begin to accept its status in life. Its ultimate ranking within the pack will be decided. This process will be reflected in the domestic dog too.

THE FIFTH AGE: OVERVIEW

The ten-month period the dog is now entering is one that will have a fundamental influence on the adult that emerges at the other end of it. By the end of it the dog will have reached full physical maturity, with the skeleton fully developed. Mentally, the dog will be as alert and highly attuned to its surroundings as it ever will be. During this period too, around the two-year mark, the dog will also reach the ideal age to begin breeding.

Developmentally, however, it still has to pass through a crucial phase. In the wild, a dog of this age might be preparing itself to challenge for the leadership of the pack. The domestic dog may be making its bid for its desired status too. During this period it is the equivalent of an ambitious 24-year-old trying to establish him or herself in the world. It is ready to take on that world and challenge it until it gets what it wants. For this reason it is a time for particular vigilance and one during which a number of behavioural problems may arise.

Challenging times

People often talk about the terrible twos, a period in their dog's development when its behaviour seems to go through a really bad patch, when all manner of mischief and bad manners crop up. Of course, the comparison with a child passing through its terrible twos is completely misleading. A dog, after all, is the equivalent of 24 years old at this point. Yet there is a human comparison; one that is helpful in understanding – and dealing with – this very tricky phase in a dog's development.

If we think of a 24-year-old human, we think of someone who is establishing themselves as a mature adult. He or she is working hard to do this, both in their career and in their personal life. It is the time when people confirm where they are heading in life, and they focus on this with great drive and determination.

Something very similar is happening in the dog. In the wild, this phase is the one when the young pack member ends its apprenticeship.

By the end of this period it will be initiated as a fully fledged member of the hunting pack. This is where the dog sees itself in life as well.

The upshot of this is that even if you have got your dog convinced of your leadership, this is the period when you are going to face some of the sternest challenges. The dog believes it is now ready to assume leadership and is all set to take that job away from you, so much of its misbehaviour will be directed at defying and challenging you on a daily basis. It is important you deal with each of these challenges effectively and correctly.

Leadership challenges

Rather like a politician involved in an election contest, a dog that is competing for the leadership of its domestic pack will look for weaknesses in its opponent's defences. And, predictably, it will tend to look first at the key battleground areas, the four aspects of day-to-day life where leadership is constantly defined. Of the four areas, the most potent and symbolic from the dog's point of view are the walk and mealtimes – however,

Leadership contest: just like their relatives in the wild, dogs compete over status by standing up to each other.

throughout this phase you must remain vigilant in retaining control of all four key areas. The cumulative effect of controlling each of these will keep the dog's challenge at bay.

CHALLENGES ON THE WALK

Even if it has been a well-behaved companion until now, a dog of this age will tend to start challenging you on the walk. It may begin at home, where it might be more exuberant at the first sign of you gathering its lead. If this happens, postpone the walk until you have re-established that it is you – and only you – who decides when the walk happens.

The dog may begin to barge through in front of you as you prepare to go out through the door. This cannot be tolerated. Calmly and gently remove the dog from the door and ask it to wait. If it doesn't calm down and insists on nudging up against the door, again postpone the walk for an hour or so. Even if the walk is foregone altogether it is important that the dog has time to assimilate what has happened. It needs to understand the consequences of its actions.

Pulling on the lead is perhaps the most common signal of a dog's burgeoning self-confidence. At this point your dog may start trying to pull your arms out of their sockets on occasions. This can't be allowed to happen. If the dog does start trying to haul you down the road you must stand your ground. Don't try to pull it back towards you. It will see this as a tugging contest and believe you are acknowledging at least the possibility that it is worthy of challenging for the leadership. Instead, ask the dog to come back to heel. Do so calmly but authoritatively. Use some food reward if necessary, to remind the dog you are the provider.

The dog should return to your side. If it doesn't and it continues to jerk at the lead you have to take the ultimate sanction and cut short the walk. At this point in its life more than at any other time, the dog needs to receive crystal-clear information about its status. By doing this you are telling it two things: firstly, there is only one leader on this walk, and it is not the dog. Secondly, you are reminding the dog that misbehaviour comes at a price.

The most common sign of a leadership challenge at this time, however, will be a reluctance to come back to you when the dog is off the leash. It may be a small-scale rebellion, but equally it could become a major attempt to shake things up in terms of the leadership. Sometimes they will simply bolt off and disappear for a period. In really extreme cases they will disappear for longer.

None of these situations can be tolerated, of course. If this does happen, the dog cannot be given another chance to repeat it. Once you have retrieved the dog, you must go home and prepare to take a completely different tack next time.

Wait a day or so, then return to the same spot, this time with the longest lead you can find. This can be a length of rope attached to the conventional lead if necessary. The main thing is that it gives you control over your dog and its movements. The dog needs to learn that freedom comes with responsibility – and that responsibility includes doing what its guardian asks of it.

STEP BY STEP   THE WALK

- With the lead at a length of no more than a few feet, practise the basic steps of the recall, inviting the dog to join you then rewarding it with a tidbit if it does so.
- If it doesn't conform, cut the walk short. Let the dog know that defiance is going to get it nowhere.
- If it does return to you, reward the dog by extending the length of the rope or lead by a few feet and go through the process again.
- Build on this until the dog is running around at the full length of the lead or rope.
- Each time it responds properly to your recall, reward the dog.
- Ensure the rope remains slack by using a combination of pressure and release. If you feel a tautness on the line, release the pressure so that the dog notices it. Then take the line back without tugging but with enough pressure for the dog to know the difference. You are giving the dog the choice of working with the line taut or slack. It will quickly learn that it prefers it when the line isn't taut. It will exercise self-control to ensure it stays that way.
- When you are ready to end the exercise, position yourself near the gate so that the dog knows you are heading homewards.

> • If when you ask it to come to you the dog tries to bolt or stand its ground, don't tug on the line, simply wait. Don't make a single step back to the dog either, as this will be seen as deference.
> • Stand your ground until the dog comes back to you, using food reward as an incentive.
> • When it does finally come to you be warm in your praise. Let it know that it has been a 'very good dog' in returning.

Continue with this for a few days. When the dog's behaviour both here and at home merits it, give it another chance to run off the lead. If it shows any signs of reluctance to return to you do not hesitate to return to the long lead again.

It may be a war of attrition, but it is one you must win.

CHALLENGES AT MEALTIMES

Food is perhaps the most powerful signal of status to the dog, so it is entirely predictable that an ambitious young dog will become fixated on mealtimes as an area where it can assert its authority.

A dog can challenge your leadership at mealtimes in several ways. It can become agitated while you are preparing the meal, sometimes jumping up at you as if to say 'come on, hurry up'. It can also be reluctant to let you near its bowl when the meal is over. Again, the signal here is clear – the dog is saying: 'I decide when I'm finished, not you.' Of course, this cannot be allowed.

The most extreme way of underlining your control of feeding time – and hence your leadership – is to apply a variation of gesture-eating that I call Power Gesture Eating. If a dog of this age is persistently defying you at mealtimes it may be necessary to implement it.

'Hurry up': challenges for control of the food supply are common during this phase.

STEP BY STEP   MEALTIMES 2

- Approach mealtimes as you would if you were going to practise normal gesture eating, but this time divide the dog's meal up into smaller portions, distributed between three or four bowls.
- Prepare a corresponding number of snacks for you and any other members of the family that are present.
- As with normal gesture eating, eat one snack in full view of the dog.
- If the dog becomes over-excited or agitated slow the process down. Make it realise it will have to wait. If it becomes aggressive or snappy remove the food altogether and go away for half an hour or so.
- If the dog calms down, place one of the dog's bowls on the floor, giving it plenty of room to eat in peace. Don't crowd the dog. Imagine how nervous you would feel if you had a waiter hovering over you while you ate in a restaurant.
- When the dog has finished, place another bowl in a different part of the room.
- Continue with this until each plate and bowl is empty.

The ultimate sanction – countering challenges to your leadership

This can be a tough period for an owner. The dog is empowered by a real sense of self-confidence at this phase of its life. As its experience of life grows, it feels it can conquer the world. It is vital that you don't allow the dog to win any battles that occur now, and this may entail using the ultimate sanction – removal from the pack.

Once more, the key to this lies in understanding the dog's hard-wired belief in the pack system. Challenges such as the one the 'pretender' is making at home happen on a regular basis in the wild, and they are dealt with in the most direct way. Faced with unacceptable behaviour or insubordination, an alpha wolf may physically eject a younger wolf from the den. The cast-out wolf would be forced to live on the outskirts of the pack, scavenging on leftovers and barred from joining in the hunts. It would only be allowed to rejoin the pack once it showed it had learned its lesson. Any attempt to reclaim its place prematurely would be met with more aggression.

Ultimately, this ploy almost always works. Such is the wolf's inherent belief in the pack system as its only means of surviving in the world, it will fall into line with whatever rules it needs to follow to be a member of that pack. The only other option is for the wolf to head off in the hope it can form a pack of its own.

Domestic dog owners don't need to put their dogs out on the street to convey a similar message; they can do it simply by separating the dog from the rest of its pack.

WHEN AND HOW TO BANISH A DOG

As with all the most powerful weapons, banishment must be used sparingly. There are two reasons for this. Firstly, it will come as such a shock that the dog will not fail to pay heed to it. Secondly, once it has been used, the dog will be armed with the knowledge that it may be used again.

It is something owners find difficult, but it is vital they remember they are working with the dog's overriding need to survive. A dog knows it is in trouble on its own; it knows it needs to be part of a pack environment in order to survive.

Banishment should be used whenever the dog is being openly and persistently defiant, and the length and severity of the separation should be increased according to the strength of that defiance. During this challenging phase, a dog can look at its owner with contempt, as if to say, 'Who do you think you are calling?' So you have to make that dog question his attitude, and the way to do that is to treat it with something approaching the contempt with which it is treating you.

If you decide to implement this, the dog should be cut off from the rest of the pack for the remainder of the day. It should still eat, of course, although it must do so using gesture eating, but it should not be walked or played with. It should not even have its presence acknowledged during these 24 hours.

Some people find this very severe, but what are the alternatives? The old-fashioned way to get this message across would have been to shout and holler and shake the dog. How much of that is going to mean anything to the dog? Isn't it far better to talk to it in a language it understands and threaten it with a sanction that really impinges on its quality of life?

Previously, in really severe cases of defiance I have asked owners to ignore their dogs for two, three or even four days. It has been extreme – but it has worked.

Breeding

There is a real joy to witnessing the wonder of new life. And, provided it is approached from the right perspective, breeding can be a hugely fulfilling process for both dog and owner. It has certainly been so for me on the occasions when I have bred from my own dogs. Yet breeding is a big step for any dog owner, no matter how experienced. It requires responsibility, planning and a solid, well-informed understanding of what lies ahead. No one should go into it lightly.

TO BREED OR NOT TO BREED?

By this age a dog is physically and mentally in perfect condition to start breeding. But that doesn't mean that all dogs are suitable for breeding, or that even if they are good specimens their owners should jump into producing puppies. Some important questions have to be answered first.

1. Is your dog going to pass on inherited illnesses?

If there is one overriding priority when breeding it is that the process improves the canine gene pool. By this I mean that all owners should try to breed from healthy dogs that are going to, in turn, produce good-quality puppies. By breeding from dogs that do not meet these standards, owners run the risk of doing serious harm to the individual breeds.

By this stage all dogs should have been examined for the key congenital disorders, eye and ear problems, displasia and other bone diseases. If a dog does have a problem then it should not be used for breeding. The probability of one or all of its offspring inheriting this condition is extremely high.

2. Does your dog have the right temperament to breed?

To me this is as important as the physical quality of the dog. There are certain temperaments that, to my mind, make them unsuitable for breeding. If you have a dog that is a nervous character then you should not breed from it. There could be hereditary factors which would reflect themselves in a litter of nervous pups.

Equally, if a dog is very aggressive it shouldn't be used for breeding. A lot of people ascribe aggression to breeds, wrongly in my opinion. Yes, some breeds, such as pitbulls, have been bred by humans to be aggressive. But that doesn't mean that all pitbulls are devils, just as not all Labradors are angels. Within every breed there are different personalities. If a dog has a bit of a mean streak, it is not a good candidate for breeding no matter what type of dog it is. It is far better to select dogs that are calm and well-adjusted, as they are much more likely to produce puppies with a similar disposition.

3. Are you sure you are prepared for the hard work and expense?

Breeding a litter of puppies requires a lot of time, effort and money. While the mother is carrying the puppies she will need extra attention, not to mention additional food and vitamins. She will also need to be seen by a vet on a regular basis and to undergo treatments like worming. Even if nothing goes wrong in the pregnancy it is a major commitment. In financial terms alone, stud fees can cost up to £1000, with vet fees and extra food costing up to another £500 between them.

If things go wrong then there will be even more demands on the owner's time and money, and there is always the possibility that a female could lose her entire litter. Before going ahead, owners have to ask themselves: Are you prepared to pay £1000 or more and have nothing to show at the end of it?

4. Are you prepared to keep all your puppies?

Even if things do go perfectly, there is still the problem of finding good homes for the puppies that result. And if good homes are found, there is always the possibility that the puppies will, for whatever reason, not adjust to life there and be returned by their owners. In this situation it is the breeders' responsibility to take the puppy back. So this raises the question, in the worst-case scenario, are owners prepared to keep all the puppies that are produced? Bearing in mind that females can produce up to 20 pups, it is a major consideration and not one that should be dismissed lightly.

FINDING THE RIGHT PARTNER FOR YOUR DOG

If, after considering all the pros and cons, you decide to go ahead with breeding from your female, then the first thing you need to do is find the right mate. Matching your bitch with a suitable male 'stud' dog is an art in itself and requires a lot of time, effort and – sometimes – money, so it is best to start planning well in advance, adhering to a few golden rules along the way:

1. Know your breed

If you feel your knowledge about your breed is in any way deficient, your first job is to start researching it. This is important because, as a responsible owner, you need to be aware of all the issues concerning your breed. These would include:

- The ideal shape for the breed, as set out in the breed standard.
- What breed disorders you need to look out for.
- How to gauge whether a stud dog is carrying a disorder.

The best way to do all this is via the Kennel Club, who will be able to point you in the direction of the appropriate breed secretary. They will provide you with all the information you need – and after that they will also give you a list of good dogs available for stud.

2. Know your stud dog

Once you have chosen a potential stud dog it is important you go along and see it well before mating it with your dog. You should satisfy yourself of the following:

IS IT A GOOD BREEDING DOG?

Many owners choose a mate for their dog that has a great record as a show dog. But this is no guarantee that it is going to be a good stud dog, so it is important to make an independent check of whether the dog has a good breeding record as well as a good pedigree. The best way to do this is via the Kennel Club or the canine press, both of whom have plenty of information on the top sires in every breed.

IS THE OWNER A GOOD, RESPONSIBLE BREEDER?

A reputable breeder will be proud of their dog. So when you ask to see its documentation, they should be more than happy to produce whatever is necessary. It is, in my experience, one of the surest ways to satisfy yourself of a breeder's quality. What is more, a good breeder will want to turn the tables and check you out as well. So, just as you would expect the stud-dog owner to have all their documentation to hand, so you too should be able to provide everything they would expect of you as a responsible breeder. Again, you should be proud to be able to do this.

DOES THE DOG MEET THE BREED STANDARD IN TERMS OF APPEARANCE?

You should know your breed well enough to be familiar with what its Kennel Club breed standards are. Give the stud dog a thorough examination to make sure it conforms. Any deviations from the norm will only be exaggerated in the puppies, so it pays to be picky in this regard.

HAS THE DOG GOT THE CLEARANCES IT NEEDS?

Knowing that the stud dog is clear of the congenital disorders and diseases that afflict its breed is hugely important. For instance, if you are considering mating a breed with a history of hip dysplasia you should check its hip-scoring certificate, ensuring it has a combined score for both hips of less than 20. Equally, if there is a tendency to develop eye diseases within a breed, the stud owner should be able to produce an eye-test certificate. Remember the golden rules here. You can't breed with a dog that is affected. You should only breed with a dog that has been classified as clear.

Don't accept someone's word that the dog is 'clear'. If a stud-dog owner can't produce a current certificate then alarm bells should ring immediately. Everyone is issued with one.

HOW OFTEN TO BREED?

A female can produce pups for most of her life, often from the age of nine months until she is well into double figures in terms of years. So, in theory, a fit, fertile female could produce tens of litters during the course of her life. In practice, however, this would be the height of cruelty. A female is not a puppy factory. In general, a dog shouldn't produce more than three litters; the number it would have in the wild. By restricting her breeding to this number, you are also giving her the best chance of producing healthy, high quality puppies that will, in turn, make good potential parents, which is – after all – one of the main objects of the exercise.

SUCCESSFUL MATING – GETTING IT RIGHT

Having chosen a stud dog you must now begin planning for the mating. The key to this, obviously, is timing, so the first thing to do is monitor the female closely.

How to Spot if the Female is Ready

There are a variety of tests you can do with your vet, but the best way to test whether a female is ready is to do so yourself manually. You can do this by running your hand across her back towards her tail, then putting your fingers between the tail and the vulva and giving it a slight rub. If she lifts her vulva up to meet your hand and at the same time puts her tail to one side then she is 'presenting' and is ready.

You now have up to five days to take advantage of this. To give yourself the best chance of conceiving it is best to take your dog to the stud dog as early as possible within this window. It may also be helpful to warm the female at this stage.

This is where it can become very disappointing for owners. Dogs aren't automatically going to want to mate with each other. They are, let's not forget, sensitive, living creatures, probably strangers to each other, and there are all sorts of factors that can put them off. Females, particularly 'maidens' who are breeding for the first time, can be very difficult. They can let the stud dogs know they are not interested in mating, and do so in no uncertain terms. Equally, even the most reliable stud dogs can be put off by a nervous or a reluctant female. So it is vital that the mating is conducted under supervision. Many stud-dog owners insist on the owners of visiting females leaving them to it. This is fine, providing you are sure they are experienced and know what they are doing.

The tie

If all goes according to plan, the male and female will execute a 'tie'. This will happen in three distinct stages:

FOREPLAY

The two dogs should be given time to get to know each other. If they are interested in mating they will begin a little foreplay, playing around and sniffing at each other. There should be nothing aggressive or confrontational about this. The longer they do this the stronger the indications are that things are going to work out.

PENETRATION

If the female is ready she will present herself and stand quietly waiting for the male. He will then mount her, inserting his penis into her vagina and holding himself in position by clasping her hips with his front legs. He will then ejaculate inside the female.

THE TIE

The bulbourethral gland on the male's penis will now swell inside the female, stimulating the vulva to contract around it and preventing it from withdrawing. This is nature's way of flushing through the semen. Every thirty seconds or so the male will release fluid to flush the semen further into the female. While this is going on, the dogs will change position so that the male is now facing away from the female but is still 'tied' to her. You shouldn't pay a stud fee unless you know mating has occurred, so even if you have been asked to leave the room you should ask to see the dogs tied together. Even if it is a brief moment, this will act as proof.

The mating dogs stay this way for, on average, twenty minutes or so. But it can be less – or, indeed, much longer. I have experienced a tie that has gone on for three and a half hours. You must never interfere, regardless of how long the tie goes on, but it is important that whoever is supervising keeps a close eye on this phase. A prolonged tie can be distressing and painful to the female and she may get aggressive towards the male at this point. When the tie is finally broken, both male and female will vigorously groom their genital areas to rid themselves of any harmful bacteria.

MAKING A DETAILED BIRTH PLAN

The average canine pregnancy lasts just over nine weeks, or 64 days. There will be few obvious signs of anything happening during the first half of this. Indeed, some pregnant females don't show any signs of being pregnant until they produce puppies. But it is important that as soon as mating is achieved you begin to prepare for the days, weeks and months ahead by putting together a detailed birth plan.

The first thing to do is work out the date the female is likely to produce her puppies. This is done simply enough by calculating 64 days ahead, or referring to a whelping chart such as the one below. You can then begin adding other key landmarks ahead, such as scanning and, if it is still to be done, worming, as well as the beginning of the countdown to the big day itself when you will need to start preparing a whelping box.

Pregnancy

THE PUP'S PROGRESS

Fertilisation occurs in the fallopian tubes. Six to ten days later the fertilised eggs then move down the two tubes into the uterus, which is made up of two thin tubes or 'horns'. The fertilised eggs – or 'zygotes' – are then spaced out symmetrically so that they each have an equal chance of being nourished by the placenta. By the end of the first two weeks the embryo will have developed its main features and will have become a foetus. Even at this point some foetuses will have an advantage over others, however. Those positioned near the middle of each horn will have better access to the nutrients that will fuel their development over the weeks ahead.

SERVED JAN	WHELP MAR	SERVED FEB	WHELP APR	SERVED MAR	WHELP MAY	SERVED APR	WHELP JUN	SERVED MAY	WHELP JUL	SERVED JUN	WHELP AUG
1	5	1	5	1	3	1	3	1	3	1	3
2	6	2	6	2	4	2	4	2	4	2	4
3	7	3	7	3	5	3	5	3	5	3	5
4	8	4	8	4	6	4	6	4	6	4	6
5	9	5	9	5	7	5	7	5	7	5	7
6	10	6	10	6	8	6	8	6	8	6	8
7	11	7	11	7	9	7	9	7	9	7	9
8	12	8	12	8	10	8	10	8	10	8	10
9	13	9	13	9	11	9	11	9	11	9	11
10	14	10	14	10	12	10	12	10	12	10	12
11	15	11	15	11	13	11	13	11	13	11	13
12	16	12	16	12	14	12	14	12	14	12	14
13	17	13	17	13	15	13	15	13	15	13	15
14	18	14	18	14	16	14	16	14	16	14	16
15	19	15	19	15	17	15	17	15	17	15	17
16	20	16	20	16	18	16	18	16	18	16	18
17	21	17	21	17	19	17	19	17	19	17	19
18	22	18	22	18	20	18	20	18	20	18	20
19	23	19	23	19	21	19	21	19	21	19	21
20	24	20	24	20	22	20	22	20	22	20	22
21	25	21	25	21	23	21	23	21	23	21	23
22	26	22	26	22	24	22	24	22	24	22	24
23	27	23	27	23	25	23	25	23	25	23	25
24	28	24	28	24	26	24	26	24	26	24	26
25	29	25	29	25	27	25	27	25	27	25	27
26	30	26	30	26	28	26	28	26	28	26	28
27	31	27	May 1	27	29	27	29	27	29	27	29
28	Apr 1	28	2	28	30	28	30	28	30	28	30
29	2			29	31	29	Jul 1	29	31	29	31
30	3			30	Jun 1	30	2	30	Aug 1	30	Sep 1
31	4			31	2	31		31	1	31	

WHELPING TABLE

WHELPING TABLE

SERVED	WHELP	SERVED	WHELP	SERVED	WHELP	SERVED	WHELP	SERVED	WHELP	SERVED	WHELP
JUL	SEP	AUG	OCT	SEP	NOV	OCT	DEC	NOV	JAN	DEC	FEB
1	2	1	3	1	3	1	3	1	3	1	2
2	3	2	4	2	4	2	4	2	4	2	3
3	4	3	5	3	5	3	5	3	5	3	4
4	5	4	6	4	6	4	6	4	6	4	5
5	6	5	7	5	7	5	7	5	7	5	6
6	7	6	8	6	8	6	8	6	8	6	7
7	8	7	9	7	9	7	9	7	9	7	8
8	9	8	10	8	10	8	10	8	10	8	9
9	10	9	11	9	11	9	11	9	11	9	10
10	11	10	12	10	12	10	12	10	12	10	11
11	12	11	13	11	13	11	13	11	13	11	12
12	13	12	14	12	14	12	14	12	14	12	13
13	14	13	15	13	15	13	15	13	15	13	14
14	15	14	16	14	16	14	16	14	16	14	15
15	16	15	17	15	17	15	17	15	17	15	16
16	17	16	18	16	18	16	18	16	18	16	17
17	18	17	19	17	19	17	19	17	19	17	18
18	19	18	20	18	20	18	20	18	20	18	19
19	20	19	21	19	21	19	21	19	21	19	20
20	21	20	22	20	22	20	22	20	22	20	21
21	22	21	23	21	23	21	23	21	23	21	22
22	23	22	24	22	24	22	24	22	24	22	23
23	24	23	25	23	25	23	25	23	25	23	24
24	25	24	26	24	26	24	26	24	26	24	25
25	26	25	27	25	27	25	27	25	27	25	26
26	27	26	28	26	28	26	28	26	28	26	27
27	28	27	29	27	29	27	29	27	29	27	28
28	29	28	30	28	30	28	30	28	30	28	Mar 1
29	30	29	31	29	Dec 1	29	31	29	31	29	2
30	Oct 1	30	Nov 1	30	2	30	Jan 1	30	Feb 1	30	3
31	2	31	2	31		31	2	31		31	4

The key moments in the foetus's development from here on are:

3 Weeks

This is roughly equivalent to the three-month mark in a human pregnancy. By now all of the key tissues and organs will have developed.

5 Weeks

The main body characteristics will now be apparent. The legs, mouth, eyes, ears and tail are all in place.

6 Weeks

The foetus will now have formed itself into a miniature dog. Its eyelids, claws, hair and skin colour are distinct by now. The pup's skeleton will now be visible on an x-ray. Its skull will also be detectable by feeling the abdominal wall.

6–9 Weeks

The formed foetus will now grow steadily, although its internal organs are still developing. The lungs, for instance, are not capable of taking in oxygen. Instead, right until birth the foetus will still rely on the placenta for its sustenance.

THE MOTHER'S PROGRESS

Morning Sickness

Just like humans, some dogs experience morning sickness during the early phases of pregnancy. There is nothing alarming in this, it is merely nature's way of expelling the toxins that may potentially affect the foetuses within her womb, but you should monitor it to ensure it does not drain the dog of its energy, thereby endangering the puppies. It should also fade away by the middle phase of the pregnancy. If in any doubt, consult your vet.

Feeding

It is important to get the feeding of the pregnant female right. Most of the weight gain happens in the last four weeks of pregnancy as the puppy inside really begins to increase in size. Overfeeding a dog before this can lead to excess fat and may even cause problems during labour.

As a rule of thumb, the amount of food the female is eating should be increased by between 10 and 15 per cent per week from the beginning of the fifth week until whelping. So by the time the litter is ready to arrive she should be eating roughly 50 per cent more than she was before mating.

Inside the womb: in the space of the first six weeks of the nine-week pregnancy, an embryo develops into a foetus and then a tiny dog, ready to be delivered. The diagrams above show the progress within the womb (left to right) during the first two weeks, then at three and finally six weeks.

It is important, however, to feed the dog small meals and to use a more concentrated and palatable food. The reason for this is simple. With the growing uterus taking up so much of the female's stomach, it simply isn't able to expand as much as it would normally when it takes in food.

Scanning

Many owners want to know firstly whether the mating has been successful and – if it was – whether to expect a small or a large litter. Modern medicine provides the option of giving the female an ultrasound scan midway through the pregnancy. This is best conducted just the once, around the five-week mark.

Blooming

Five weeks or so into the pregnancy the female should be blooming. There should be no more morning sickness and she should have the sparkling eyes and generally happy demeanour of a dog that knows nature is performing its wonders within her. She will also have begun to show in terms of weight. She will have lost her waistline, and the areas behind her ribs and in front of her hips should have significantly widened.

Exercise

Pregnant females need to remain fit, not least because they will soon have to face the challenges of whelping and raising their litter. But at the same time owners should be careful not to over-exercise pregnant females. Exercise should be light, and guided by the female's responses. If she needs to rest during or after a walk, then let her rest. There should definitely be no pounding of the roads. Agility work should also be put on hold until after the puppies arrive. It is important to ensure females don't stretch too much, so behaviour like jumping up is even more undesirable during this phase.

Worming

All pregnant females are prone to suffering from worms, in particular roundworms. These tend to become active six weeks or so into the pregnancy, when because of the hormonal changes affecting her, the female and her natural immune system fail to deal with them as they normally would. The roundworm larvae cross via the placenta into the pups, where they infest the liver. Some also settle in the mother's mammary glands, ready to cross into the pups when they get their first drink of colostrum. It is vital that you protect the pups as much as possible from this, so it is advisable to give the mother regular doses of a worming treatment during the final three weeks or so of the pregnancy. Ideally the doses should begin at around six and a half weeks, and be repeated every five or so days until the puppies are born.

'Gentling'

There is lots of evidence to suggest that petting the belly of the pregnant female produces puppies that are more docile and receptive to being touched and stroked from an early age. The thinking behind this is that the puppy develops some of its tactile instincts even before birth and can feel its mother being stroked while inside the uterus. When it emerges into the world it is less of a shock to its system and it responds less fearfully to human touch. This gives the puppy a good start, making it more likely it will go on to be amenable to human interaction sooner rather than later in its life.

PHANTOM PREGNANCIES

In the wild it is not just the breeding alpha female who becomes 'broody' during pregnancy. The subordinate wolves also experience a physical change, produced by the hormone prolactin. This readies them for the job of becoming surrogate parents when the pups emerge from the den at three weeks of age.

The domestic dog doesn't live in the pack environment any longer, but there is physical evidence that their bodies are still pre-programmed to act in this subordinate, surrogate-parent role. It is why some believe that many dogs experience phantom pregnancies.

When she is going through oestrus, a female often goes through the hormonal changes normally connected with pregnancy despite the fact she has not mated. She can put on weight, her teats can change shape and her behaviour can alter significantly. She can be snappy, disinterested in eating and begin making dens where she 'mothers' her toys. She can, in some cases, even begin producing milk in readiness for her babies' arrival.

It is only when the nine weeks pass and she enters the post-oestrus phase that the dog returns to normal. You should, of course, have a very strong idea whether your dog really is pregnant. But if for whatever reason you are unsure, there are only two real options: having a scan or waiting for nature to take its course.

THE FINAL COUNTDOWN

By six or seven weeks into the pregnancy the puppies are entering their final growth spurt. In the last two weeks they will almost double in size. As a result of this the mother-to-be will show unmistakable signs of latter-stage pregnancy. Her belly will drop under her and she will probably put on a significant amount of weight.

There are several things you need to begin to think about now. And the first of these is where she is going to give birth.

In the wild, wolves take great care planning and preparing their dens. They ensure they are near a plentiful supply of water, and they make very clear boundaries so that the pups will not be able to wander far from their mother during their first weeks. Your domestic dog is going to be just as meticulous about where she wants to give birth. With a little planning you can lead her to the right decision.

The Whelping Box

There are two main types of whelping boxes. For smaller breeds an enclosed box is more suitable. This can be constructed easily at home from a cardboard box if necessary. It should be between 60–90 cms (2–3 feet) square. All you have to ensure is that there is lots of light and ventilation, that the floor is lined with plenty of newspaper or another absorbent lining, and that the mother – but not the puppies – can get in and out as she pleases. For larger breeds, a bigger, drawer-like box is better. This should be between 1.2–1.5 metres (4–5 feet) square and fitted with a guard rail set in between 7.5 and 15 cms (3–6 inches) from its inner edges to protect the puppies from being laid on by their mother. The guard rail should be set at a similar height off the floor.

The whelping box should be placed somewhere quiet and removed from where the main activity of the house takes place. This replicates the behaviour in the wild, where the alpha female marks out her dens, so that they are isolated from the rest of the pack, where she knows she will be safe for the next three weeks.

You should begin to introduce the female to the whelping box as early as possible, perhaps three weeks before the puppies are due. She will have been planning where she intends to have her puppies during the final days of her pregnancy, so to suddenly spring your idea of the location any later than this may result in her rejecting it.

Delivery day – helping your dog through whelping

Dogs are generally very reliable in delivering their litters on time. Occasionally a female will go into whelp a few days early, but in the main they produce like clockwork. As delivery day draws near it is vital that you are ready and fully prepared for the big event.

ITEMS TO HAVE TO HAND

- clean towels
- fresh bedding
- notebook and pen for timing events
- scissors
- thermometer
- some formula newborn-puppy milk in case of feeding problems
- a small feeding bottle or eye-dropper
- emergency telephone number for vet

HOW TO SPOT THAT WHELPING IS ABOUT TO BEGIN

The lead-up to whelping usually begins some 36 hours before the first arrival. The telltale signs are:

- At this point the mother-to-be's temperature begins to drop. By the time she is ready to deliver it will have dropped from the normal 38°C to around 36°C before whelping.
- As she senses labour approaching the mother may refuse food.
- She may also begin vomiting and shivering. Don't overreact, just keep her comfortable.

WHELPING

As labour begins there will be a series of obvious signals from the dog:

- She will begin turning around in circles or lie down.
- There will be obvious signs of contractions and straining.
- A sac of fluid or 'waters' containing the first pup will begin to protrude through the vulva and burst. This is a sure sign that the first arrival is around two hours away.

In most circumstances a dog will be able to deliver its pup naturally. When the first one emerges the mother will lick off the membrane surrounding the puppy and sever the umbilical cord with her teeth. Soon afterwards the placenta, or afterbirth, passes through accompanied by a dark green fluid. There should be one of these for each of the pups. The mother will eat this. This is nature's way of giving her a real dollop of nourishment, because the mother won't want to leave the den for the next few days at least. In the wild the mother will eat the placentas of all its pups, maybe eight of them. It will keep her going for five days, storing up the nutrients she knows she will need during the demanding days and weeks ahead.

The mother will then lick the pup vigorously, warming and drying the newborn dog but also stimulating it to breathe. Soon afterwards she will offer it its first milk, or colostrum, and its life should be safely underway.

When precisely the next puppy will follow is hard to gauge. It may arrive within ten minutes, or it may take longer, even hours. The key is to ensure that the dog is not in distress. If a dog is clearly pushing but no pup emerges, alarm bells should start ringing. If this goes on for an hour a call to the vet is definitely in order, as there is clearly a risk of a puppy being blocked or breached, and this will put both the mother and the puppy at risk.

As the mother passes through her multiple deliveries there will be a lot of knocking around of the pups in the whelping box. With the mother

The miracle of life: a mother attends to a new arrival during whelping.

liable to twist and turn as she forces each new arrival out, the first pup in particular is going to get moved around a lot during the intervals between each birth. At this point it is vital that the pup remains close to its mother's teats, not least because she is its main source of warmth. If a pup becomes disconnected the mother should draw them back in. If she does not, however, and the puppy's own instincts don't kick in, you should put the pup back to the teat.

LITTER SIZES

As a rule, the bigger the breed, the bigger the litter size. Small breeds like Yorkshire Terriers tend to have three puppies, while larger ones like German Shepherds can produce as many as twelve puppies. There is every chance in these bigger breeds that a mother may produce more puppies than she has teats. This is natural selection at work in its most fundamental form. Comp-etition for places on the teats is intense and only the strongest will survive. In this circumstance what to do is up to the owner. Some may want to leave nature to take its course. Others will want to intervene and hand-feed.

PROBLEM DELIVERIES

Most dogs are able to deliver their litter unaided if necessary. Some, however, will have problems for a variety of reasons.

A major cause of problems is selective breeding. A female may, for instance, have been mated with a much bigger male for breeding reasons. The large pups she then produces may not be physically capable of passing through her birth canal. This can also often be a problem with smaller breeds whose birth canals have, through generations of breeding, become too narrow and restrictive to pass any pups into the world.

The other related problem concerns dogs that are too immature to produce. Selective breeding has succeeded in producing females who go into puberty younger and younger. But while they are physically capable of getting pregnant and producing babies they are nowhere near ready to do so emotionally. When it comes to the whelping process these dogs can get very distressed indeed. This can then have a knock-on effect, complicating the pregnancies or leaving the mother so emotionally drained she is incapable of delivering the pups inside her.

In all of these cases, the only option is a Caesarean section conducted by your vet. If any of these situations occur, contact the vet instantly.

As with humans, the decision to have a Caesarean should not be taken lightly. The mother will be inhibited after the operation and may not be able to care for the pups as well as she might. There can also be problems in terms of bonding between the pups and the mother. Ordinarily a chemical reaction occurs within the mother when she passes pups through the birth canal and then licks them clean of the membrane and mucus. With a Caesarean this doesn't happen. The dog's natural maternal instincts can fail to kick in as a result.

WHEN TO CALL THE VET

Giving birth is a precarious operation for the dog. Generally it passes off without problems, but there are many serious complications that can set in. If this happens your vet should be called in to tackle them.

The following are situations where the vet should be called:

- If the dog has gone past the 64-day point in her pregnancy without going into labour.
- If the first stage of whelping (vomiting, disinterest in food, etc.) has gone on for more than 36 hours without a puppy appearing.
- If the dog is in labour and has been straining and pushing to produce a pup for more than an hour without any success.
- If a pup appears but doesn't pass through the birth canal within 20 minutes.
- If the number of placentas is less than the number of pups, suggesting the mother hasn't expelled all the afterbirth inside her.
- If the discharges from the mother are dark, bloody or foul-smelling.
- If the mother continues to reject a particular pup for more than three hours.

Puppies are extremely vulnerable during their first hours. There are a number of telltale signs that may indicate a newborn is suffering from a problem. Some will require you to call a vet, others can be dealt with directly. The key concerns are:

Flat Puppy Syndrome

Some pups are born with weak muscles and come out flat-chested. They resemble swimming turtles, hence their nickname 'swimmers'. It is particularly common in pups from the giant breeds. With proper exercise the problem can be overcome so that by the time the puppy is three months old it looks normal.

Hernia

If the pup has a swelling on the navel or groin it may have suffered a hernia during birth. There are two possibilities here. If it is a small reducible hernia it needs no treatment. However, if the swelling is hard and painful when pressed, it is likely to be a strangulated hernia, which is a serious problem, and the dog should be taken to the vet immediately. Some breeds such as Lhasa Apsos and Shih Tzus are prone to hernias.

Vitamin K Deficiency

Vitamin K allows the blood to clot properly. It should be produced by the mother and passed on to the puppy. Undernourished mothers, however, may not produce enough vitamin K, causing the puppy to bleed easily. If you notice a puppy bleeding, take it to the vet where it can get a vitamin K injection.

Infected Navels

The remains of the umbilical cord should shrivel and fall off within a few days of birth. In some cases, however, infections can set in, leaving the navel area looking red and swollen. This can be cleaned with an antiseptic, but it may be necessary to consult the vet if the problem persists.

Cold Puppies

If a pup feels cold to the touch it needs immediate attention. A puppy whose body temperature falls only a couple of degrees can quickly fade away and die. Either return it to the warmth of its mother, or – if she is rejecting it – place a warm hot-water bottle near the pup.

HELPING OUT: HOW TO HELP THE MOTHER

Dogs are very resilient and determined creatures, especially when it comes to doing something as natural – and important – as giving birth. The mother will probably have no difficulties in producing babies herself, but in some circumstances, however, you will need to help.

One of the most common situations when this occurs is with a young, maybe first-time mother who becomes exhausted. Alternatively – in the most extreme circumstance – you might be needed because a mother does not survive the ordeal of labour.

The key things you should do are these:

- Pick up the newly delivered puppy with a warm towel or cloth and wipe away all the mucus and membrane surrounding it, taking particular care to clean the nose and mouth.
- To stimulate the pup to start breathing, hold it tightly in the towel or cloth then tilt it so that any excess birth fluid comes out, then gently rub its chest.
- If the dog does not start breathing immediately, give it artificial respiration by placing your mouth over its nose and breathing hard. If this doesn't work call the vet immediately.
- Using a piece of gauze or cotton thread, tie the umbilical cord 1 cm (half an inch) from the pup's stomach. Then, with heated and sterilised scissors cut the cord between the tie and the placenta.
- If the mother is with you, place the pup in with her, encouraging her to feed it by nuzzling the newborn's head against her stomach.
- If the mother isn't present or isn't able to feed the dog, prepare some formula milk and feed it to the pup through a small bottle or eye-dropper.

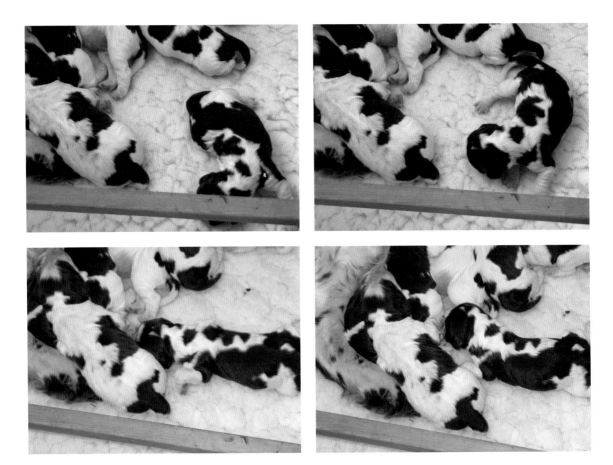

1. Basic Instincts (top left): a day-old puppy finds itself ejected from its mother's teat.
2. (top right): instinctively it turns towards the warmth of the litter.
3. (bottom left): the pup paddles its way back towards the family unit.
4. (bottom right): home again, it fixes itself on its mother's teat.

You also need to be particularly careful with large litters. A dog is hugely resourceful. If a bitch has a large litter she may well split them into two groups and feed them alternately. It's amazing to see how she instinctively organises her litter. Despite this, however, you still need to be vigilant on the new litter's behalf during these first few hours. The physically strongest pups tend to get to the teat first. As they do so, these stronger pups can push weaker ones away by paddling forward with their feet. It's not a deliberate thing, simply that most natural phenomenon, the survival of the fittest.

If you have a pup that's repeatedly being knocked off the teat, in nature this would be one of the pups that perished. They need that first feed of colostrum, and if they don't get it they lose ground very quickly. A pup without nourishment in the first twelve hours will be hard-pressed to survive.

Listen out for the mutting sound a pup makes when it is distressed. If you see one has been knocked away and isn't finding its way back naturally, act quickly to return it to its mother.

Diet

The new mother's demand for energy and nutrition will rise significantly while she is rearing her puppies. At the peak of her feeding, around the third week, she will be giving between four and seven per cent of her body weight to her puppies every day in the form of milk, so her diet will need to be increased accordingly. As a rule, a new mother will need to eat up to three or four times her normal amount of food. She needs this not just to make sure she can produce enough milk for the puppies but to maintain her strength and her own good health at the same time.

At this point you can feed the dog as much as she wants. Such are the demands being made on her that it is highly unlikely she will over-eat. Once more, however, meals should be relatively small, made up of highly palatable food and spread out over three or four meals during the day as well as a night feed. Just as importantly, the mother must always have an unlimited supply of fresh water available.

THE SIXTH AGE

protector

28 MONTHS TO AROUND 7 YEARS

'The sixth age shifts
Into the lean and slipper'd pantaloon,
With spectacles on nose, and pouch on side,
His youthful hose well sav'd'

IN THE WILD

By the age of two and a half, a wolf is fully developed – both physically and mentally. It is at the height of its powers, able to draw on its experience to deal with all that life throws at it. Whether it is an alpha or a subordinate wolf it will remain here – unless challenged – for five or more years. During this phase it will be completely at ease with itself and its role.

If it is an alpha it will live certain in the knowledge that its job is to provide for and protect the pack. It also knows it's up to it to ensure the continuation of the pack's bloodline. The buck stops with it. There is no delegation.

A wolf ranked elsewhere in the pecking order will get on with its job too, content in the knowledge that it is a vital cog in the machine that is the pack.

There will be times of danger, of course, but it no longer has any worries about leadership, food, or how threats to the pack will be dealt with. It is now free to relish its life.

A domestic dog that has accepted life in the same way is a happy and contented one. Ideally, this is the state of mind dog owners want their pets to reach at this stage. For some dogs, however, life is far removed from this relaxed idyll.

Leader of the pack: an alpha wolf exudes authority, strength and confidence.

THE SIXTH AGE: OVERVIEW

The dog has now reached physical and mental maturity. It is in its prime and ready to enjoy the best years of its life. Just as in the wild – where this stage marks the moment when the wolf is fully integrated into the pack – the dog has mentally settled for its position in life. It will be comfortable in its own skin; it will know its environment and its place within it. If the dog is well-adjusted this phase will be a rewarding one for its owner. It will be a time to revel in the age-old relationship between man and his best friend.

Unfortunately, if the dog reaches this point having decided it is leader of the pack, the owner will face severe problems. The dog's belief that it is responsible for the domestic pack will now be firmly established and its role as protector will be taken quite literally. A variety of behavioural difficulties can now arise as a result.

The die is cast

The dog, just like the wolf, will enter this new phase of its life convinced it has reached a crossroads. The insecurity it felt about its status during the pretender phase will have passed. Instead it will have decided the die has been cast in terms of its position in life. It will have told itself 'this is the way things are'. If it is a well-adjusted dog then it will see its role as subordinate to you, its human leader.

It will still make small daily challenges to your status, perhaps giving a little tug on the lead so as to double-check the leadership remains with you. All in all, however, it will be confident in your ability to make the right decisions.

This leaves it free to enjoy what should be the best days of its life. During this phase of its life the dog will generally become an altogether happier animal. It will usually enjoy its walks and its playtime more. It will interact with other dogs more easily. It will also tend to become a more caring dog. As a puppy it had little concern for anyone else; it was too wrapped up in its own world, and its need for food, sleep and play. Now it is more empathetic and more attuned to the needs of others around it, whether canine or human.

Typically during this phase, dogs tend to look after fellow dogs more, licking at wounds if they get hurt, for instance. They also become much more aware and responsive to human needs and emotions. I know from personal experience that if an owner is going through a bad time, a mature dog is capable of being the best friend you could ever wish to have. It is a magical phase in this sense.

The best days of their lives – helping your dog enjoy its prime

With its adolescence long behind it, the mature adult dog can relax and get on with the business of enjoying its life. It has placed its trust in its human owner, it doesn't go hungry, and potentially dangerous situations are dealt with calmly and efficiently by its leader. It knows where it stands. The next five years or so should be the happiest and most fulfilling of its life.

Happy days: freed from the stresses and strains of adolescence, a mature dog is ready to enjoy life to the full.

All dogs are different of course. For some, perfect happiness is a day made up of a good long walk in a favourite spot followed by a decent meal and a sleep in front of the fire. And there is very little wrong with that. But for dogs – and indeed owners – who want to get more out of their life together there is now a dizzying variety of sporting and competitive activities to suit all breeds, personalities and athletic abilities.

In the UK, the Kennel Club licenses almost 5,000 different canine competitions every year, ranging from breed shows to field and working trials, obedience to agility competitions.

Here is a guide to some activities a dog may enjoy:

FIELD AND WORKING TRIALS

This is something that will appeal to those breeds developed specifically for working roles, the gundogs and pastoral dogs in particular. They may not all be working on grouse shoots on Scottish estates or herding sheep on a Welsh hillside, but their instincts are still there and they will enjoy putting them to the test.

As with all sports there are rules and regulations governing dogs that can and cannot compete. In the UK, the Kennel Club is a good starting point for gathering the information you will need.

AGILITY

One of the most exciting sports a dog can take part in is Agility. This fun activity was introduced to the UK at Crufts in 1978 and has since caught on hugely, with hundreds of clubs now competing.

In Agility, teams of dogs and owners run around an obstacle course against the clock. Courses are made up of a combination of 16 obstacles, each designed to pose the dog a different challenge. These range from hurdles that the dog must clear without knocking over, to a table which the dog must lie down on for a set time; as well as a long jump, a water jump, a seesaw, weaving poles and two different types of tunnel. It is a fast and frantic activity that is also hugely entertaining for audiences to watch.

Fun and games: agility classes provide even the unlikeliest dogs with an opportunity to show off their athleticism.

As they improve, dogs move up to different levels from Elementary, Starters, Novice, Intermediate, Seniors, Advanced and Open.

To make sure some smaller and less athletic breeds aren't disadvantaged there are different competitions: for Standard Dogs, measuring over 432 mms (17 inches) at the withers; Midi Dogs, measuring between 432 mms (17 inches) and 381 mm (15 inches); and Mini Dogs, measuring under 381 mm (15 inches). Because it is so demanding physically and requires a lot of training, the sport is recommended for mature dogs, and no dog under 18 months of age can compete.

FLYBALL

Flyball arrived in the UK in 1990. Teams run against each other and the clock in relays. Each dog has to leap over a series of hurdles to reach the Flyball box, where it presses a pedal that projects a tennis ball into the air. The dog must catch the ball in its mouth then race back over the hurdles to the finish line. Once it has done so the next team member sets off. The winners are the first team to have each member successfully complete the course.

Huge fun, and a genuine test of the dog's agility, speed and intelligence, Flyball races are very popular with audiences at the major dog shows. The dogs clearly love them too, as the loud barks they deliver when competing testify.

OBEDIENCE COMPETITIONS

These hugely popular competitions test how well dog and owner work together. Some of the tests include the sort of standard controls most owners use, such as the sit, stand or lie down (each delivered from a distance), and heel work done at different speeds and incorporating a variety of manoeuvres. As the standard rises, however, there are more tricky challenges, such as scent discrimination, where the dog must use its power of smell to retrieve an article from a selection laid out in the ring. Owners can compete at a variety of standards but the emphasis throughout is on informality and on the dog working in a natural and happy way.

DOG SHOWS

By far the most popular form of activity for dogs, these are effectively beauty pageants for the canine world. They climax in the major events like Crufts in the UK and the Westminster Dog Show in the US.

In essence, a dog show is a simple affair. The Kennel Club has a 'Breed Standard' for every breed of dog, which represents the ideal conformation and characteristics for that breed. At shows, the judge must compare each dog with the breed standard to find the dog nearest to that ideal picture of the breed. Yet the truth is that, with its seemingly endless number of categories and grades of competition and baffling jargon, the show world can be a bewildering place for newcomers.

To help owners who plan to 'show' their dogs there are many clubs that specialise in 'Ringcraft'. Their classes teach owners how to prepare and present their dogs so as to make the best impression when they enter the show ring.

Alternatively, owners can start showing at small, local shows where the entry requirements are less stringent and everybody is more friendly and relaxed, and work their way up from here.

DOING WHAT COMES NATURALLY

Dogs derive huge fun from using their exceptional natural abilities. Another popular activity, for instance, is tracking, where owners get their dogs to utilise their amazing sense of smell and direction. Objects are strategically placed to form a trail that the dog has to successfully follow. In many cases, dogs that excel at this go on to work as search and rescue dogs. Other activities allow particular breeds to show off their natural assets. The Newfoundland, for instance, is a great swimmer, and owners of this breed organise competitions in which they simulate rescuing humans out at sea. This, again, often leads to dogs working closely with emergency services like the Coast Guard in the UK.

Muddled-up dogs

For a dog that is properly adjusted to its role in the human world, middle age is a real pleasure. The dog that is not so well adjusted, however, is going to have a completely different time of it.

A dog that is convinced of its leadership status at this point is going to be in a real muddle. It has been living with the wrong information for a long time. So, if it is used to ripping up the mail when the postman delivers it each morning it will by now have convinced itself this is normal. It will have said to itself: 'This is what I do.'

Therefore, an older dog with a developed personality can display a whole range of behavioural problems. And these problems will be subtly different from those displayed during the pretender phase. Then the dog was challenging for the role of leader. Now the dog believes that challenge has long since gone. It is convinced it is the leader and becomes fixated on fulfilling that role. And as it fails to do that job its behaviour can become a mixture of the extreme and the eccentric.

For instance, it is very common for dogs at this stage to become obsessive in their behaviour. Tail-chasing, feet-chewing, motorbike-chasing and assorted other habits are at their most common during this phase. You may also see excessive licking of people, an inability to leave visitors alone when they come to the house, or perhaps an obsessiveness in collecting or protecting toys.

Equally, it is common for a dog to 'shut down' at this point. It will appear outwardly quiet and calm, yet inside the dog will be overwhelmed by the challenge of doing a job it is hopelessly unequipped to carry out. It is feeling that it simply can't cope. This is something that doesn't usually happen before this age, and it can be a nightmare for the owners, but is also purgatory for the dog.

Again, however, the remedy for each of these behavioural problems is rooted in the same pack-leader principles. The dog must be stripped of its belief that it is in charge.

Potential behavioural problems

A dog that has reached this point still believing it is the leader of its pack can behave in any number of undesirable ways, depending on its personality. It can be highly protective and react strongly, possibly aggressively, to ensure its 'children' aren't harmed or upset in any way. Alternatively, a dog of this age can feel completely 'out-jobbed'. The sheer strain of being responsible for its pack – and in a world it doesn't understand – proves too much. This can result in odd obsessive behaviour, and it can also lead it to almost fall apart mentally. The following are some of the typical problems I have encountered during this phase of the dog's life:

SEVERE AGGRESSION

Dogs who have reached this stage in their life under the impression they are the leader of their domestic pack may well be reacting excessively as they carry out the various duties they associate with the job. In particular,

On the attack: left with the wrong impression of their leadership status, adult dogs can become extremely aggressive.

at times of perceived danger they can become extremely hyperactive and aggressive. The stronger the personality, the stronger the tendency. They will also tend to focus on one particular problem, perhaps the delivery of the post in the morning or the ringing of the telephone. Their preoccupation with these issues can become obsessive.

Helping dogs who have got themselves into this position is not easy. By relieving such a dog of its role as perceived leader, you are cutting off the supply of attention it is used to getting. It is not going to react well to this, but it has to be done. You must blitz a dog with all four elements of canine communication, beginning with the reuniting-after-separation technique.

A dog faced with a situation like this will opt for one of the three Fs: it will freeze, flee or – in the worst-case scenario – fight. There is every chance it will bark loudly, jump up into the owner's face and even bite.

For this reason you should be prepared. Owners who have dogs with strong personalities like this should think about putting a collar on the dog before beginning. They should also prepare a room or an area of the garden where the dog can be safely excluded if necessary. If there is the remotest chance of the dog becoming hyperactive and 'trashing' the room, then this room must be cleared out in advance.

If, as is likely, the dog reacts in an unacceptable way when you ignore it, you must take it by the collar and lead it to the exclusion zone. This is a crucial moment. The dog hasn't been used to being ignored, let alone being excluded from the pack. It is getting a powerful message. That message is going to come through even more strongly if you demonstrate all the qualities of a good leader at the same time. Do not shout or scream or get upset in any way. Don't speak to or acknowledge the dog, and do everything firmly and decisively. Close the door to the exclusion zone behind you and leave the dog to absorb the signal it has just been given. It may well go ballistic. Let it do what it needs to do.

Sooner or later the dog will have to calm down. You must be vigilant and listen out for this because almost immediately after it has happened you need to reunite with the dog again. Within five seconds or so of things going quiet you should reopen the door to the exclusion zone and let the dog back into your space. If the dog goes back into its repertoire, take it straight back to the exclusion zone and wait for it to calm down again. This time, when things go quiet, wait a little longer, say 10 seconds, before leading the dog back in. If it starts playing up again, repeat the process, keeping the exclusion period to around the same length. Carry on like this, rewarding the dog with reunification until it gets the message that, if it gives you what you want, you will give the dog what it wants.

It will be tough but it will happen. Each time it is banished the dog should reduce the intensity of its protests. As this happens the length of time it remains quiet while waiting to be released should be extended.

If the dog is prone to biting, owners should work with a lead attached to the collar. The dog should be led back and forth from the main room to the exclusion zone at a safe length. If the dog is so agitated it is difficult to even lead it out of the room, leave the room yourself. The effect will be almost as powerful.

As before, this process must be repeated until the dog has conceded defeat and relaxed. And throughout you must remain quiet. The dog must be given time to assimilate what is going on. By speaking you will only block its ability to do so.

It can be very hard work. I have worked with owners who have had to go through this routine up to twenty times. But I cannot over-emphasise how important it is to remain determined. The lessons the dog is learning at this point are life-changing. By the end of the process it should have redefined its status within the domestic pack.

SEPARATION ANXIETY

Dogs can get terribly upset when they are separated from their owners. I have encountered dogs who have turned their homes upside down the moment their human companion has walked out of the front door. I have come across owners who have returned to find furniture ripped and soiled and the entire contents of their wardrobe strewn across the floor. It's a problem that can escalate too. Dogs can become obsessed with chasing after their owner and start chewing furiously at the doorway through which they leave. Because a dog's endorphin levels rise while this is happening, acting like an adrenaline rush to dull the pain, in the most extreme cases it can result in the dog inflicting serious harm on itself.

This is something that can manifest itself at younger ages, but it is particularly prevalent in mature dogs in the protector phase, and is hardly surprising, given what is going on inside the dog's mind. An unadjusted dog believes it is responsible for the welfare of everyone within its extended pack. So when it sees its owner leaving it is immediately thrown into a panic. It is the equivalent of a parent seeing its child walking out the door without an explanation of where it's going. Viewed from this perspective, it's hardly surprising the dog can get itself worked up into such a frenzy.

To overcome this problem you must let the dog know that you – as the leader – are free to come and go as you please. You do not need its permission to do this. What's more, because you are leader it is for you to

Desperate housemates: mature dogs can suffer from extreme separation anxiety when their owners are away from home.

worry about your welfare while you are away from the home. The dog shouldn't give it a second thought.

By implementing the four main elements of canine communication the dog should be relieved of its status as leader. But to underline the process owners can practise 'gesture leaving'.

- Make sure the dog and the atmosphere within the house is calm.
- In full view of the dog, put on your shoes and coat.
- Leave the house, preferably by using a door or exit other than the front door.
- After a minute, re-enter the house, preferably through the front door.

- Ignore the dog when you reappear, underlining the fact that this is no big deal.
- Repeat this process, extending the length of time you remain outside by a minute each time. Repeat it as many times as possible. The more often the dog sees you doing this, the quicker it will get the message.

NERVOUS AGGRESSION AT MEALTIMES

Protector dogs tend to focus their misbehaviour on small, very specific areas of their daily life, and food is one that is a particular favourite. Rather than eat its meal, a dog can simply patrol its bowl. This is particularly likely if its owners are in the habit of giving it snacks or leaving permanent supplies of accessible food around the house. What it is doing here is saying, 'This food is the symbol of my status. I decide who eats from this supply and when.' But it has become so fixated on its power and preserving or reinforcing it that it will not eat its power base.

Alternatively, a dog can snap or even bite its owner as they place their food in the bowl. Their fear here is clear: the owner is going to take that food before they are. This is particularly common in rescue dogs, who can snarl and snap at anyone who comes near them at mealtimes. It is, of course, easy to see why they behave this way. Often these dogs arrive at sanctuaries or rescue centres having been starved close to death. When they are given food they are desperate to hang on to it, and anyone approaching them is seen as a threat that might take that food away.

Whatever the dog's background, however, it cannot be allowed to continue its attempts to exercise control over mealtimes. That control has to be exercised by you, the owner, the only leader the household can have. Owners must take complete control of feeding time, deciding where and when it takes place. At all times dogs must be reminded of the key points about feeding time:

- Food does not just turn up, it has to be earned.
- The person who provides the food is the surrogate protector it is looking for.
- There are certain ways to behave when food is being eaten.

So the following situations must be avoided:

- Dogs should never be left bowls with food or snacks.
- Meals should always be prepared on worktops, not on the floor where a dog can intervene.
- If a dog with a food problem tries to dictate a mealtime by standing at their bowl at a set time, change the mealtime. It cannot be allowed to dictate.
- If a dog who is misbehaving at mealtimes gets too excited when you are preparing the meal, put the meal on hold.
- If a dog walks away from its meal, remove that meal immediately and do not replace it. The dog must learn that it cannot control events. It will have to wait until the next mealtime.

To underline all this, practise 'gesture eating' by allowing the dog to see you taking a snack before placing its meal on the ground.

TOILET TROUBLES

Most dogs journey through life without having too many toilet troubles. This is because their natural instincts tell them they should remain clean and perform their bodily functions in an outdoor environment anyway. An owner's job should really be to work with this nature, to lead them to the correct routine and to reward them when they get there.

Life, of course, isn't always as straightforward as this, and some dogs have problems with toilet training. If this remains unchecked when the dog enters the neurotic protector phase it can manifest itself in a lot of unpleasant behaviour.

Some of the blame for toilet troubles may lie with the owner or breeder for not having trained the dog during the crucial three- to eight-week period when it begins to go to the toilet on its own. But the more serious problems are rooted in the dog's mistaken sense of its place within the pack. If a dog believes it is leader and is responsible, it will become anxious and nervous. This in turn can cause it to mark out its territory or lose control of its functions, hence the bedwetting or involuntary urination and diarrhoea.

*Leaving a mark: **adult dogs
can become obsessive about
their toileting.***

By the time it reaches the protector phase the downward spiral can accelerate, especially if the dog's owners react dramatically or scold when it does its toileting. This simply worsens the situation. The dog believes its job is to make its pack happy. If its toileting is doing the opposite and making its human charges distinctly unhappy, then it will try to circumvent this by disposing of the evidence.

The most common manifestations of toilet troubles are:

* Unpredictable defecating around the home
* Eating up of faeces when doing so
* Diarrhoea
* Wetting themselves.

Treating Toilet Troubles

Toilet troubles can be very upsetting for everyone involved. It goes without saying that having a dog defecate on a clean carpet or sofa is deeply unpleasant. Yet the key to curing this problem lies in masking these feelings.

RANDOM TOILETING

The key to treating a dog that is defecating at random around the house is, as always, to first remove it of its role as leader. It must be relieved of the notion that it is in charge, and with that be relieved of the anxiety it feels about being in charge.

On top of this, however, owners can help alleviate the problems further by monitoring the dog's toilet habits. First thing in the morning and at mealtimes look for telltale signs of toileting, such as circling. When you see this, give the dog the opportunity to go to the correct spot, by opening the door to the garden, for instance. If the dog does defecate somewhere it shouldn't, don't get angry, just clear it up and carry on as if nothing has happened. The worst thing an owner can do is to make a song and dance about it. By shouting, becoming agitated, or – worst of all – picking the dog up and rushing it to the correct toilet area, you are only exacerbating the problem.

If, on the other hand, the dog urinates or defecates in the right spot then it should be rewarded with food and praised as a 'good dog' or 'clean dog'. This will help renew its good association with the right spot.

With patience and calm it will soon begin using this spot all the time again.

EATING FAECES

If your dog has been eating its faeces, you need to distract it and draw it away after its toileting. The best way to do this is when it has defecated in its allocated spot, call it to you with food reward, praise it by saying 'clean dog' then remove it into the house. While the dog is inside, happy and focused on its treat, you can remove and dispose of the faeces quickly and without any fuss.

Additionally, by adding pineapple or courgette to the dog's diet you will reduce its tendency to eat its faeces. For some reason both make it unpalatable.

Again, with patience and above all calmness the problem should soon alleviate itself.

CAR CHAOS

Car chaos is a common and potentially very upsetting problem – both for dog and carer. Dogs can become extremely agitated, showing signs that vary from shivering and panting to screaming with fear. Clearly it is dangerous for the driver and awfully upsetting for the dog.

Car problems can arise at any time, but they are often a manifestation of problems to do with the phase the dog is passing through. During the playboy, protégé and pretender phases, for instance, the dog is still trying to work out its place in the world. This can make it prone to getting particularly hyper and distressed when it enters what is, after all, a very confusing and unpredictable environment. To a dog, a car is a den on wheels, a scary environment that is exposed, thanks to its glass windows, to threats from all sides. The dog's anxiety is heightened even further during the protector phase because it feels it is losing control. Unlike on its regular walk, for instance, the dog has no idea where it is going, only that it is heading somewhere. It feels even more unsure of itself, its surroundings and its place within them. When it jumps around and barks like this it is a more extreme version of a child perpetually pestering its parents with that dreaded question: 'Are we there yet?'

Tackling car chaos is a relatively straightforward matter, although it does require a lot of application. The first thing that needs to happen, as ever, is that the relationship at home must change. If the dog believes it is leader it must be persuaded to trade places with you, the owner, and take on a subordinate role. Once the readjustment has been made, then you can move on to changing the dog's bad association with travelling in the car.

To begin with you must change the dog's association with the car in general. Spend time cleaning or tinkering with the car, encouraging the dog to move around the vehicle too. Leave the car doors open and place small treats inside. When the dog is relaxed around the stationary car, you are ready to move on.

Before even making a journey you should try to get the dog used to simply sitting in the car with the doors locked and the engine running. If the dog reacts badly don't say or do anything in reaction to this, in fact do the opposite. Remain calm and do something that suggests you are completely undisturbed by the commotion, such as doing your make-up, fiddling with the radio or looking at a map. Then, when the dog has calmed down, simply climb back out of the car.

When you come to make the first journey it is helpful to have two people in the car, preferably with the companion driving and the owner travelling as the passenger. They will need to be on hand to interact with the dog. You should also put on the dog's collar and lead. Sit next to the dog, or if it is in a cage at the back of the car, sit in the rear seat with the dog's lead threaded through the wire. When the dog begins reacting, draw it to you, remaining calm and quiet. If the dog is in a cage, draw on the lead until the dog's neck is lightly touching the mesh. Do not say anything. The key here is to show the dog that it is making something of nothing. You are doing this by making nothing of nothing.

When the dog relaxes, simply remain quiet and calm. As you go through this process, try to ensure it encounters as many different types of traffic and surroundings as possible. It needs to know that whether you are passing a lorry or a bus, driving through a busy town centre or along a country lane next to fields filled with cattle, there is absolutely nothing for it to fear.

Rescue dogs

It is a harsh reality, but it is true. At this stage in their lives many dogs will face a new threat to their welfare – abandonment.

The pattern is depressingly familiar. What arrived in the home as a cuddly, fun-loving puppy that only wanted to play, sleep and eat has grown into a mature animal with a very different set of demands. It now needs regular exercise and lots more food. It may also have developed a strong personality and is causing problems that seem impossible to overcome. The owner has decided it can't carry on.

It is unforgivable, of course, but the sad fact is that the world's stray dog homes and rescue centres are disproportionately full of mature and older dogs.

What makes this even sadder is that despite the huge amount of goodwill among dog-lovers, many potential owners aren't prepared to

Another unwanted statistic: many dogs are abandoned as they reach maturity, leaving the rescue centres to pick up the pieces.

take them in because they see dogs of this age as being 'set in their ways' and untrainable.

This is simply not true. Provided you are prepared to show a little patience and perseverance, a rescue dog can be as good – maybe even a better – companion than a pedigree dog you have acquired through a breeding kennel. Apart from anything else, the pleasure it can bring to see an abused and disadvantaged dog enjoying a normal life is hard to beat.

LIVING WITH A RESCUE DOG

By definition, a rescue dog is not going to be well-adjusted. How could it be? It has been let down and perhaps even abused by its human guardian.

It is no surprise that it finds it hard to place faith in a human as a trusted friend.

It is, however, perfectly possible to transform these unhappy creatures into fulfilled and contented adults. By applying the four main principles of leadership – taking charge when reuniting, eating, facing perceived danger and walking – you can establish a bond of trust. You effectively throw a security blanket around the dog, allowing it to relax around humans, perhaps for the first time. However, there are a few points worth bearing in mind:

Give the Dog Time

Dogs are living, breathing and, most of all, feeling creatures. Like us, they develop according to their own abilities, and we must be prepared to accommodate that into our lives. So getting a dog to overcome its natural fears and fit into a human world that has let it down before is going to take time.

A useful mental approach is to think of these dogs as animals with learning disabilities, sometimes severe ones. They will learn like other dogs but they will do so slowly. And they are going to need that extra bit of patience and understanding to move forward.

Don't Get Hung Up on a Dog's Past

A mistake many people make is to analyse everything in terms of what has happened in the dog's past. More often than not this is based on guesswork. Many rescue dogs have been abandoned without any explanation as to where they came from or why they were rejected.

Regardless of whether you know the dog's background or not, this is a pointless exercise. Rather than being failures, as some people see them, rescue dogs have been failed by humans in their past. The most important thing you can do as the owner of a rescue dog is to concentrate on not failing the dog again, and you are more likely to do that by concentrating on its future than by dwelling on its past.

Make Allowances for Nervousness

You must show particular patience with very nervous rescue dogs. Rather than confronting visitors, such dogs may run away and hide. In extreme cases they may wet themselves. The crucial thing here is to leave the dog alone. Rather than freezing or fighting it has chosen the option to take flight, and this must not be removed from it. As with reuniting after a separation, these dogs must be given time to overcome their nerves. They must be persuaded that human beings are not automatically associated with pain. They must be given the time and the space to heal – and learn at their own pace.

In time, the arrival of a stranger will be greeted with a minor reaction. And with further training a simple thank you will return the dog to its usual relaxed state.

Wellbeing

Middle-age spread – overweight dogs

Middle age should be a comfortable time for your dog, but there is a danger it can be a little too comfortable. Obesity in middle-aged dogs is rife and owners need to be vigilant.

It is easy to see how dogs at this stage become overweight. Dogs are natural scavengers. Given half the chance they will feed on anything they can find. By this stage they know their environment – and their human companions – intimately. They will know how, where and when to obtain those extra morsels.

If the middle-aged dog leads a relatively sedentary life, the pounds will pile on even faster. By the time a dog reaches the upper end of this phase, around five or six years of age, their body and its organs will be beginning to slow down. As this happens, so their ability to burn off those extra calories will be reduced. Just like humans, 'middle-age spread' can creep up on a dog quickly. And as it does so it can lead to numerous health problems.

HOW TO TELL IF YOUR DOG IS OVERWEIGHT

As with the younger dog it is easy to body-score your dog. The simplest way of assessing your dog's weight is to feel its ribs with the flat of your hand. If you can only feel the ribs with difficulty, your dog probably needs to lose weight.

HEALTH

DIETING: HOW TO HELP YOUR DOG LOSE WEIGHT

Getting your dog to lose weight is going to be a joint effort involving three parties – you, your dog and your vet. It will be your vet who will set the target weight your dog needs to reach. He or she will recommend the amount of food the dog eats and may also prescribe special low-calorie products. It is important you stick to your vet's guidelines.

The length of time the dog will have to stay on the diet will depend on the seriousness of its problem. Normally, however, a dog will need between eight and fourteen weeks to reach a target weight. It might be that the vet prescribes a step programme. This might mean that having reached one target, the dog will then need to start dieting to reach another lower one.

At home the best way to help your dog meet its target weight is to follow some simple rules.

- Cut out all treats and snacks during the period of the diet.
- Make meals smaller. As a rule you should divide the dog's meal into up to four separate meals.
- Weigh your dog at least once a week and keep a record. Make sure to weigh your dog at the same time every day, perhaps immediately after it has done its toileting first thing in the morning.
- If you have more than one dog, feed the dog that is on the diet separately. It will be all too easy for it to scavenge from its fellow dogs' bowls.
- Feed your dog before your mealtime then remove it from the kitchen or dining area. This will discourage it from fishing for leftovers.
- Increase the dog's exercise, gradually introducing more vigorous games and longer walks.
- As you adjust the dog's exercise regime be careful to make sure that it doesn't go anywhere where it can easily scavenge for food. At home make sure the lids are on rubbish bins both inside and outside the house.
- Be sure to tell friends, family and neighbours about your dog's weight problem. That way they too can avoid giving it treats or scraps.
- Give the dog a plentiful supply of fresh water at all times. Water helps flush out the body.

PROBLEMS ASSOCIATED WITH OBESITY

Arthritis

Arthritis is a general term for the inflammation of the dog's joints. There are a number of causes: infection, congenital defects like dysplasia, stress and trauma to particular joints, and sometimes simply wear and tear. The other major cause, however, is obesity. When the dog begins to carry too much weight it begins to put an unnatural strain on its bones and joints.

Arthritis results in a wearing away of the cartilage inside the affected joint and a steady downward spiral. The bone beneath the cushion the cartilage provides becomes exposed and the joint becomes swollen and inflamed. Calcium deposits can build up as well.

The net result of all this is that the dog begins to suffer considerable pain when it is exercising the affected joints. Motion becomes more and more restricted, which in turn exacerbates the problem. The downward spiral can then continue, with the dog putting on even more weight, which in turn places more strain on the affected joint. If left untreated it can lead to the dog becoming crippled with pain.

HOW TO SPOT IT

Dogs are stoic creatures and don't always show any obvious signs of pain or discomfort, so it is up to owners to be vigilant in watching out for the telltale hints that arthritis might be developing. The first clue of something being awry might be a sudden gain in weight. The dog might then start sleeping more and taking less of an interest in playtime. It might also seem less alert and generally less excited when you interact with it. More obvious signs are that it is walking gingerly, perhaps when it is climbing stairs.

HOW TO TREAT IT

If you suspect your dog has arthritis, take it to the vet immediately. He or she should be able to conduct an x-ray, which will quickly tell if there is a problem with a particular joint. If arthritis is diagnosed the treatment is generally an anti-inflammatory drug. To supplement this, however, owners also have to tackle the dog's weight.

HEALTH

Diabetes

Overweight dogs are also prone to diabetes. Females carrying too much weight are particularly prone to the problem and are twice as likely to suffer as males.

A dog develops diabetes when its body fails to remove sugar from its blood. Normally this function is performed by insulin, a hormone produced in the pancreas which converts the sugar into energy. Diabetics don't produce enough of this insulin and as a result the blood-sugar levels become too high. The knock-on effect of this is that some blood sugar spills out into the dog's urine via the kidneys, making the urine more concentrated and demanding more water to be passed with it. This in turn makes the dog more thirsty and, because the blood sugar is wasted, sometimes more hungry as well.

At first diabetes can make the dog listless and it may begin to lose weight, but if left untreated there can be serious damage to the kidney and eyes. The body can also begin to use existing fat for energy, producing poisonous ketones into the system. In severe cases this can lead to death.

There are several obvious signs of diabetes:

- Abnormal thirst
- Increased hunger
- Higher than normal amounts of urine
- Signs of sugar in the urine
- Tiredness
- Weight loss

If your dog displays any of these symptoms, take it to a vet who will be able to run blood and urine tests.

HOW TO TREAT IT

Diabetes is treatable, but as a lifelong condition it requires a lifelong commitment from owners. In most cases dogs will need a daily injection of insulin. The dog's diet and exercise regime also has to be carefully planned so that its sugar levels don't drop. Urine samples should be taken on a regular basis as well. Diabetes does require vigilance on the part of the owner. If their dog's insulin levels drop too low it can result in the dog suffering hypoglycaemia. For this reason you should also keep a selection of high-sugar items like honey or syrup to hand.

Overheating

Normally dogs get rid of excess body heat by panting. They also sweat a tiny amount, through their pads rather than their skin. When it gets overweight the dog's body becomes less efficient at eliminating this excess heat. This leaves the dog prone to overheating and suffering heat-stroke.

Pancreatitis

As its name suggests, this condition affects the pancreas, the organ that produces most of the body's supply of enzymes, vital for the breaking down and digestion of fat, proteins and carbohydrates. The pancreas becomes inflamed, reducing or even stopping its ability to produce enzymes.

Acute pancreatitis is extremely painful. In severe cases it can also lead to cancer. Obesity is the biggest known cause of the condition, with middle-aged females by far the most at risk.

THE SEVENTH AGE

pensioner

AROUND 7 YEARS AND BEYOND

*'Last scene of all,
That ends this strange eventful history,
Is second childishness and mere oblivion'*

IN THE WILD

For a wolf, the final phase of its life is the cruellest. Throughout its life it has lived by the principle of survival of the fittest – and so it must be at the end.

Because their survival depends on the survival of their pack, wolves are acutely attuned to weakness within their ranks. And if they sense that there is a weak link in the chain of command – whether it is an alpha or a lower-ranked wolf – they act before their entire existence is endangered.

There is no point dressing up the situation – it is, frankly, brutal. In the wild there is no such thing as a bloodless coup. Wolves deemed to be a threat to the pack because of their weakness are either driven out or killed.

Veteran: an elderly wolf nearing the end of its life.

THE SEVENTH AGE: OVERVIEW

As the dog enters this final phase of its life, its strength begins to fade. And as its energy level drops, so it will also adopt a much slower, more sedate attitude to life. Inevitably, however, it will also become increasingly prone to illnesses and a gradual deterioration in its senses, its hearing and sight in particular. Other illnesses which might have been minor irritants when the dog was younger and stronger will begin to affect it even more. And new problems – from the relatively minor, like bad breath caused by dental problems, to the life-threatening, like cancer – will come to the fore.

The impact of ageing is also as much psychological as it is physical. The changes it is experiencing will leave the dog feeling vulnerable and liable to react nervously at times. It may also experience senility and lapse into a second childhood, behaving like a puppy once more. This may create problems around other dogs.

But the twilight years need not be any less enjoyable than the rest of a dog's life. Just as elderly humans can counter the effects of age-ing by changing their lifestyle, so dogs can learn to cope with – and indeed overcome – these problems by adjusting their daily routines.

Longevity – how long will my dog live?

It is the greatest sadness of owning a dog. Sometimes, it seems, they have no sooner arrived in our lives than they are ready to leave again.

In the UK, at least, the average life-expectancy of a dog is eleven years, but this figure changes enormously from breed to breed. As a general rule of thumb, the smaller breeds will tend to outlive the larger ones. A Poodle or Chihuahua, for instance, can live twice as long as a big dog like a Bulldog or an Irish Wolfhound, both of which can have a lifespan of less than seven years. There is also a tendency for breeds that have been heavily moulded by human interference to live shorter lives.

For this reason, the onset of the final pensioner phase is spread more widely than any other. For a large dog with a lifespan of seven years it could begin as early as six. Yet some dogs with long life expectancies can remain in their prime until they are into double figures.

AVERAGE LIFESPANS BY BREED

The most definitive study on the subject in the UK was published in 1999 by the *Veterinary Record*, the magazine of the British Veterinary Association. It unearthed a lot of interesting facts. For instance, mongrels tend to live longer than most pedigree dogs, only eight per cent of dogs live beyond 15, and 64 per cent die or are put to sleep because of illness. Cancer is responsible for 16 per cent of deaths, twice as much as heart disease.

Here are the average life spans, in years, for the most popular breeds:

Afghan Hound: 12.0

Airedale Terrier: 11.2

Basset Hound: 12.8

Beagle: 13.3

Bearded Collie: 12.3

Bedlington Terrier: 14.3

Bernese Mountain Dog: 7.0

Border Collie: 13.0

Border Terrier: 13.8

Boxer: 10.4

Bull Terrier: 12.9

Bulldog: 6.7

Bullmastiff: 8.6

Cairn Terrier: 13.2

Cavalier King Charles Spaniel: 10.7

Chihuahua: 13.0

Chow Chow: 13.5

Cocker Spaniel: 12.5

Collie: 13.0

Corgi: 11.3

Dachshund: 12.2

Dalmatian: 13.0

Doberman Pinscher: 9.8

English Cocker Spaniel: 11.8

English Setter: 11.2

English Springer Spaniel: 13.0

English Toy Spaniel: 10.1

Flat-Coated Retriever: 9.5

German Shepherd: 10.3

German Shorthaired Pointer: 12.3

Golden Retriever: 12.0

Gordon Setter: 11.3

Great Dane: 8.4

Greyhound: 13.2

Irish Red and White Setter: 12.9

Irish Setter: 11.8

Irish Wolfhound: 6.2

Jack Russell Terrier: 13.6

Labrador Retriever: 12.6

Lurcher: 12.6

Miniature Dachshund: 14.4

Miniature Poodle: 14.8

Norfolk Terrier: 10.0

Old English Sheepdog: 11.8

Pekingese: 13.3

Multiple-Breed/ Mongrel: 13.2

Rhodesian Ridgeback: 9.1

Rottweiler: 9.8

Rough Collie: 12.2

Samoyed: 11.0

Scottish Deerhound: 9.5

Scottish Terrier: 12.0

Shetland Sheepdog: 13.3

Shih Tzu: 13.4

Staffordshire Bull Terrier: 10.0

Standard Poodle: 12.0

Tibetan Terrier: 14.3

Toy Poodle: 14.4

Vizsla: 12.5

Weimaraner: 10.0

Welsh Springer Spaniel: 11.5

West Highland White Terrier: 12.8

Whippet: 14.3

Wire Fox Terrier: 13.0

Yorkshire Terrier: 12.8

Your Dog's Age in Human Terms According to Size – A Guide

EMOTIONAL OLD AGE

In the natural environment there is no such thing as the final pensioner phase. An old or infirm wolf is surplus to requirement and will be disposed of or discarded. This obviously doesn't apply to the domestic dog, yet, in a way, our pets are intuitively aware that they are entering uncharted waters at this point. They sense they are past their sell-by date and begin to feel vulnerable. As they become more and more aware of their weakness they may become snappier, more irritable and generally difficult.

This will apply to all dogs of this age, but such mental fragility can be particularly dangerous if the dog believes it is the leader of the pack. During the protector phase the dog that believes it is leader has no self-doubt whatsoever. It feels almost invincible and unchallengeable, as an alpha would in the wild. As they enter this phase, however, they come to realise they are no longer able to do the job. And as a result they become more worried and concerned and begin acting in a much more defensive manner. They have still got the job to do but they can't do it any more.

It's confusing when they are young, problematic at their peak, but now, as they get older, the responsibility is frightening.

TABLE OF RELATIVE AGES OF SMALL AND LARGE BREEDS				
	1–10 kg	10–25 kg	25–40 kg	40 kg +
5 years	36	37	40	42
6	40	42	45	49
7	44	47	50	56
8	48	51	55	64
9	52	56	61	71
10	56	60	66	78
11	60	65	72	86
12	64	69	77	93
13	68	74	82	101
14	72	78	88	108
15	76	83	93	115

Given the different life expectancies of small and large breeds, two dogs of exactly the same age may in fact be at very different stages in their lives. This table illustrates how the relative age of different-sized dogs diverges through life.

Never too old: elderly dogs still enjoy the simple pleasures of life, like rolling in the grass.

They can still benefit from being introduced to the four key elements of canine communication. Even at this late stage they can become less stressed by being relieved of the misapprehension they are leading the pack, but owners should take great care here.

INTERACTING WITH OTHER DOGS

On the Walk

One area that needs particular diligence is interaction with other dogs. Dogs sense weakness in other members of their species. And, just as in the wild, they will be completely unsympathetic to that weakness. They will also try to capitalise on that weakness. On the walk, younger dogs may be more confrontational with an older dog, particularly if it is noticeably weak, perhaps limping or displaying obvious signs of senility or poor eyesight. In the dog world the phrase 'respect one's elders' doesn't exist. For this reason it is advisable to be more selective about where you exercise an older dog like this. Avoid places where there are lots of other dogs. If this is difficult, keep it on an extended lead so that you retain control.

If there is a confrontation with another dog, the key, as ever, is to remain calm and controlled and to not get involved. Given its sensitivity your dog may well be more inclined to fight than it would have been in the past. To let it get involved now, more than ever, could be disastrous. Remove your dog from the situation immediately, picking it up if you have to.

At Home

If you have more than one dog at home, these same problems may occur in the domestic environment. There is nothing you can do to prevent a younger dog picking on an older, more infirm dog. All you can do is anticipate this and take appropriate action.

For this reason, once a dog turns eight or nine years of age it should never be left with a younger dog. And if either dog begins showing signs of aggression, such as barging, growling or snapping at the other dog, you must break them up quickly, removing the aggressor.

Sleeping and feeding arrangements should be reorganised too. Mealtimes in particular could become a breeding ground for confrontation. Far better to stagger the dogs' feeding times or feed them in separate rooms to keep the atmosphere calm.

Growing old gracefully
– looking after an ageing dog

Just as a young dog had its own requirements for a peaceful, happy environment when it first arrived in the home, so the elderly dog has its needs. Fulfilling each of them can contribute to a more comfortable – and extended – life.

PATIENCE

As it enters this final phase the dog's body begins to deteriorate. The vital organs function less efficiently than they have done. The body slows down, and with it so does the dog.

Your dog needs you to understand this. It is no longer the creature with boundless energy it once was. It needs more rest, more peace and quiet. And, in particular, it needs more patience. Specifically your dog needs you to:

- Give it more time to accomplish things. Walks, mealtimes, toileting, grooming: each of these things is going to take longer now. Be prepared for this.
- Don't expect your dog to respond to you as immediately as it has done. Its faculties are on the wane too. It is not using selective hearing, it simply may not hear you when you call it.

COMFORT

As its life slows down, so the dog's daily routine is going to change. It won't be so mobile now, so it is going to spend much more time lying around and sleeping. Ensure that its favourite spot is a good one. Make sure it isn't cold, damp or draughty, or alternatively that it isn't in direct sunlight for too long. Make sure the dog can get to it easily, at any time of the day or night. Make sure too that it is well-padded, with a decent cushion or piece of foam for the dog to rest its body on. Lying on hard, unyielding surfaces for long periods of time can take its toll on an ageing body. Dogs can develop calluses on the prominent bony bits of their body like the elbows and the hocks. Over time these can become ulcerated and infected.

ROUTINE

The dog will begin a mental as well as a physical decline during this phase. The severity of this will vary according to the dog, but in general all dogs will become much more easily disoriented. Major changes in the house, from a rearrangement of the furniture to the arrival of new faces, from major changes in its diet to new directions on the walk, can throw a dog badly. So try to keep the amount of upheaval to the daily routine it adopts during this phase of its life to a minimum. Try also to avoid leaving the dog alone for any length of time. It can easily get agitated by this.

COMPANIONSHIP

As one dog goes through its inevitable decline it is only natural for owners to begin thinking about taking in a new pet. This, again, is a step that has to be taken carefully. Elderly dogs can respond well to the arrival of a young puppy. Much like the arrival of a grandchild can breathe new life into an ageing human, so a sprightly young pup can provide an old dog with a new lease of life. The relationship can also be reciprocal. Unlike more grown-up dogs, who look at the pensioner and see weakness, the puppy sees wisdom and companionship. It treats the elderly dog as a kindly grandfather.

This isn't always the case, however. A new dog can have completely the opposite effect, so if you are thinking of getting a puppy introduce it to your pensioner beforehand. Do so on neutral territory, or at the home of the prospective new arrival, and try to allow the two dogs time to get used to each other. If they take a violent dislike to each other, rethink your plans. Elderly dogs become even more nervous, temperamental and confrontational as they get older. The new dog may be more trouble than it is worth at this stage. You can always acquire a new dog at another time.

EXERCISE

Inevitably, dogs become less active when they get older. Whereas once they would have bounded on ahead of you while out on the walk, they will now walk contentedly at your side. Whereas once it would have played with a ball for hours on end if given the chance, now it will take little interest in toys.

Exercise is important, however. The dog needs to keep fit in both body and mind, so you need to make adjustments that take account of their age. It is particularly important that you give your dog mental stimulation during this stage. Senility is a big problem at this age and it has been proven that activities which keep the dog alert mentally can stave off mental decline.

There are a wide range of toys designed for older dogs that stimulate their brains but also reflect their waning powers. For dogs suffering from fading mental abilities there are toys that can have treats inserted inside and then require the dog to work out how to release them. For dogs suffering from poor eyesight or deafness there are balls that glow or make a noise when they bounce or roll around on the ground.

Diet

ADAPTING THE DOG'S DIET TO OLD AGE

A dog's dietary needs change significantly as it gets older. The main change is that it requires less energy as it exercises less and its metabolism slows down. This means the amount of calories a dog needs to fuel itself drops, usually by up to 20 per cent. At the same time, however, the dog should still get the right balance of nutrients to maintain its body in good health.

Its diet is also going to be influenced by its physical state. It no longer has teeth strong enough to chew at bones or crunch kibbles so it is going to need a much softer diet. It may also have more difficulty in digesting raw meat, so owners feeding the BARF diet, for instance, should be prepared to modify the dog's meals accordingly.

So, regardless of whether it is on a complete, complementary, home-made or BARF diet, the dog's diet needs to reflect its advanced stage of life. Fortunately, the food companies have done a lot of research into this and there are many specialist elderly dog foods on the market. Equally, dog welfare organisations have advice for those using the other options.

OVERWEIGHT AND UNDERWEIGHT DOGS

Elderly dogs suffer more from being underweight than they do from being overweight. (One study in the US found that while five per cent of 12-year-old dogs were overweight, twelve per cent were underweight.) Once again, it is easy to check whether a dog is carrying too much or too little weight. Feel its ribs with the flat of your palm. If it's hard to find them, your dog needs to lose weight. If, on the other hand, the ribs are very prominent, or in the case of a short-haired dog you can see them plainly, it needs to put on some pounds.

COAXING OLD DOGS TO EAT

Elderly dogs tend to have poor appetites. The ravenous creature that used to eat anything and everything that was put in front of it is transformed into a picky slow eater that rarely cleans its bowl. Yet the need to eat well has never been greater. Here are a few tips on how to get your elderly dog to eat:

- Feed them tasty, easily digestible food.
- If they like something in particular, don't be worried about giving it to them almost all the time.
- Make the meals smaller and more frequent. Feed the dog up to four times a day.

- Only warm the food to body temperature.
- Make sure the dog has a quiet corner for eating. If there are other younger dogs in the house, feed the old dog separately so that it is left in peace.

SPECIAL NEEDS

There are a range of diets specially designed to help manage particular illnesses or disorders, and you should always consult your vet before embarking on one of these. They include:

- A low-phosphorous/fibre-rich diet for kidney disease
- A low-sodium diet to prevent heart disease
- A balanced-fibre diet for bowel problems
- A low-mineral or low-protein diet to prevent bladder stones
- A low-calorie diet for weight loss
- A high-fibre diet for diabetic dogs
- A high-fat/low-carbohydrate diet designed to aid cancer treatment
- A balanced fatty-acid diet to aid skin diseases
- High-energy/high-calorie diets for convalescence from surgery or weight gain

An elderly dog's best friend
– the importance of the vet

Visits to the vet become all too familiar experiences during this phase of the dog's life, but their importance should never be underestimated. They can mean the difference between life and death.

You will need to see your vet for several reasons. Booster vaccinations to protect your dog against the key diseases are as important now as ever. The older dogs get, the less effective their immune system becomes, and the harder it is for them to fend off infections and disease. Visits will also be useful as a means of getting your dog checked out thoroughly by a professional. Your vet should be able to make assessment of the major organs such as the skin, heart, kidneys and liver. Any abnormal lumps or abrasions can also be looked at, as can the condition of the dog's mouth and teeth. Urine samples will help detect problems such as kidney diseases, so it is always a good idea to prepare one before each visit to your local surgery. Always make sure the sample is placed in a clean, dry and sealable container, such as a screw-top jar.

Your vet will also be able to monitor your dog's weight and advise you on a suitable diet geared to your dog's specific needs. Last but not least, your vet can advise you on how regularly your dog should be checked and whether its breed is prone to particular problems that you should look out for.

It may seem like a chore, travelling back and forth, but at this stage in your dog's life it is vital.

Grooming

Grooming is important throughout a dog's life, but it becomes an absolute priority during this final phase.

Helping hands: monitoring a dog's health during grooming becomes even more important as it reaches old age.

First of all, it is genuinely good for the dog. Brushing helps to improve the circulation to the skin and keeps the coat shiny and tangle free. This will help the dog feel more comfortable. But of course it also allows you to keep an eye out for the signs of deterioration and illness that occur at this time. By being diligent – and working in conjunction with the advice you get from regular visits to the vet – you can help your dog head off many serious problems.

WHAT TO LOOK FOR

Outwardly there will be plenty of obvious signs of old age. As with humans, a dog's hair can dry out and turn grey, losing its youthful lustre. Their stomachs can begin to sag and look flabby, and they become stiff and more ponderous as they move. They will also be more lethargic. But many of the biggest threats to its health lie beneath the surface, hence the importance of regular grooming. It is also advisable to bathe your dog more often when it is older. This too will give you a good opportunity to check for problems, in particular skin disorders.

The areas you need to look at are the same as they have been throughout: skin, ears, eyes and teeth in particular. But there are now specific things for which you need to monitor your dog closely:

Skin and Coat

As the dog gets older so its skin becomes thinner and less elastic than it used to be. The coat too starts to deteriorate, becoming less shiny and patchier. This is exacerbated by the fact that the dog begins to lose the pride it used to have in itself. It will no longer groom its coat in the way it used to, something that may also be down to the fact its stiffening joints make it a more painful process.

During old age, dogs also begin to secrete more from the sebaceous glands that keep their skin healthy. But rather than maintaining the skin and hair, this results in either oily or flaky skin. In turn, this can make their coats smell of that very distinctive odour we all know as 'doggy smell'. Some breeds, such as the Cocker Spaniel, are particularly prone to this unpleasant condition.

In general it is advisable to bathe the dog more often when it gets older, but it is a particularly good idea in this case.

When grooming keep a particular lookout for signs of skin infections. One of the main victims of ageing is a dog's immune system. During its early life it is there to fend off bacteria or viruses, and does so very efficiently. As the dog reaches this veteran stage, however, it becomes less reliable. And as it does so the dog becomes liable to more problems, and skin infections are among the most common.

Teeth and Mouth

As the dog's body deteriorates it becomes less able to fight diseases and infections. Given that it is the main route into the dog's body for most exterior bacteria, it is not surprising that teeth and gums are prime sufferers as a result of this.

TELLTALE SIGNS OF PROBLEMS

The regular check of the teeth and mouth during grooming will reveal the more obvious problems, such as discoloured teeth or build-ups of tartar. But there are other, less apparent problems that a dog of this age can develop. The best way to spot these is by observing the dog and watching out for telltale signs. The main ones are:

Eating

If the dog is eating more slowly and is being generally pickier about what it puts into its mouth, it may be troubled by something within its mouth. Similarly, if it is tilting its head to one side during mealtimes this is a good indication that there is a problem on one side of the mouth. In both cases, if there is nothing visible consult a vet.

Drooling

A few breeds with slack lower lips, such as the St Bernard, drool large amounts of saliva naturally. But in most other breeds 'hypersalivation', as it is known, is a sign of some kind of problem. It might be that the dog is about to vomit or has an alien object stuck in its mouth. Equally it may indicate a variety of gum and mouth diseases, such as periodontal disease or gingivitis.

Jaw Problems

If the dog is having trouble opening its jaw, this again might be cause for concern. Potential explanations are a head, neck or jaw problem, or an abscess or alien object lodged somewhere in its mouth.

Bad Breath

This is the most obvious sign of a problem. Halitosis can indicate not just mouth conditions but can also be an indication of a stomach condition. Furthermore, it might be a sign of a kidney condition called uraemia. If it is this then it will probably lead to them demonstrating other telltale symptoms including excessive thirst, loss of appetite and weight, lethargy, vomiting and diarrhoea. If any of these manifest themselves then go to the vet immediately.

Wellbeing

Medical problems

A lot of people deliberately avoid taking their older dogs to the vet for regular check-ups. In some ways their attitude is understandable. They fear it might be the last time they make the journey, that the vet will discover something serious and recommend the dog be put out of its misery there and then. In reality that hardly ever happens, and the truth of the matter is that regular trips to the vet are more essential than ever if a dog is to enjoy as long a life as possible.

A dog should see the vet at least twice a year. But owners should also be acutely aware of their dog's health, so that if needs be they get them to the vet quickly. I have seen many instances where failure to pick up a life-threatening condition at an early stage has meant that a dog has been taken to the vet too late.

In general there are a few telltale signs to look out for:

- Loss of appetite and weight
- Coughing or breathing problems
- Growths and lumps on the body

HEALTH

- Unusual discharges
- General weakness, lethargy and disinterest in exercise
- Increased thirst
- Increased urination
- Diarrhoea or constipation
- Increase in breathing rate
- Fever or fast heart-rate

CANCER

Cancer – in the form of malignant tumours – is the biggest killer of dogs. Some breeds are more disposed to develop it than others. Breeds at high risk, for instance, range from big breeds like the Irish Wolfhound, Rottweiler and Old English Sheepdog to smaller breeds like the Standard Poodle. Those facing the lowest risk include the German Shepherd and Cocker Spaniel, the Border Collie and the Yorkshire Terrier. As the dog reaches old age, however, cancer becomes more common across the breeds. This is mainly because the dog's immune system has become less efficient, but it is also down to the fact that cancers, at their simplest level, are formed when cells reproduce at abnormal rates, and when the dog reaches old age their cells have simply had more time to develop abnormally.

Tumours can range from benign lipomas to malignant ones like osteosarcomas, or bone cancers. Any signs of unusual lumps or bumps should always be referred to the vet.

Telltale Signs of Cancer

As with humans, treatment of cancer is improving all the time. Dogs can be treated with surgery, radiotherapy and chemotherapy, with ever-improving effectiveness. The key to successful treatment is early detection. The most obvious signs of cancer are tumours on the skin, which can be spotted during grooming. Lumps are not always cancerous, of course. Many are simply lipomas, benign fatty tumours that form under the skin, particularly common in older females who are overweight. However, the vet should be involved in assessing anything that looks unusual.

Other key signs include:

- Loss of appetite
- Breathing irregularities
- Unusual swellings
- Lack of stamina or lethargy
- Bleeding from any of its openings
- Significant weight loss
- Signs of straining or discomfort when toileting
- Strong and unpleasant body odours

SENILITY

Just like humans, many dogs show signs of senility when they pass into the later stages of their life. Just like humans they will become forgetful or clumsy. You may find your dog standing at the wrong door expecting to go out for its walk.

Up to 50 per cent of dogs display signs of Cognitive Dysfunction Disorder (CDD). The most obvious clues that your dog is suffering from the onset of this are:

- A change in sleeping patterns
- Weakness and trembling
- Lethargy and a general loss of interest in life
- Compulsive behaviour, such as circling the house, whining, paw-licking and barking 'absently'

It is a condition that will only get worse if it is not treated. Medication and even diet can help counter the effects, but perhaps the most positive thing you can do to help is keep the dog stimulated mentally. You should play with it regularly and you should make the games you play as mentally stimulating as possible.

You can, for instance, play hide-and-seek games by secreting bits of food reward around the house or garden. You can also buy toys that have been designed to stimulate the dog mentally. The key is to keep the dog thinking.

HEALTH +

HEART CONDITIONS

Second only to cancer as the main killer of elderly dogs, heart conditions account for almost one in four dog deaths. As with humans, weak hearts can be inherited and there are a number of breeds which are predisposed to problems, among them the Cavalier King Charles Spaniel and the Doberman. As the body weakens, the strain on the heart increases, eventually placing too great a burden on it.

Heart conditions can be spotted early by your vet. They can also be helped by good, regular exercise and by incorporating marine fish oil into the dog's diet.

BOWEL AND BLADDER PROBLEMS

Bowel Problems

Incontinence and constipation are common conditions in dogs throughout their lives, but they become particularly prevalent during old age.

CONSTIPATION

Dogs suffering from constipation either defecate much smaller amounts of faeces or stop producing them altogether. Left unchecked it can lead to more serious intestinal problems, but if spotted early it can be treated easily with laxatives.

One of the most common causes of constipation in older dogs is a lack of water, so to prevent it make sure your dog drinks plenty of water throughout its day. At the same time make sure its food is moist and that it doesn't eat things that are hard to digest, such as grass or leftovers. Small amounts of mineral oil (liquid paraffin) can be added to meals to help digestion.

Exercise is also a good way of fending off constipation.

INCONTINENCE

As well as everything else, the dog can also lose control of its bowels at this stage in its life. This can be caused simply by a loss of control of the sphincter muscles, but it can also be a side effect of other problems such as tumours, inflammations and infections and disorders of the nervous system, including dementia.

If your dog does start defecating in an erratic and uncontrolled way, consult your vet.

FLATULENCE AND BURPING

Older dogs can develop unpleasant habits. Burping and flatulence are among the least loveable of them. The smell produced can be quite awful.

Diet plays a big part in producing the gases that cause wind. Food that is more difficult to digest, such as carbohydrates and vegetables, can increase the most noxious of the internal gases the body produces, hydrogen sulphide.

There are a couple of ways of combating this problem. You can give the dog less to digest by giving it smaller, more frequent meals, and cut out high-fibre foods. You can also add charcoal to the dog's diet. This has the effect of reducing the odour produced when the dog suffers from flatulence. It can make a big difference.

Bladder Problems

There are a few telltale signs that an elderly dog is having bladder problems:

CHANGING HABITS

Any changes to the dog's toileting habits should be treated with suspicion. In particular you should be concerned if they produce more or less urine. If the dog begins passing much more urine it could be suffering from a variety of conditions, including kidney diseases, diabetes and liver disease. If, on the other hand, it begins going to the toilet less frequently, this too should be taken as a warning signal.

When it is younger a dog can go up to 12 hours without urinating, but if an elderly dog goes this long without passing water there may be something wrong. A dog of this age should urinate once every six to eight hours.

Dogs can also suffer from urinary incontinence. Small amounts of urine can 'leak' out when they are sitting or lying down, leaving unwelcome stains. There are medical treatments to control it.

HEALTH

SIGNS OF PAIN

Owners should be on the lookout for signs of pain or distress when the dog is urinating. If a dog is suffering from relatively minor problems, such as a burning sensation when it passes water, it will tend to hold its position after finishing. If the problem is more serious the dog may strain, make whimpering noises or even cry out when urinating.

Owners should also watch out for their dog excessively licking its penis or vulva. In each of these instances the vet should be consulted.

BLOOD IN THE URINE

The colour and concentration of the dog's urine can tell you a lot. An orange tinge can indicate liver problems, as can a brown or black colouration. A milky whiteness to the urine can be a sign of inflammation or a metabolic problem.

The surest sign of a problem, however, is blood in the urine. This can be caused by a large number of conditions, including bladder or kidney stones, severe urinary-tract problems, kidney disease or tumours. Any sign of blood, therefore, should be acted upon. Consult the vet immediately.

Sight and sound – the senses fade

LOSS OF HEARING

How to Detect Your Dog is Going Deaf

The most obvious signs of deafness are the dog being hard to wake up when it is sleeping, failing to respond to requests, or being startled when you approach it from behind. Owners often make the mistake of putting some of these symptoms down to 'selective deafness'. They believe the dog is simply turning a deaf ear. There is, of course, no such thing.

There is an easy way to check for deafness. Simply clap your hands or make a loudish noise near to the dog and see if it responds. A dog's natural preference is for peace and quiet, so that it can hear any signs of approaching danger. If it responds suddenly to this noise then there is nothing wrong with its hearing.

There isn't much you can do to treat loss of hearing, although it is worth visiting the vet to see if it is temporary and related to an ear infection. However, there are a few steps you can take to help the dog deal with its poor hearing.

- Take extra care when near roads: the dog may no longer be able to hear cars approaching.
- Have them on a lead or long line at all times.
- Be careful around children: the dog may react badly if approached from behind, even if the child is being playful.
- Start to give signals by hand rather than verbally.

Hand Signals

Because they naturally rely on body language to communicate with each other, dogs respond well to hand signals. If your dog does begin to lose its hearing, these may become invaluable when you are out and about together. The signals are best learned in conjunction with the verbal requests. There are no formal instructions, the precise signal you use is entirely up to you, but it is worth bearing in mind a few guiding principles.

- Don't block your face with your signals: the dog will look to your expression as an extra clue what to do.
- Make sure you can deliver the signal in one single, uninterrupted move.
- Make each signal distinct from the others you develop.
- Make sure each signal is going to be clear from a distance.

SUGGESTED HAND SIGNALS

- **Sit:** Begin with your signalling arm at your side then move it upwards, with your hands open and palm up towards the side of your face.
- **Down:** Reverse the sit, moving your hand from its starting position against your cheek down to your side.
- **Stay:** Begin with both hands on the front of your chest with palms facing outwards, then bring them forward at 90 degrees in a pushing movement.
- **Come:** Bend your knees slightly then bring both hands down palms first in a patting action. If your dog isn't suffering from acute loss of hearing, the noise you make can act as an additional element to the signal.

HEALTH

The key to using all these signals is that they must be sharp to ensure the dog will respond to them crisply and cleanly. If you see your dog is in danger you need to be sure it is going to react immediately to your signals. It might mean the difference between life and death.

LOSS OF SIGHT

Most dogs suffer from deteriorating eyesight in their later years. This is in many cases, however, nothing to do with disease, just a general symptom of ageing – as indeed it is in humans. The aging of the retina reduces the dog's vision. This in turn will leave the dog less responsive to visual stimuli, and owners must take account of this. It is also very common for the lens of the eye to develop a cloudiness. This is caused by a nuclear or lenticular sclerosis, a hardening of the lens. When they see this, many owners mistake it for cataracts, a much more serious condition. Unlike cataracts this may not require surgical intervention.

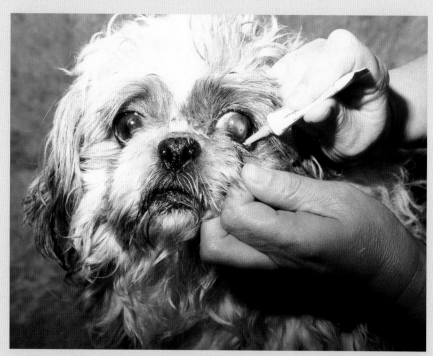

Medicine time: many eye conditions are treatable with ointments and creams that can be easily applied by owners.

How to Spot When Your Dog is Losing its Eyesight

It can be very straightforward to spot a dog's diminishing eyesight. It can begin bumping into objects, failing to retrieve toys while playing or using its nose to guide itself to the food bowl. If the problem is relatively mild, however, it can be hard to detect. Dogs are very clever at memorising their way around the domestic environment. If you suspect your dog does have a problem, the best way to test it is to simply rearrange some of the furniture and turn the lights down a little. A few telltale bumps will tell you all you need to know.

How to Help a Dog with Fading Eyesight

There is nothing you can do physically to arrest the dog's loss of sight. Unlike humans, they can't be prescribed glasses. And also, unlike humans, they can't benefit from having another dog dedicated to guide them. So it is up to the owner to act as the guide and protector the dog needs.

In general terms, the most important thing to bear in mind is that the change the dog is going through will leave it feeling very vulnerable. It won't know specifically that it is losing its sight, but it will know that there is something missing in its sensory makeup, and it will be feeling unsettled and uncertain about this. Always remember this. However, there are a number of simple, practical steps you can take to make your dog's life easier when its sight fails:

- Don't move the furniture around the house. The dog is going to rely more and more on memory to get around, so even the slightest change to the layout within the home and the garden can throw it.
- Don't approach the dog from behind or come over the top to greet it. With its vision restricted the dog will not be able to see you coming and this will startle it. Always approach so that the dog can see you, or at least be aware of something coming towards it. Underscore this by speaking to the dog as you approach: always, of course, in a steady, reassuring and non-threatening tone.
- Don't change your normal smell. With the failure of one of its senses the dog will come to rely more and more on its other two main ones, smell in particular. By suddenly changing your perfume or aftershave you will confuse the dog and make it jumpy around you.

HEALTH

- Don't touch the dog on the top of its head. If you want to stroke or touch the dog, do so on the side of the face, taking care to signal you are about to do so. Again, the sudden feeling of a hand on its body may make the dog jump. By approaching slowly and speaking, and also allowing it to scent your smell, the dog will know you are coming.
- Don't leave them unsupervised around other dogs, even those within their own home.
- If you have to leave the dog in the house, give it a safe area, a space where it knows it will be secure. Make sure everyone in the house knows this is its haven and walks around that area quietly and calmly.
- Make sure the dog responds to its name, if necessary practising the come.
- If there are other dogs in the house, feed the elderly dog separately. Food, as we know, is an area of intense significance for dogs. The rest of the pack will sense the older dog's vulnerability and may act upon it.
- When out on the walk never let the dog off the lead. Even if it is running in a field it must be kept on a long line. You must also be vigilant to watch for other dogs approaching. Blindness is regarded as a disability in our world, but in the wild it is regarded as a liability, and a fatal one. So a dog with poor eyesight is going to receive no sympathy whatsoever from its fellow canines. In addition, dogs with cloudy eyes are sending out confusing signals, which again may cause other dogs to react. You have to be prepared for that.
- Let other dog owners know your dog has poor eyesight or is blind by using a white collar, a white lead and wearing a white sash yourself.
- If a dog is less responsive to requests it will be a lot jumpier and more easily spooked. At the same time their other senses will be heightened.

The loss of its eyesight can be a catastrophic thing for a dog. Many of the worst conditions, such as cataracts, are operable these days, but there are some progressive eye problems that are not. Blindness or partial blindness is inevitable.

If the problem cannot be rectified and it is clear the dog is unhappy or is not coping with its disability, then you have to ask yourself some big questions about its quality of life. Most owners would prefer their dog had eight happy years rather than their life be ruined by six bad months at the end. Euthanasia may be the only humane answer.

The final farewell

The time will come when you will have to say goodbye to your dog. It will be a testing time, no matter what the cause of the dog's death. Some dogs will live to the full extent of their life expectancy – there are examples of dogs surviving beyond twenty years of age – and eventually pass away quietly of natural causes. About one in twelve dogs will make it to the end in this way.

Others, sadly, will die of illness or in accidents. One in three dogs dies because of an illness, while around one in twenty dogs dies accidentally. Road accidents are the biggest killer of all, claiming far too many lives.

More than half our dogs, however, die with their owner's help.

EUTHANASIA

The word euthanasia has its roots in Greek language, *eu* meaning good and *thanatos* meaning death. It is appropriate then that it is much more commonly – and openly – used in the dog world than the human one. Whereas for us the subject, and indeed the word, carries a controversial weight with it, when it comes to our dogs we are in universal agreement. Every dog deserves a good death.

About one in five dogs are euthanised because of old age. Just under a third of dogs are put down because of illness before they reach this point. Sadly, a number are put down because of behavioural problems, usually because they have attacked or harmed a human. This happens despite the fact that their behaviour can be controlled.

Ultimately the decision is the owner's, but in many cases they are guided towards their choice by their vets. Both have their own criteria for making their decisions.

Why Vets Advise Euthanasia

There are certain circumstances under which it is always going to be the vet's advice that a dog is put down. The main ones are:

- The dog has suffered such severe physical injury it cannot be rehabilitated. This may apply if a dog is involved in a car accident or suffers another extreme trauma.
- Through disease or wear and tear the dog's body has deteriorated to such a degree it can no longer control its bodily functions.
- Disease has progressed to such an extent that the dog's pain and suffering cannot be controlled any longer.
- The dog is carrying a disease that is dangerously contagious and threatens humans.
- The dog has a condition so serious that even if it recovers it will not be able to lead anything like the life it led before illness.

Why Owners Choose Euthanasia

Life isn't always cut and dried, of course. The medical advice may be clear, but the human factor means the decision to put a dog down isn't always an automatic one. An owner faced with a severely ill or disabled dog has to weigh up their own options. The main considerations are:

- Are you capable of providing the care the dog will need even if it recovers?
- Is the task of looking after the dog going to have adverse consequences for your life and that of your family?
- Can you handle the financial implications of keeping your dog alive?

The one thing you cannot introduce into the decision-making process is selfishness. No owner relishes the prospect of losing their dog – the loss is going to be heavy, and it is going to mean a lot of heartache – but that cannot be a consideration. There are only two options: either the dog is going to be in pain or you are. It should never be the dog.

Saying Goodbye: The Process of Euthanasia

In practical terms, euthanising a dog is very straightforward. A vet will give it an anaesthetic drug, introduced intravenously in a highly concentrated form. The dog loses consciousness within seconds. Seconds after this it is brain-dead.

Faithful friend: even at the end of its life, a dog needs its owner to look after its best interests.

On an emotional level, however, it is much less straightforward. It is a hugely powerful moment for any owner, one that can affect many people deeply.

Everyone is going to handle the experience differently, but there are a few pieces of advice worth sharing:

- Try to be there with your dog as the procedure happens. Dogs are emotionally intelligent animals and have a sense of what is happening to them. Make sure the last thing it sees in this life is the face of its closest friend.
- If you know or even suspect in advance that the dog may be euthanised, try to have someone with you. You will need support afterwards.
- Don't hide the truth from children. This is a mistake that many people make, and it is wrong. Children form deep attachments to dogs and deserve to know the truth. Yes, of course they will be upset, but so will they be if they find out you have not been honest with them. It will also help them in the long term, preparing them for the other losses that sadly but inevitably they will have to deal with later in life.

A FITTING FAREWELL: WHAT TO DO WITH YOUR DOG

How you deal with your dog's corpse is, of course, a matter of personal choice. Some people favour cremation, others burial. Some opt for burial in a designated dog or pet cemetery, others prefer to lay their dog to rest somewhere more personal, perhaps in their garden or close to a favourite tree, where their memory can be honoured on a more daily basis.

If you do choose to bury your dog yourself, there are one or two points to bear in mind:

- Ensure the dog is wrapped up in material that will be absorbed into the earth. Choose something biodegradable – such as cotton sheeting. Don't use anything synthetic.
- Ensure the grave is deep enough. Other animals may be attracted to the burial site and dig up the body. A grave should be at least one metre (roughly three feet) in depth.

The loss of a beloved dog is a terrible blow. Many people feel more grief-stricken about losing their canine companions than losing a human friend or relative, yet many people also feel guilty about admitting how upset they are. They shouldn't. Loss and grief are complicated emotional issues and can be hard for other people to understand. That is not your concern. To deny your sense of loss is to deny the love you had for your dog, and that is not right.

You have hopefully spent many happy years doing what is right for your dog. The right thing to do when your canine friend passes away is to honour its memory, look back on the good times you shared, and be honest about how much you miss their company.

A fresh start

Everyone has said it; I know I have. The pain of losing a faithful friend is so great, you can't imagine yourself putting yourself through it again. 'I will never get another one,' you say. But you do, of course. It's a fact that, in a large percentage of cases, owners do find themselves new dogs, and do begin the process of sharing the joys of life with them once more.

How soon after the loss of your dog this happens is, it goes without saying, a purely personal decision. There is no right time. If you feel the need to replace your dog immediately, then that is what you should do. There is no need to feel guilt over this. Equally, if you want to take time to let the wounds heal, that is fine too. Whenever you decide to choose a new dog, however, it is worth bearing in mind a few, final thoughts.

Firstly, take the positives from your last relationship. The best way to honour the memory of the dog you have lost is to use the lessons it taught you as a means to improve your relationship with your new dog. Use the knowledge you have gained to make your new dog, if possible, an even happier pet. You will make mistakes, of course, but with luck they will be different ones from those you made last time around.

Don't get frustrated if you can't master certain aspects of life with your new dog as easily as you did with your last dog. Accept the fact that we all make mistakes. Just try to make them different ones. Don't expect your new dog to replace the old one: that is impossible. And to expect your new dog to be an exact replica of the dog you have lost is simply unfair. So don't get frustrated if you can't master certain aspects of life with your new dog as easily as you did with your last one. Again, the key is to focus on the positive aspects of your relationship with your new dog. It is going to have a personality of its own, one that will bring you very different pleasures, but will also set you very different challenges. Relish each of them and you will enjoy as rich and rewarding a life with your new dog as you did with your last one.

Further information

While I hope this book has covered all the main subjects that will concern an ordinary dog owner, there is no way it can claim to answer every conceivable question. With so many breeds and so many minor ailments and conditions in existence beyond those I have outlined in the preceding pages, that is inevitable. The good news, however, is that there are a number of respected institutions and bodies which between them can provide answers to 99.9 per cent of the issues an owner is likely to face. And if they don't know the answer, they can certainly refer you to someone who does.

I have drawn on the expertise of many of them myself in the compilation of this book. Listed below is a selection of some of them, along with the major international points of contact that will act as ideal starting points for dog lovers around the world.

CONTACTS IN THE UK

British Small Animal Veterinary Association
Woodrow House
1 Telford Way
Waterwells Business Park
Quedgeley
Gloucester
GL2 4AB
Tel: (01452) 726700
www.bsava.com
Enquiries: adminoff@bsava.com

British Veterinary Association
7 Mansfield Street
London W1
Tel: (020) 7636 6541
Fax: (020) 7436 2970
www.bva.co.uk
Enquiries: bvahq@bva.co.uk

Dogs Trust (formerly the National Canine Defence League)
17 Wakley Street
London
EC1V 7RQ
Tel: (020) 7837 0006
www.dogstrust.org.uk
Enquiries: info@dogstrust.org.uk

The Kennel Club of Great Britain
1–5 Clarges Street
Piccadilly
London
W1Y 8AB
Tel: (020) 7493 6651
www.the-kennel-club.org.uk
Enquiries: info@the-kennel-club.org.uk

OVERSEAS CONTACTS/KENNEL CLUBS

Australia

AUSTRALIAN CAPITAL TERRITORY
ACT Canine Association Inc.
PO Box 815
Dickson
ACT 2602
Tel: (02) 6241 4404
Fax: (02) 6241 1129
www.actca.asn.au
Contact: administrator@actca.asn.au

NORTHERN TERRITORY
The North Australian Canine Association Inc.
PO Box 37521
Winnellie
NT 0821
Phone: (08) 8984 3570
Fax: (08) 8984 3409
www.users.bigpond.com/naca1/
Contact: naca1@bigpond.com

NEW SOUTH WALES
Royal New South Wales Canine Council Ltd
PO Box 632
St Marys
NSW 1790
Tel: (02) 9834 3022 or 1300 728 022
(NSW Only)
Fax: (02) 9834 3872
www.rnswcc.org.au
Contact: k9council@rnswcc.org.au

QUEENSLAND
Canine Control Council (Queensland)
PO Box 495
Fortitude Valley
Qld 4006
Tel: (07) 3252 2661
Fax: (07) 3252 3864
www.cccq.org.au
Contact: dogsqld@powerup.com.au

SOUTH AUSTRALIA

South Australian Canine Association Inc.
PO Box 844
Prospect East
SA 5082
Tel: (08) 8349 4797
Fax: (08) 8262 5751
www.saca.caninenet.com
Contact: info@saca.caninenet.com

TASMANIA

Tasmanian Canine Association Inc.
The Rothman Building
PO Box 116
Glenorchy
Tas 7010
Tel: (03) 6272 9443
Fax: (03) 6273 0844
http://tca.freeservers.com.au/
Contact: tca@iprimus.com.au

VICTORIA

Victorian Canine Association
Locked Bag K9
Cranbourne
VIC 3977
Tel: (03) 9788 2500
Fax: (03) 9788 2599
www.vca.org.au
Contact: office@vca.org.au

WESTERN AUSTRALIA

Canine Association of Western Australia Inc.
PO Box 1404
Canning Vale
WA 6970
Tel: (08) 9455 1188
Fax: (08) 9455 1190
www.cawa.asn.au
Contact: k9@cawa.asn.au

Belgium

Fédération Cynologique Internationale
13 Albert Place
B-6530 Thuin
Belgium
Tel: 071 59 12 38
Fax: 071 59 22 29
www.fci.be

Brazil

Confederaçao Brasileira de Cinofilia
Tel: (24) 9279 1915
www.cbkc.org
Contact: imprensa@cbkc.org

Canada
Canadian Kennel Club (CKC)
89 Skyway Avenue
Suite 100
Etobicoke
Ontario
M9W 6R4
Tel: (416) 675 5511
Fax: (416) 675 6506
www.ckc.ca
Contact: information@ckc.ca

Czech Republic
Ceskomoravská Kynologická Unie
Jankovcova 53
CZ-170 00 Praha 7
Tel: 234 602 273, 602 216 874
Fax: 234 602 278
www.cmku.cz

Denmark
Dansk Kennel Club
Parkvej 1
2680 Solrød Strand
Denmark
Tel: (56) 18 81 00
Fax: (56) 18 81 91
www.dansk-kennel-klub.dk

Finland
Finnish Kennel Club
Kamreerintie 8
FIN-02770 Espoo
Tel: (9) 887 300
Fax: (9) 8873 033
www.kennelliitto.fi
Enquiries: fihs9cd9@ibmmail.com

France
Société Centrale Canine
155, avenue Jean Jaurès
93300 Aubervilliers
Tel: 01 49 37 54 00
www.scc.asso.fr

Germany
**Verband für das Deutsche
Hundewesen (VDH)**
Westfalendamm 174
44141 Dortmund
Tel.: (0231) 56 50 00
Fax: (0231) 59 24 40
www.vdh.de
Contact: info@vdh.de

Hungary
**Magyar Ebtenyésztök
Orszagos Egyesülete**
Tétényj ut 128/b-130
Budapest
H-1116
Tel: 0036 1 208 2300
www.meoe.net

Ireland

The Irish Kennel Club
Fottrell House
Harold's Cross Bridge
Dublin 6W
Tel: (01) 453 33 00/(01) 453 23 09/(01)
453 23 10
Fax: (01) 453 32 37
Contact: ikenclub@indigo.ie

Italy

**Ente Nazionale della Cinofilia
(ENCI)**
V. le Corsica 20
20137 Milano
Tel. 02 700 20 324
www.enci.it
Contact: info@enci.it

Japan

www.jkc.or.jp

Netherlands

**Raad van Beheer op Kynologisch
Gebied in Nederland**
Emmalaan 16-18
1075 AV Amsterdam
Postbus 75901
1070 AX Amsterdam
Tel: 0900 – 7274663
Fax: (020) 671 08 46
www.kennelclub.nl
Contact: info@kennelclub.nl

New Zealand

New Zealand Kennel Club
Prosser Street
Private Bag 50903
Porirua 6220
Tel: (04) 237 4489
Fax: (04) 237 0721
www.nzkc.org.nz
Contact: nzkc@nzkc.org.nz

Norway

Norsk Kennel Klub
PO Box 163
Bryn
0611 Oslo
Tel: 21 60 09 00
Fax: 21 60 09 01
www.nkk.no
Contact: info@nkk.no

Poland

Zwiazek Kynologiczny W Polsce
Zarzad Główny
ul. Nowy Swiat 35
PL-00-029 Warszawa
Tel: (022) 826 05 74
Fax: (022) 826 46 54
www.zkwp.org.pl
Contact: zg@zkwp.pl

Portugal

Clube Português de Canicultura
R. Frei Carlos, 7
P-1600 LISBON
Tel: 1 799 47 90
Fax: 1 799 47 99
www.cpc.pt

Spain

**La Real Sociedad Canina
de Espana**
Calle Lagasca 16
Bajo dcha
28001 Madrid
Tel: 914 264 960
Fax: 914 351 113
www.rsce.es
Contact: administracion@rsce.es

Sweden

Venska Kennelklubben
Svenska Kennelklubben
S-163 85 Spånga
Sweden
Tel: 8 795 30 30
Fax: 8 795 30 40
www.skk.se
Contact: info@skk.se

USA

The American Kennel Club (AKC)
51 Madison Avenue
New York
NY 10010
Tel: (212) 696 8200
www.akc.org
Contact: info@akc.org

United Kennel Club
100 E Kilgore Rd
Kalamazoo
MI 49002-5584
Tel: (269) 343 9020
Fax: (269) 343 7037
www.ukcdogs.com

The Westminster Kennel Club
149 Madison Avenue, Suite 803
New York
NY 10016
Tel: (212) 213 3165
Fax: (212) 213 3270
www.westminsterkennelclub.org
Contact: write@wkcpr.org

INDEX

A

abandonment 262, 264
abdomen 135-6
abscesses 117, 179, 287
accidents 50-1, 75, 177-8
Afghan Hounds 19, 81, 109
aggression 252-5, 257-8, 278
agility 248-9
Airedales 20
Alaskan Malamutes 16, 19
allergies 38
alphas
    pensioner stage 272, 277
    pioneer stage 88-9
    playboy stage 124, 144, 150, 166, 173
    pretender stage 210, 217, 231-2
    protector stage 244
    protégé stage 188, 198-9
    puppy stage 24, 30, 54
American Cocker Spaniels 18, 112
amniotic fluid 26
anaemia 56, 116-17
anal sacs 114, 126-7
anoestrus 164
anti-inflammatory drugs 114
antioxidants 39
anxiety 51, 54, 96-7, 140, 147, 158, 192,
    255-8, 261
apprentices 62, 170, 172, 212
arthritis 38, 46, 134, 267
artificial respiration 239
assistance dogs 165
Australia 57, 103, 180, 303-4
Australian Shepherds 19

B

baby teeth 124, 162
'back' command 142
bad breath 46, 124, 274, 287
balance 29
banishment 217-18, 254
Banzejis 155
barking 29, 185-6, 201, 253, 261
Basenjis 20
basic controls 91-3
baskets 72
Basset Hounds 20, 118, 120, 134, 154, 159,
    182, 205
bathing 110-12
Beagles 134
beans 46
bedding 50
beef 46
Belgian Shepherd Dogs 19
Belgium 302
Bernese Mountain Dogs 19, 205
Bichon Frises 20, 81, 109
birth 26-7, 226, 236-7
biting 35, 48, 66, 95-6, 179, 185, 254, 257
bladder 291-2
bleeding 180, 238, 289
blindness 58-61, 294-6
blocked tear-ducts 120
Bloodhounds 20, 59
blooming 229
body language 24, 34, 53
    playboy stage 138, 142, 146-57
    protégé stage 188, 193, 201-2
body scoring 134-6
body temperature 28, 103, 238-9, 283

bolting 215-16

bonding 26, 32, 63, 105, 122, 144, 236

bones 40, 42, 45-7, 62, 96, 122, 133,
    137, 182-3

Bones and Raw Food (BARF) diet
    45-7, 282

boosters 104-5

Border Collies 19, 288

boundaries 68-9, 87-101, 137-8, 172, 231

bowel problems 290-1

Boxers 19, 107, 112, 125, 152-3

brain 16

Brazil 304

breeders 222

breeding 16, 18-21, 60-2

    pioneer stage 80-1, 120, 125

    playboy stage 150-7, 165-6

    pretender stage 212, 219-26

    protégé stage 204

bristle brushes 106, 109

Britain see United Kingdom

British Veterinary Association (BVA)
    61, 175, 204-6, 302

broken bones 182-3

broken teeth 125

brushes 62, 106

Bull Terriers 20

Bulldogs 152, 274

Bullmastiffs 19

burping 289

C

Caesarian section 236

cages 72, 161, 262

Cairn Terriers 20, 134

calamine lotion 114

calcium 40, 42, 44-5

Canada 305

cancer 38-9, 275, 288-9

Canis familiaris 14, 16

Canis lupus 14, 16

carbohydrates 41, 44, 291

cars 72, 160-2, 261-2, 293

castration 165

cataracts 59-60, 294, 296

Cattle Dogs 19

Cavalier King Charles Spaniels 20, 134,
    152, 290

cereals 46-7

certificates 61, 223

challenges 212-18, 244, 246, 251

charcoal 291

cherry eye 59

Chesapeake Bay Retrievers 18

chickens 46, 101

Chihuahuas 81, 152, 274

children 293, 299

Chinese Crested 154

choking 40, 46, 141, 183-4

Chow Chows 21

circling 260

claw clipping 63

clearances 222-3

'close' 142

coats 107-9, 134, 285-6

Cocker mouth 125

Cocker Spaniels 18, 59, 112, 118, 120, 125,
    285, 288

Cognitive Dysfunction (CD) 289

cold puppies 238-9

colitis 46

collars 254, 262, 296

Collie Eye Anomaly (CEA) 60-1

Collies 60-1, 81, 109

colostrum 27, 102, 232, 236, 240

combs 106

'come' command 91, 177, 191-5, 202, 216, 293

comfort 279-80

commissar 149, 153

communication 88-93, 150-7, 201, 253, 278, 293

companionship 76-7, 280-1

competitions 248-50

complementary food 42-3

complete food 42-3, 47

confrontations 157-8

conjunctivitis 59, 120

consequences 36, 214

constipation 288, 290

cooking oil 107, 185

Corgis 107

cotton buds 119

courgettes 260

cross-packing 157

Crufts 248, 250

crying 96-8

curled tails 155

curly coats 109, 118

cuspids (canines) 62, 128, 162

cut-off points 36

cuts 180

Czech Republic 305

D

dairy products 38-9

Dalmatians 21

dandruff 115

danger 89, 186, 194-7, 200, 264

Daschunds 20, 107, 114, 134, 154, 182

deafness 119, 292-4

deciduous teeth 62

decisiveness 201

defecation 28, 36, 49, 69, 193, 260, 291

defiant pups 54

dehydration 75, 102-3

delivery 234-41

demodex 114, 118

Denmark 305

dens 72

dental health 62, 121-4, 274

depression 103

dermatitis 114

dew claws 126

diabetes 134, 268-9, 291

diagnoses 178, 205, 267

diarrhoea 48, 55, 57, 75, 102-3, 258-9, 288

diet 16, 37-47, 75, 96, 240, 281-3, 289

dieting 266

difficult dogs 185-7

directions 145, 200

discharges 118, 120, 126, 237, 287

discipline 72, 138, 172, 185-7

dislocations 182

distemper 102, 104, 120

distichiasis 59

DNA 16, 21, 61, 191

Dobermans 19, 114, 290

docked tails 155-6

The Dog Listener 13

dogs

  foods 36, 39, 42-3, 122, 282

  shows 250-1

  types 16-21, 82-6, 133, 159-60, 221, 236, 249, 275-6

domestication 16, 203

doorbells 194-6

doors 145, 194, 200, 214

'down' command 293

down hair 106

drooling 286

dry eye 59

dry food 43

dysplasia 61, 134, 202-7, 219, 222, 267

E

ears 29, 118-20, 147-8, 151-2, 292-3

eating 48, 89-90, 93-5, 133

   pensioner stage 282-3, 286

   pretender stage 228-9, 232, 241

   protector stage 257-8, 264, 278-9

   protégé stage 187, 197-9

ectropion 58

eggs 38-9

Egyptians 19

elbows 202-7, 280

Elkhounds 20, 155

emaciated dogs 135

encephalitis 181

English Mastiffs 205

English Setters 18

entropion 58

essential fatty acids 38

Europe 20, 180

euthanasia 297-300

evolution 16-21, 30

exclusion 254

exercise 80-1, 133, 136-40

   pensioner stage 278, 281, 290

   pregnancy 231

   protector stage 266

   protégé stage 177, 181, 205

expense 220

extended pack 29-31

eyes 28-9, 33, 294-6

   body language 147-8, 152

   contact 33, 97, 190, 193, 199, 201

   diseases 219, 222

   feeding 48

   personality tests 52-3

   problems 120

   softening 192-3

   testing 58-62

F

facial expression 24, 98

fading eyesight 294-6

faeces 259-60

farewells 297-300

fat 38, 41-2, 44

fear 147-8, 158-9, 261, 264

feeding *see* eating

feet 32, 63, 125-6, 137, 179-80, 252

females 163-5, 223-4, 228-41, 268-9, 288

fibre 41, 44

Field Spaniels 18

field trials 246

Finland 303

Finnish Lapphunds 19

first journeys 143-51, 262

first-aid kits 178

fish 38-9

fits 56

five-minute rule 191

flat puppy syndrome 239

flatulence 291

fleas 56, 113-16

floppy ears 118, 120, 156

flu 103

flyball 249-50

foetal development 228

food 89, 93-5, 133, 240, 281-2

food reward 139-41, 157, 159

    pensioner stage 289

    pretender stage 214, 216

    protector stage 260

    protégé stage 177, 191, 197

foreface 149, 152-3

foreign objects 119, 122, 178, 286-7

foreplay 224

formula milk 233, 240

Fox Terriers 20

fractures 182

France 305

free radicals 39

fruit 46

furniture 73-4, 96

G

gardens 72-3, 100

genitals 107, 225

gentling 232

German Shepherds 19, 81, 106, 109, 204-5, 236, 288

German Shorthaired Pointers 18

Germany 305

germs 28

gesture eating 199, 216-18, 258

gesture leaving 256-7

Giant Schnauzers 39

gingivitis 43, 122, 124, 286

glaucoma 60

Golden Retrievers 18, 205

Gordon Setters 18

grains 38

graves 300

Great Danes 81, 205

Greyhounds 20

grief 298

grooming 32, 80-1, 90

    coat types 107-9

    pensioner stage 279, 284-7

    pioneer stage 105-31

    playboy stage 162

    tools 106

growling 28-9, 34, 100, 278

growth 132-3, 232

guard hair 106

guide dogs 165, 295

guidelines

    bathing 111-12

    broken bones 182-3

    choking 183

    deafness 293

    delivery 237

    euthanasia 297-8

    fading eyesight 293-4

    farewells 298

    foot injuries 179

    gesture leaving 255-6

    grooming 107

    hand signals 293

    losing weight 266

    mealtimes 257-8

    mouth checks 122-4

    newborns 240

    off-leash walking 176

    over-amorous dogs 167

    patience 278

    pensioner health 283, 287-8

    walking 157-8

    whelping 235

gum disease 43, 122-4, 286

gundogs 18, 80, 139, 248

H

hackles 149, 154

hair dryers 112

hair loss 113

halitosis 124, 287

hamsters 101

hand signals 293-4

hand stripping 81

hand-rearing 47-8, 197

handling 31-3, 53

hardpad 102

harnesses 161

health 55-63, 112-33, 139

    pensioner stage 274, 283-99

    playboy stage 174

    pretender stage 219, 223, 241

    protector stage 267-9

    protégé stage 186, 202-7

hearing 28, 119

heart 38-9, 133-4, 275, 284, 290

heartworms 57

heat-stroke 269

heel work 138-40, 144-5, 214

hepatitis 56, 102-3

herbs 46

herding dogs 19, 81

hernia 243

hierarchy 24, 30, 35, 47

    pioneer stage 66, 69, 88, 90, 106

    playboy stage 124, 148

    pretender stage 210

    protégé stage 170, 199

hips 61, 202-5, 222, 224, 231

home vet 112-33

homemade dens 72

homemade food 41-2

hookworms 56, 181

hound gloves 107

hounds 19-20

Hungarian Vizslas 18

Hungary 303

hunting 88-90, 170, 172, 187, 213, 217

hypersalivation 286

I

ice balls 184-5

ideal weight 135

immune system 39-40, 286, 288

impalements 181

incisors 62, 122, 162

incontinence 290-1

independence anxiety 96-7

industrialisation 45

infections 113-14, 116

    pensioner stage 286, 291, 293

    pioneer stage 118, 120

    playboy stage 133-4, 164

    pretender stage 239

    protégé stage 178

inherited illnesses 219

injuries 179-84, 297-8

insulin 268-9

introductions 159-60

Ireland 306

Irish Setters 18

Irish Terriers 20

Irish Wolfhounds 20, 77, 205, 274, 288

Italy 306

J

Japan 180, 306

Japanese Akitas 21

jaundice 103

jaw problems 287

journeys 160-2, 261-2

jumping 177, 181, 203, 216, 230

juvenile pyoderma 118

K

Kennel Club (KC) 61, 165, 204-6, 221-2, 248, 250, 304

kennel cough 103-4

kennels 72

Keratoconjunctivitis Sicca (KCS) 59

kidney disease 46

kidney worms 57

knocking at door 194-5

knotting 108

L

labelling 42, 48

Labradors 18, 81, 107, 134, 204-5, 220

lamb 122

lameness 179, 202, 204

lapdogs 20

leadership 35, 51, 54, 74

   pensioner stage 277

   pioneer stage 88-91, 93-4, 100

   playboy stage 144-6, 157, 163, 165

   pretender stage 212

   protector stage 244, 246-7, 251-2

   protégé stage 172, 186-208

   rescue dogs 264

leads 100, 132, 137-8

   pensioner stage 278, 293, 296

   playboy stage 140, 157

   pretender stage 220-2

   protector stage 262

   protégé stage 200

   removing 175-8, 214

leaving home 144-5

leptospirosis 103

letterboxes 195

Lhasa Apsos 21, 109, 239

lice 115

lifespan 82-6, 275-6

limping 179, 205, 278

lip-fold inflammation 125

lips 25, 125

litter sizes 236

long coats 108-9

long tails 154-5

longevity 274-6

losing weight 266

lungworms 57

Lyme disease 116, 181

M

machine-clipping 108

maidens 223

mail deliveries 195, 251, 253

males 107, 162-3, 268

malocclusions 124-5

Maltese 20, 81, 109

marrow bones 40, 122

maternal instincts 26, 29, 238

mating 163-4, 210, 223-5

mealtimes 197-9, 213, 216-17, 241, 257-8, 278-9

meat 38-9, 42, 46-7, 56, 221

medical demands 87

mentors 30

metabolism 133, 281

metoestrus 164

Mexican Hairless 21

middle-age spread 265-9

milk 39, 41, 47

minerals 39-44

Miniature Poodles 16, 21

misbehaviour 185-7, 212-14, 252-62

mites 113, 115, 118

molars 62

morning sickness 228

mosquitos 57

motion sickness 161

mouth 122-5, 147, 193, 284, 286

mouthwashes 124

mutting 240

N

nails 180

names 33-4, 202, 296

navel 239

neck 191

nervousness 51, 53-4, 79

    pensioner stage 274, 281

    playboy stage 158

    pretender stage 220, 224

    protector stage 257-8, 264-5

neutering 132, 165-7

New Zealand 180, 306

newborns 26-8

Newfoundlands 205, 251

newspapers 50

nicitating membrane 59

nights 71, 98

no-go zones 73-4

noise 79, 158-9, 194, 200-1, 292

non-moulting coats 109

non-sporting dogs 21

North America 57, 103

Norway 306

Norwegian Buhunds 19

nose 29, 47

nuts 46

nymphs 117

O

obedience competitions 250

obesity 134, 267, 269

occlusion 124

oestrus 164, 231

off-leash walking 175-8, 214-16

offal 45-6

Old English Sheepdogs 16, 19, 81, 109, 156, 288

Omega-3 38, 44

Omega-6 38, 44

otitis externa/media 118

otodectes 118

over-amorous dogs 166-7

over-feeding 48

overweight dogs 133-6, 181, 265-9, 282, 288

ovulation 164

P

pack instincts 14, 24, 69

    pensioner stage 272, 277, 296

    pioneer stage 76-7, 88-91, 100-1

    playboy stage 124, 149, 157, 165

    pretender stage 210, 213, 217-18, 231

    protector stage 244, 252-62

    protégé stage 170, 172, 186-201

padding 50

painful ears 119

palm-of-the-hand test 53

pancreatitis 269

panic 69-70, 78, 100, 158-60, 165, 255

parasites 55-8, 113, 115-18, 181

partners 221-3

parvovirus 103-4

pastoral dogs 19, 80, 248

patience 91, 139, 159, 260, 263-4, 279

pecking order 89, 99, 191, 244

pedigree 175, 222, 263

Pekingese 20, 81, 153

penetration 224

pensioner stage 270-99

periodontal disease 130, 286

Persians 19

personality 24, 28, 51-5, 197, 247, 254, 262, 301

phantom pregnancies 231-3

phobias 160

physical demands 80-1

picking-up process 31-2, 53

pineapple 260

pioneer stage 64-121, 173

Pitbulls 220

placentas 26, 56, 228, 231, 236, 238, 240

plaque 43, 122

play 24, 30, 34-6, 53
  pensioner stage 289, 293
  pioneer stage 66, 69, 73, 90, 96, 100
  protector stage 246, 267
  protégé stage 184, 187

playboy stage 128-67

pneumonia 56, 102

Pointers 18, 80

Poland 306

police dogs 35

Polish Lowland Sheepdogs 19

Pomeranians 20, 81, 154-5

Poodles 81, 109, 118, 274, 288

poop-scoops 56

pork 46, 122

porridge 47

Portugal 307

post-oestrus 232

postal deliveries 195, 251, 253

posture 201

poultry 46

power eating 216

praise 34, 48, 75, 91
  playboy stage 139, 141
  pretender stage 216
  protector stage 260
  protégé stage 191, 202

predators 66

pregnancy 220, 225-33, 236

premolars 62

prepared foods 42-3

preservatives 43

pretender stage 208-47, 251

pro-oestrus 164

problem deliveries 236-7

professional groomers 108-9

Progressive Retinal Atrophy (PRA) 60

projection 201

prolactin 24, 231

protector stage 242-69

protégé stage 168-201

proteins 38, 41-2, 44-5

puberty 124, 132, 162-4, 236

Pugs 112, 152

puppies
  birth plan 225
  classes 159
  cold 238-9
  companionship 280
  formula milk 233, 240
  handling 31-3
  homes 220-1

pregnancy 166, 225-8

stage 22-63

Pyometra 164

Pyrenean Mountain Dogs 19

R

rabies 180-1

random toileting 260

rank 24

rashes 115

'recall' 172

red skin 114-15

removing leads 175-8

rescue dogs 165, 198, 257, 262-5

resistance fighters 54

retained baby teeth 130, 162

retinal dysplasia 61

Retrievers 81, 134, 205

reuniting 89-90, 187-94, 253-4, 264-5

ribs 135-6, 230, 282

ringcraft 250

ringworm 114, 181

rivalries 99-101

Rottweilers 206, 288

roundworms 55-6, 230

routine 280

rules 98, 172, 218

breeding 222

feeding 93-4

five-minute 191

play 35-6

trials 248

walking 137

weight loss 266

running 181, 203

S

safety 72-3, 98, 164

St Bernards 19, 59, 206, 286

Salukis 19

Samoyeds 19

sanctions 217-19

sarcoptes 118

sarcoptic mange 115

sashes 296

scabies 115

scanning 225, 230, 232

Schnauzers 107, 118

Schwarzenegger, Arnold 153

scissors 106-7, 109, 178, 233, 240

scratches 119

scratching 113-14

scruff of neck 32

seasons 164

sebum 106, 110, 112

security blankets 78

sedatives 114

seeing 29

senility 287

senses 29, 77-80

separations 89-90, 97, 187-94, 253, 255-7, 265

Setters 18, 80

settling-in process 70-1, 98

sexual identity 124

shampoo 111, 115, 117

Sharpeis 112, 152

Shetland Sheepdogs 60

Shih Tzus 239

showing dogs 165, 250-1

shyness 51, 53

Siberian Huskies 16

sighing 193

signals 88-9, 147-57, 234
    pensioner stage 293-4, 296
    pretender stage 216
    protector stage 254, 262
    protégé stage 186-7, 190, 192-4, 199-200
silky coats 109
single-litter mothers 166
Sit command 91-2, 202, 293
size 82-6
skin 39, 46, 113-15, 134, 284-6
skull 16
sleeping 27, 29, 36, 50
    pensioner stage 278, 280
    pioneer stage 69, 71, 74, 98
    protector stage 267
sleepy eyes 120
smell 78, 94, 111, 119, 251, 285, 295
smooth coats 107
snacks 133, 137, 199, 217, 258
snow 184-5
soap 111
socialisation 32, 124, 157, 159, 210
sound 79-80, 158-9, 194, 200-2, 292
Spain 307
Spaniels 18, 20, 59, 81, 109, 112, 125, 156
spatial demands 81
spaying 165-6
special needs 283
sperm 132, 162
sporting dogs 18, 80, 125, 139
sprains 181-2
Springer Spaniels 18, 80, 152
Staffordshire Bull Terriers 153
stairs 267
stalking 170
stance 149, 153
standards 222, 250

status 24, 28, 34-5, 47
    pioneer stage 88-90, 93, 100, 106
    playboy stage 150, 165
    pretender stage 212, 214, 216
    protector stage 245, 251-52, 255-7
    protégé stage 188, 196, 199
'stay' command 172, 202, 293
step by step
    claw clipping 63
    Come command 91, 191-2
    first walk 144-6
    hand-feeding 47-8
    handling 31
    heel work 139-40
    leads 141-3
    mealtimes 199, 217
    noise training 79
    off-leash walking 177
    personality tests 53-4
    Recall command 174-5
    Sit command 91-2
    Stay command 173-4
    toilet training 50
    walking 215-16
strains 181-2
stress 31, 78, 252, 267, 278
stud dogs 221-4
stud fees 220, 224
suckling 24, 27-8, 30, 36
Sweden 305
swellings 119, 179, 181, 289
swimmers 237

T

tail 29, 98, 146-7, 252
    base 135-6
    body language 150, 159

mating 223

types 154-5

tapeworms 56, 118, 181

tartar 43, 121-3, 286

teats 27-8, 36, 52-3, 231, 235, 240

teeth 16, 40, 43, 46-7

  body language 149

  pensioner stage 282, 284, 286-7

  pioneer stage 95-6, 121-5

  playboy stage 152-3, 162

  puppy stage 62-3

temperament 220

Terriers 20, 81, 107

testes 107, 162-3

testosterone 165

tests

  dysplasia 202-3

  eyes 58-62, 120

  mating 223

  personality 51-4

thanks 196-7, 265

thinkers 53-4

threshold 144-5, 200

Tibetans 20

ticks 113, 116-17, 181

tie 224-5

toileting 193, 279, 289

  problems 258-60, 291

  training 34, 36, 48-50, 74-5

tone of voice 34, 201-2

tools

  delivery 233

  first-aid kits 178

  grooming 106

tooth decay 46

toothpaste 63, 124

towels 112, 161, 233

toy dogs 20, 81, 87

Toy Poodles 77

toys 73, 96, 100, 231, 252, 289

training 79

trauma 70, 75, 181, 266, 298

travelling 160-2, 261-2

trichiasis 58

trust 26, 32, 63, 79, 90

  pioneer stage 105, 122

  playboy stage 140, 144

  protector stage 247, 264

  protégé stage 192

tugging 35, 96, 141, 212-16, 246

tumours 288-9, 290-2

turning 141-2

U

ulcers 58-9

umbilical cord 27, 235

underfeeding 48

underweight dogs 134-5, 137, 282

United Kingdom (UK) 20, 61, 175, 180, 185, 248-50, 274, 302-3

United States (US) 250, 282, 307

uraemia 287

urination 28, 36, 49, 193, 258-60, 288, 291-2

urine samples 284

utility dogs 21

V

vaccinations 69, 102-5, 137-8, 160, 283

vegetables 38, 41, 46, 291

ventilation 118, 120

vets 32, 57-8, 61, 75, 87

  arthritis 267

delivery 238-90

diabetes 268

dieting 266

euthanasia 297-8

home 112-33

newborns 238-9

pensioner stage 283-99

pioneer stage 126

playboy stage 134, 162-7

pretender stage 220, 228, 233, 235-6

protégé stage 180-2

weight 137

visitors 194-7, 252, 264

visual impairment 294-6

Vitamin K deficiency 238

vitamins 39, 41-2, 220

vomiting 55, 102-3, 161, 287

vulva 164, 223-4, 235, 292

W

Wait command 143, 177

walking 50, 132, 143-57

to heel 132, 139-40, 144-5, 214

leads 139-40

off-leash 175-8, 214-16

pensioner stage 278

pregnancy 230

pretender stage 213-16

protector stage 246

protégé stage 172, 187, 200

rescue dogs 264

water 38, 43, 232, 241, 290

weaning 26, 34, 36-48, 90, 197

weeping eyes 120

weight 48, 55, 57, 132-8

pensioner stage 287, 289

pretender stage 229, 233

problems 136-8

protector stage 265-9

Weimatraner 18

wellbeing 202-7

West Highland Terriers 20, 59

Westminster Dog Show 250

wet food 43

whelping 234-5

whelping box 29-31, 36, 49, 225, 232-3

Whippets 107

whipworms 57

wiry coats 107-8

wolves

body language 148-50, 152

breeding 166

pensioner stage 272

pioneer stage 66, 76, 90, 106, 110, 121

playboy stage 124

pregnancy 232-4

pretender stage 210, 217-18

protector stage 244, 246

protégé stage 170, 188, 190, 200, 202-3

puppy stage 13, 16, 21, 24, 30, 42, 62

wood shavings 50

working dogs 19, 126, 165, 248

working trials 246

worming 55-8, 220, 231-2

Y

yeast infections 118

Yorkshire Terriers 20, 109, 236, 288

Z

zoonotic diseases 180-2

zygotes 225